Lady Lucy
Houston DBE

This book is dedicated to the memory of the pioneering publisher Leo Cooper, and to all entrepreneurs who succeed in making their convictions take flight.

Lady Lucy Houston DBE

Aviation Champion and Mother of the Spitfire

With a Foreword by Lord Craig, Marshal of the Royal Air Force, GCB, OBE

Miles Macnair

Pen & Sword
AVIATION

First published in Great Britain in 2016 by
Pen & Sword Aviation
an imprint of
Pen & Sword Books Ltd
47 Church Street
Barnsley
South Yorkshire
S70 2AS

ISBN 978 1 47387 936 2

Typeset in Ehrhardt by
Mac Style Ltd, Bridlington, East Yorkshire
Printed and bound in India by
Replika Press Pvt. Ltd.

Pen & Sword Books Ltd incorporates the imprints of Pen & Sword
Archaeology, Atlas, Aviation, Battleground, Discovery, Family
History, History, Maritime, Military, Naval, Politics, Railways, Select,
Transport, True Crime, and Fiction, Frontline Books, Leo Cooper,
Praetorian Press, Seaforth Publishing and Wharncliffe.

For a complete list of Pen & Sword titles please contact
PEN & SWORD BOOKS LIMITED
47 Church Street, Barnsley, South Yorkshire, S70 2AS, England
E-mail: enquiries@pen-and-sword.co.uk
Website: www.pen-and-sword.co.uk

Contents

List of Illustrations

FIGURES – Within Text

PLATES – Black and White

PLATES – Colour

Foreword

In the late 1920s and early 1930s, the Royal Air Force was fighting for its very survival. Government defence policy was focused on disarmament. Funding was extremely tight. The British aircraft industry, fragmented between a number of relatively small private companies, had to compete for any prototype of a new aircraft specified by the Air Ministry. For cost reasons, specifications tended to concentrate on multi-purpose roles. It was not an environment to inspire innovation or experimentation.

Against this depressing background, the Government decided to give no support for Britain to partake in the 1931 Schneider Trophy air race. This was a prestigious competition that other countries valued as the perfect showcase for their technical achievements in aviation. It was only through the most generous, patriotic and timely gift by Lady Houston that Vickers/Supermarine could afford to develop the record breaking S6.B airframe, later to become the Spitfire, and Rolls Royce could increase the performance of their engines leading to the iconic Merlin used so extensively to power aircraft in World War II. Only a couple of years later she sponsored the successful first ever flights over Everest. These major sponsorships not only gave a highly valuable technical boost to important aspects of aviation; they also raised Britain's status in the eyes of the world. Her vision of the increasing importance of air power in future conflicts, and her anticipation of the horrors of the blitz led her to offer to buy fighter aircraft for the defence of London. Her generosity was spurned, curtly dismissed by government ministers.

Without her foresight and personal generosity in the early 1930s, the outcome of the Battle of Britain in 1940 may well not have been the great victory that Winston Churchill celebrated in his famous speech in honour of 'the few'. So I am delighted to add my appreciation to this well researched new biography of a truly unique and remarkable lady.

Lord Craig, Marshal of the Royal Air Force, GCB, OBE,
former Chief of the Defence Staff.

Acknowledgements

My sincere thanks wing their way to the descendants of Lucy's lover and her sundry husbands who have been kind enough to reply to my enquiries, particularly Sir Roderick Brinckman whose grandfather was Lucy's first husband. I am most grateful for the ready help I have received from librarians and archivists at the following institutions: Warwickshire Yeomanry Museum (Philip Wilson), the British Library, Mary Evans Picture Library, *The Times* photographic archives, the National Archives, the National Portrait Gallery, the British Film Institute, the Royal Geographical Society, the Royal Aeronautical Society, the RAF Museum, Hendon and, particularly, Solent Sky Museum, Southampton.

For much of the information in Appendix II, I acknowledge my gratitude to the ancestry.com website and to the other researchers who have made their family trees accessible to the public.

David Wilson is a very talented marine artist and his painting of the Supermarine S6.B, with Lucy's yacht *Liberty* in the background adds a wonderful touch of colourful spontaneity to the triumph of the 1931 Schneider Trophy race (see PLATE C12).

Authors without an established reputation and a portfolio of favourable reviews have to accept rejection slips as a natural hazard of their trade. So I was delighted that Pen & Sword Books found sufficient merit in my draft offering to assign me a commissioning editor under their aviation imprint. Laura Hirst could not have been more helpful or encouraging, so I now express my deep gratitude to her. Likewise to Barnaby Blacker, who then took on the editorial baton and has been a wise and knowledgeable counsellor. It was a happy coincidence that his grandfather was a key member of the successful Houston–Mount Everest expedition and could add family items to the chapter on this heroic venture.

A special word of thanks goes to my neighbour Dr Tom Winnifrith, former Professor of English at Warwick University, who has been a good friend by reading draft chapters and making helpful suggestions on matters of grammar, syntax and punctuation. Finally, my dear wife Juliette, who has a voracious appetite for quality historical novels, has been a great help with enhancements to those ephemeral aspects of 'pace' and 'readability', while having to live for three years in a 'ménage à trois' with the ghost of the beautiful, enigmatic and eccentric Lucy.

Introduction

The life of Lucy Radmall, known to her family and close friends as 'Poppy' and later as Lady Houston DBE, must surely rank as one of the most romantic, fascinating and intriguing stories of the last 150 years. As a window onto the history of the turbulent years between the two world wars it is not only very significant but also highly controversial. Yet now she is completely unknown and her achievements utterly forgotten and unrecognised. She rose from quite humble birth and a brief spell as a teenage actress on the London stage to become the richest woman in England, a scourge of the political establishment and arguably the single person who did more than anyone else to help win the Battle of Britain. Between her birth in 1857 and her weird death in 1936, she had one youthful, scandalous love affair with a supposedly married man, and then three marriages of her own, each to men of completely different character. She seduced and schemed her way to the pinnacle of the British aristocracy, while attaining sufficient wealth to fund her numerous acts of charity as well as her forthright political and journalistic ambitions. She was a renowned beauty with a stunning figure. She had charisma, a sharp wit and a feisty charm that could entrance both men and women, and alarm them in equal measure. For her work on behalf of nurses in the First World War she was honoured by King George V as one of the first five women to be made a Dame of the British Empire. With all this she should be a biographer's dream.

But there are problems. For one thing she never had any children who might have preserved material about her. The descendant families of her lover and her three husbands have responded to my requests for information with polite encouragement, but one and all have confessed that nothing tangible in the way of personal letters, photographs or other memorabilia remains in their possession; except for the occasional anecdote or half-recalled reminiscence. The only two biographies of Lucy, written by men who worked for her and became her confidants in the last years of her life, are unsatisfactory. The first, published in 1946, is a slim volume written in a somewhat Victorian style in which the author uses his own experiences to provide padding, a background of places and events in which she was not necessarily involved (Warner Allen, *Lucy Houston DBE – One of the Few*, Constable, London, 1947). The second, written by a much younger man, an experienced biographer and journalist who later became the editor of the magazine *Country Life*, is far more comprehensive and decidedly more readable, but only one fifth of this book relates to the first seventy years of her life (James Wentworth Day, *Lady Houston – The Richest Woman in England*, Allen Wingate, London, 1958).

Both of these books, long out of print, do have the outstanding merit that they quote personal reminiscences by Lucy herself, as she told the authors stories from her early life and recalled, often inaccurately and sometimes with exaggeration, her recollections of people, places and events. In this field the two books overlap. Lucy did write numerous articles and letters that were published in the newspapers and her own weekly journal, but she confined her personal correspondence predominantly to telegrams, telephone calls – often in the small hours of the morning when she could not sleep – and notes to her staff scrawled in purple ink. None of these have survived.

So in trying to write a new, fair, balanced account of Lucy's extraordinary life, with its manifold contradictions and eccentricities, I have had to try and unearth untapped primary sources, the most important of which have turned out to be newspaper archives. They have proved to be a gold mine. Landmark events regarding Lucy can be found in *The Times*, while the often more fascinating, gossipy and revealing items are lurking in the columns of provincial newspapers. Some of these relate to local events when Lucy was actually in that part of the country, while others are syndicated items from the popular London newspapers and journals. Several items that were not available to either Warner Allen or James Wentworth Day have been extracted from the National Archives, collections at Churchill College, Cambridge, the British Library and the Royal Geographical and Aeronautical Societies.

I confess that I have rather fallen in love with Lucy. I hope this admission has not blinded me to her faults, which were legion; that I am not too sympathetic to her engagement with fascism, not in its brutal Nazi incarnation in Germany, but that extolled by Benito Mussolini in Italy and by many sincere, intelligent people on the right wing of British politics at the time. I trust that I have given due credit to the many other people who contributed to her great achievements. One of her enduring charms was her 'common touch', being equally comfortable in conversation with tramps as she was in discussions with statesmen, poets and peers, and indeed the Prince of Wales, later King Edward VIII. At times, Lucy could be infuriatingly obstinate and self-willed, but I sincerely believe that she deserves to be better known and recognised as a beautiful, charitable, perceptive, captivating and, above all, patriotic lady.

Chapter 1

Beginning at the End

29 December 1936. Lucy had not left her bed for several days. She was in her eightieth year and although there was a bitter wind blowing across Hampstead Heath she had ordered her staff to keep all the windows in the house wide open. The tray of food that had been brought up to her was untouched – again. Lucy had decided that she no longer wished to live. The world outside that she had enlivened with her feisty glamour and vitality for seven decades was crumbling around her and she knew that her country, the England she loved and that she had fought so hard to defend against its own politicians, was heading for another catastrophic war. One of the richest and most generous-hearted women in the country had decided to starve herself to death.

As she slipped in and out of consciousness, one can imagine that past memories from her eventful life would have flitted through her mind. Her heart had been truly broken only once before, when the love of her life, the man she had lived with in Paris for ten years since she was 16, had died in her arms in 1883. What a glamorous, carefree time she and Frederick Gretton had shared together! Now, as her unseen neighbours prepared to celebrate the New Year, she was in mourning over another bereavement, not a mortal death but the end of a romantic illusion that collapsed when she heard a broadcast on the wireless a fortnight before. That was the day when her adored idol King Edward VIII announced his abdication and his intention to marry the American divorcée Wallis Simpson. How could he be so weak-willed? How could he have allowed himself to be bullied by the Prime Minister and the Archbishop of Canterbury into renouncing the throne and deserting his country? He had even come to visit her in person recently. For Lucy, who saw patriotic duty as a moral priority above selfish indulgence, his abdication was the last straw.

Perhaps, above the noise of wind and the billowing curtains, she might have heard the sound of an aircraft flying overhead, even one powered by the revolutionary new Rolls-Royce 'Merlin' engine. She would have read about the first flight of the prototype 'Spitfire' fighter the previous March and she could enjoy a glow of satisfaction to think that neither would have been developed so quickly without her bold, impulsive initiative five years earlier. At last it seemed that the dunderheaded politicians she despised so much had heeded her prophetic warnings, men like Ramsay MacDonald, to her mind a secret communist lurking under the disguise of a so-called socialist, and Stanley Baldwin, an indecisive nonentity who was leading the Conservative party, where precisely? Thank goodness there were still some talented men who retained a patriotic vision of a Great Britain with its great Empire, men like Lord Lloyd and her hero Winston Churchill. Ah, dear Winston! – her mind doubtless wandered back to the day in 1927 when she had wheedled her way to a flirtatious encounter in his office at the Treasury.

The daylight had faded and soon the country would be swallowed up in the darkness of a winter night, in the same way that Lucy saw the whole British democratic process. She could recall another era, when she had been an ardent suffragist and a passionate advocate of votes for women. It was surely just reward for their hard work and sacrifices during the terrible Great War. She had seen not only wounded soldiers coming back from the front, but also the brave young nurses who had treated them in dressing stations behind the lines, and who had been traumatised by the experience.

She had to do something just for them. And what, she must have wondered, had that grim conflict been fought for anyway? A flawed Treaty and the setting up of the ineffectual League of Nations? To Lucy the League had never been more than just a toothless talking-shop, particularly after the United States had opted out and slunk back into isolationism. There had been one man who seemed to her to have at least some of the answers, a man of strong convictions who had a dream of combining centralised capitalism with social justice, at the same time stemming the tide of communism. Most important to Lucy was that this vision of national economic resurgence would be managed under a reconstituted monarchy. Benito Mussolini had seemed like the role-model of a politician for the third decade of the twentieth century. Now, however, he had gone a step too far with his invasion of Abyssinia, threatening to apply a pincer grip on Britain's interests around the Suez Canal. Her one-time political hero had proved as untrustworthy as the rest of them, and if he now cosied up to that brute Adolf Hitler, Lucy did not want to live to see the outcome. How often had she warned of another catastrophic war, even worse than the last, with London in flames and terrified children running screaming through the streets?

The maid had come up to turn the lights on in the bedroom but had been dismissed. Lucy never knew any of their names nowadays and there seemed to be a different one every week. She was becoming delirious and knew that she must be close to death. Lying in the darkness her mind may have wandered back to her three weddings and the three men she had enticed to the altar. How different they had been from one another. Theodore Brinckman had been a true gentleman, and we could possibly have been so happy together if only I had been able to have children and he had not been unfaithful. And then there had been bankrupt, 'red-nosed' Lord Byron, great-nephew of the illustrious poet and scandalous roué. Ah, poor George, what a liability you were for all those sixteen years we were together. So different from Robert Houston! He had been a real man, once upon a time so handsome, with his black beard and penetrating dark eyes. By 1922 'Black Bob' was in poor health and more cantankerous than ever; but he did have one cardinal virtue, and that was that he was rich – very, very rich indeed. Getting him to the altar, against the advice of his few friends and relations, had been a real challenge. At least I only had to put up with living with him as his nurse for fifteen months; his death had certainly set the tongues wagging.

A few last moments perhaps to reflect on all the other challenges she had faced, the myriads of people who had benefited from her charity, the political battles she had fought, her journalistic crusade, and the great patriotic adventures she had inspired and financed. And her own childhood, happy days in a loving family, when she had been allowed to run wild through the back streets of the city of London, streets that echoed to the clarion call of the bells of St Paul's Cathedral …

Chapter 2

The Dancing Nymph and a Teenage Love Affair

It would be quite wrong to think that the girl christened as Fanny Lucy Radmall had been a street urchin, a child brought up in rags and poverty. She had been born as far back as 1857, on 8 April to be precise, though she kept her true age a closely guarded secret throughout her life. Her birth certificate states that she was born at number 13 Lower Kennington Green, in the district of Lambeth, South London. The road no longer exists but the area, on the edge of Camberwell, was of bourgeois respectability at the time. It seems to have been a very temporary address anyway.

Back in 1840 her father, Thomas Radmall, had married Maria Isabella Clark, who had her own career as a 'wardrobe dealer' – which meant clothes rather than furniture – while his profession throughout the 1840s and 50s was described as 'warehouseman'. Their first four surviving children, three daughters and one son, had been born in Islington, but by 1861 the family address was 13 Newgate Street in the parish of Christchurch, close to St Paul's Cathedral. Lucy's father was now described as a woollen draper and it seems that he had moved his family to live 'above the shop', so that the premises could become store, counting-house and home all in one. Lucy was the seventh child, two more sons having been born in 1850 and 1852, and the last child, another daughter, Florence, would arrive in 1863 when their mother was 45. In 1871, Thomas Radmall was recorded as a 'picture-frame maker', employing a joiner and a spoke-shaver, living with his wife Maria at 21 Church Lane, in the parish of St Mary, Whitechapel. There is however no mention of any of the children at that address, though little Florence is noted as staying with one of her elder, married brothers, Thomas G. Radmall, a wine merchant in Croydon, and his wife. Lucy seems somehow to have evaded the census collectors completely.

So much for the known facts about Lucy's family background as a child growing up in London. Her parents seem to have been moderately prosperous, providing a happy environment for all their children, and the sons were certainly given good educations, two of them going on to professions in the City as commission agents in stockbroking firms. It seems likely that Lucy was the wild-child of the family, by her own admission much happier scampering round the backstreets of the city and playing hide-and-seek around the gravestones of St Pauls than taking lessons. She may have had a governess, but in later life she had a wholesome contempt for education. 'Too much,' she said, 'addles the brains,' adding that in her case it inhibited her sort of active, seeking mind – 'the world was my university and humanity my perpetual mentor.'[1]

Lucy was a very pretty girl, 'a creature of tremendous vitality and utterly roguish charm, with tiny hands and feet, a wasp waist … and large impish eyes.'[2] There is just one surviving photograph of Lucy as a teenager, most discretely dressed and looking rather prim, with magnificent hair. [see PLATE B1] It is significant that this is a portrait from the studio of the society photographer Bassano.[3] And it is Lucy's dark, wide-apart eyes that captivate the viewer, along with her very pretty mouth. She herself claimed that she had become a ballet dancer, but Sir Arthur Pinero is quoted as saying that he had once encountered her as 'a small part actress'.[4] There is no doubt that by the age of 16 in 1873 she was on the stage of some theatre or music hall as a dancer or chorus girl, possibly in pantomime. The most famous impresario of such productions was Augustus Harris at the Drury Lane theatre, and Lucy claimed that she had been taken on by him when she turned up at his office with no introduction, no appointment, no influence and just refused to go away until he had offered her a job.[5] In her later life, Lucy's recollections were somewhat muddled concerning precise events and dates, and this particular story was probably a distortion of the facts because Harris did not return to England from France until 1877; and by this time Lucy had already made the same journey, but in reverse, four years earlier.

Precisely where Lucy performed is immaterial anyway; the important point is that this was the era when pretty young chorus girls played out a special role in the London entertainment scene. Young men – and some not so young – could ogle the tightly corseted girls through their opera glasses as they cavorted around the stage, exposing flashes of shapely legs and a hint of pert, well-rounded bosom. Young army officers and city gents, the 'mashers' in their top hats, white ties and tails, with a white scarf casually thrown over the shoulders, would tip the theatre staff to deliver notes to the dressing rooms during the intervals, and then throng around the stage door to whisk their pick of the evening out to supper in some intimate restaurant. It provided a liberating safety valve from the Victorian stuffiness under which such young men had been brought up.

Lucy may have only been enjoying such adulation for six weeks since she had been launched 'on the boards' when a particular admirer came into her life. Frederick Gretton was older than the typical 'young blood' and offered more than just dinner at a nearby restaurant; he took her to Paris. There they would live together for the next ten years as man and wife, losing themselves in a love affair of pure romantic indulgence. She was just 16 and he was 34, and what may have made the whole business more scandalous was that there were rumours that he might have already been secretly married. (This was speculated at the time, though there seems to be no record of any official wedding, but it may explain why Frederick never agreed to marry Lucy, the girl he was so obviously in love with.)

Frederick Gretton had been born in the spring of 1839, the second son of John Gretton, a partner in the brewery firm of Bass, Radcliffe & Gretton in Burton-on-Trent. In 1861 it was recorded that John Gretton employed 1,084 men and 83 boys in what was probably the largest brewery in England, if not the world. His eldest son, also called John, was then aged 24 and was in the business, while the 22-year-old Frederick was described as 'Gentleman, Lieutenant in the 8th company of the Staffordshire Rifle Volunteers'. In his twenties, Frederick had taken quite a keen interest in the family business, particularly the more scientific aspects such as quality control, and he was made a partner in 1867 on the death of his father, with two shares that represented 12½ per cent of the issued capital.[6] But in the long term the mashing of malt and the brewing of beer were not the life for Frederick, who got his intoxication from gambling on the 'the sport of kings' at Ascot, York and on Newmarket Heath. His father had left an estate of £80,000 and Frederick invested his share of the cash element in building up his own string of racehorses, including the famous stallion *Isonomy*. [see PLATE B3] Over the next fifteen years he would become one of the most famous owners in the country, respected for his judgement, admired for his flamboyant betting and no doubt secretly envied by many for his unconventional lifestyle. Probably leaving Lucy at their apartment in Paris, he would return to England for the main events of the flat racing season. Readers who are interested in Frederick Gretton's contribution to this sport are referred to Appendix I.

Back to Lucy and her life in Paris, or rather to the frustration of our knowing very little about the years she spent with the man she often referred to as the 'true love of my life'. In later years she would always treat his birthday as a very special occasion. 'Mrs Gretton, as she became known, was a beautiful young coquette, with direct, impudent speech and a tiny waist, who became expert in Parisian fashions and manners. During their riotous partnership, Gretton gave her many gifts.'[7] [see PLATE B2] Their unconventional relationship meant that socially they were 'cut' by the English aristocracy residing in the city, unlike their French friends for whom the idea of a rich 'milord' and his beautiful young mistress was quite normal and one to be applauded. Paris in the 1870s was coming to terms with a Third Republic after the military disaster of the Franco-Prussian War, which had culminated in the Battle of Sedan and the capture and exile of the Emperor Napoleon III. While the military suffered the legacy of disgrace, there was an explosion of artistic vitality, in music and theatre, in sculpture and particularly in painting. 'The Impressionists' had held their first exhibition in 1874 and artists' studios and galleries became the prime places for the well-to-do of Paris to see and be seen.

It was in the studio of the painter Édouard Detaille, famous for his battle scenes, that Lucy was introduced to Edward Prince of Wales, the man known to his friends as 'Bertie' and later to be crowned as King Edward VII.[8] 'Bertie' was a hugely popular figure in Paris, cheered by the crowds in public and applauded by audiences at the theatre when he appeared in his box arm in arm with his latest mistress. 'From 1877, Bertie kept an apartment in a building on the Avenue de l'Opéra, an address he relished because it was the Right Bank's epicenter of vice, then dubbed by one British aristocratic roué, Lord Hertford, as "the clitoris of Paris".' Lucy never joined the ranks of his intimates like the actress Sarah Bernhardt, but her meeting with 'Bertie' made a lasting impression on her and gave her a deep admiration and respect for the concept of a popular monarchy, one that through a combination of charm and diplomacy could exercise a power and authority beyond that of mere politicians. When, as we will see later, she attended his coronation in 1901, she was not just a mere member of the congregation, but had her own seat among the peers of the realm. Much later in her life she would lavish her devotion for the monarchy on another Prince of Wales, Bertie's glamorous but wayward grandson Edward – with fatal consequences.

Nor was it only in the visual arts that these new expressions of originality were on show in Paris in the 1880s. The same skill and inventive energy was being put into couture dress-making, and into the kitchens of hotels, restaurants and private houses, where chefs were perfecting the classic cuisine for which the French would become famous the world over. Given Frederick Gretton's wealth and flamboyance, he and Lucy probably dined out almost every night before going on to the opera or theatre. Lucy quickly became fluent in French and the glamorous couple would have been welcome guests at the tables of the Paris 'haute-monde', including the many Russian aristocrats who had made Paris their second home. Lucy's biographer Warner Allen was himself a considerable gourmet and a noted expert on wines, but the chapter he wrote about the couple's time in Paris was mere padding, largely given over to his own recollections of Parisian cuisine in the Edwardian era.[9]

It was in the studio of Édouard Detaille that Lucy struck up a lasting friendship with the dynamic Madame de Poles. This eccentric personality, 'one of the most remarkable women in a Paris full of remarkable women' was neither beautiful nor even pretty. She was at least ten years older than Lucy and had started out as a governess, but by the end of the 1870s her salon in the Avenue de Jena was a mecca for painters, poets and writers, the well-bred and the well-heeled, and her chef was renowned. (Madame de Poles is now best remembered for her magnificent collection of furniture and objets d'art that was auctioned on her death in 1927.) She had chosen her lovers not only for their money – she had been the mistress of one of the Meunier brothers, the renowned chocolatiers, as well as a banker in the Rothschild empire – but also for their manners. From her, Lucy learnt that anyone, irrespective of breeding, could, by charm, intelligent conversation and business acuity, achieve anything they ever wished for. It was a lesson that Lucy would put to good use later, though for the time being she just enjoyed being a protégée of one of the great characters of the age.

Then disaster struck. Frederick was back in England in August 1882 when he suffered a stroke and was advised to draw up his will. A telegram to Lucy brought her hotfoot back to London to her lover's bedside at 22 Thurloe Square, South Kensington. The man known to later generations of the Gretton family as 'naughty Uncle Fred', lingered on for a few more weeks but died on November 15. *The Times* recorded: 'One of the most prominent owners of race-horses on the turf … Frederick Gretton had won not less than £120,000 by the different successes of *Isonomy*. He had been ailing for some time, but the rupture of a blood vessel was the cause of his death.'[10]

On New Year's Day 'the most important sale of bloodstock since the disposal of the Duke of Westminster's horses in training' took place at Tattersall's auction ring. 'The attendance was far larger than on that occasion, however, and the extensive yard has never been so inconveniently thronged. The "great unwashed" predominated and their Cockney jabber became so overwhelming that Mr Tattersall had difficulty in making himself heard. It was with great difficulty the various lots could make their way through the mob to come beneath the auctioneer's hammer.'[11] Over two days a total of 55 horses, mares and foals came under the hammer. Perhaps because of the crowded conditions, the prices were generally rated to be very disappointing, with many lots going for less than Frederick had paid to buy them. *Isonomy* was the star item, achieving 9,000 guineas, but even this was less than the 10,000 that had been expected. After the sale, the executors had to trace everything else that Frederick had owned and were staggered by the diversity; houses and stables in different parts of the country, a 283-ton steam yacht at Southampton, several smaller yachts at Cowes and the lease of a shooting lodge in Scotland, quite apart from his shares in the brewery. At Bladon House near Burton the cellar was stocked with over 7,000 bottles of wines and spirits, while there were 2,000 more on the steam yacht. One wonders if Frederick and Lucy had sometimes slipped back across the channel to enjoy time together on board, and whether her experience of such healthy freedom inspired her with an ambition to own, at some time in the future, a luxury steam yacht of her own. She would not be disappointed.

Frederick's will was proved four months later on April 26, showing a total estate of £412,659, a figure reduced to £350,910 after the executors had paid off his debts. He left Lucy 'the clear yearly sum or annuity of six thousand pounds British Sterling per annum during her life, free of legacy duty, income tax and all other duties whatsoever.' This was in addition to a further one thousand pounds per annum that he had already pledged to Lucy by a bond dated 10 April 1880. To his manservant William Pawsey he left an annual life pension of seventy-five pounds. The balance of his estate was to be divided between his two unmarried sisters, with a reversionary interest going to his nephew and nieces, the children of his other sister Mrs Mary Hegan.

In terms of present day (2016) money, adjusting only for inflation, Lucy's legacy was worth approximately £750,000 a year, making her a considerable heiress (see Appendix IV, which may be referred to when 'converting' other quoted sums of money).[12] She was ravishingly beautiful and still only 26 years old, with a complexion that made her look even younger. The world lay at her feet and she set out to conquer it.

Chapter 3

The Toast of London and Mrs Brinckman

Lucy now made a new home in London, inviting her younger sister Florence to live with her at a smart town house that she leased in Portland Place. Here she acquired the trappings of a rich young lady of fashion, taking on a butler, a lady's maid, a footman and a coachman for her two carriages.[1] She became the toast of the town once again, with young men in the Brigade of Guards, the 'stage-door Johnnies' and the bucks of White's Club drinking her health and swooning at her feet. One of her lifelong friends, Eva Woodward, who later married the Irish artist Harry Jones Thaddeus, had known Lucy in Paris and has left an engaging pen portrait of the impact she made.[2]

> She caused a sensation by her extreme youth and beauty. Small, exquisitely made, with a tiny waist and beautiful shoulders, her carriage was superb, her head proudly carried; her taste in dress was infallible, coming up to the highest standards of Parisian elegance. The great couturier Worth once said of her; 'Madame, you say you designed the dress you are wearing yourself – let me tell you that I could not do better myself.' Spontaneous and natural, she possessed the rare gift of wit, which rendered her conversation a delight.

'When I drove into the carriage sweep at Claridges,' Lucy recalled later, 'people climbed up the iron railings to look at me.' She was taken out to dinner at the Trocadero, the Savoy and the Café Royal, to Scott's and Kettner's, though she declined Romano's as being too boisterous. If she was to be escorted to a restaurant she didn't know, she would demand to be told the colour of the decor in advance so that she could chose a dress that was complementary.[3]

She broke young men's hearts, including that of explorer, pioneer aviator and author Henry Landor, grandson of the famous, irascible, poet Walter

Savage Landor. Eva Thaddeus described how he had come to see her in utter despair, threatening to commit suicide because Lucy had refused to marry him (Henry Landor, perhaps still carrying a torch for Lucy, never did marry and was killed in 1925 when he was run over by a bus). Lucy was determined that the man she would marry would have to have a title, or at least be the heir to one. Within nine months she had made her selection, though the young – very young – man she chose already had a rather chequered background in matters of the heart.

Because she was still in Paris at the time, she probably never saw the announcement of an engagement between two members of the English aristocracy that had appeared in the social columns of various newspapers on 11 October 1881:[4]

A marriage is arranged to take place between Theodore Francis Brinckman, the eldest son of Sir Theodore Brinckman Bart. and Miss Honywood, eldest daughter of the late Sir Courtenay Honywood Bart.

The Brinckmans had first arrived in England from Hanover with Baron Brinckman, a nobleman in the retinue of the newly appointed King George I around 1720. He had married Anne Bingley, the granddaughter of a family who had been granted the Manor of Monk Bretton in Yorkshire.[5] Three generations later, in 1842, Theodore Henry Brinckman was created a baronet, and it was his grandson, Theodore Francis born in 1862, who was to be the teenage bridegroom in the above pronouncement. His fiancée, Annie Mabel Honywood, was a couple of years older, but for some reason or other the engagement did not run smoothly. An item in the newspapers on 19 May the following year informed the public that the wedding was not now going to take place before the first of July, only to be followed up by a further notice on June 30 that the marriage had been finally called off. The jilted Annie Honywood would still be a spinster when she died in 1934; her younger sister Violet never married either.

Five months later the young, impulsive Theodore was engaged again, this time to 'Miss Matheson, the daughter of Sir James Matheson of Achany, Sutherlandshire.'[6] Theodore's mother had died when he was 15 and he was craving the love and affection of another woman, one who was preferably a little older than himself. The Brinckman family motto was *Perseverando* and if he had not succeeded on the first occasion he was determined to try again. But within six months that engagement was off as well.[7] One can only guess at the reasons why both commitments had been cancelled, though in the second case there is a possible motive, and that is that he had met Lucy and been utterly captivated by her beauty, her vivacity and her worldly experience. History does not record how, when or where this might have happened but it seems highly probable that it was on some racecourse. Theodore's widowed father, an army officer who had been the MP for York, was well known in racing circles, always with a string of horses in training and often competing against those of Frederick Gretton. Young Theodore had followed his father into the military, gaining a commission in the East Kent Militia (the 'Buffs') and soon had several horses racing in his own colours. He was an enthusiastic cricketer and had been at Lord's cricket ground in July 1880 when his friend Lord Herbert Vane-Tempest had become involved in a drunken brawl with a policeman.[8] He himself was a good bowler, taking eight wickets in a match between his regiment and the West Kents in May 1883 and helping his team to a win by an innings and 25 runs.[9] Lucy, though still grieving over the death of her lover, may well have found this tall, handsome, athletic young army officer, and heir to a title, irresistibly attractive.

On 3 September 1883 Theodore Brinckman, bachelor, of 40 Berkeley Square, was married by special licence to Lucy Radmall in the church of the Holy Trinity, Brompton, in the county of Middlesex. [see PLATE B5] His age is correctly given as 21, but Lucy, a 'spinster of 22 Thurloe Square',[10] declares her age as only 24, a fairly modest understatement compared to some of her later examples of being economical with the truth about her birthday. Her father is stated as having been a 'gentleman', which was certainly an exaggeration, though he seems to have risen up the social ladder to some extent by the time he had died in the parish of St Margarets, Twickenham in 1876. A journalist would later write that young Theodore was 'credited (or discredited according to taste) with having made a romantic match … to an orphan lady, unknown to Society.'[11]

The newlyweds were in Donegal in early October, staying with the Marquis of Conyngham, the family of his late mother, when the Marquis, his brother-in-law and Theodore himself were all struck down with typhoid fever, probably from drinking contaminated water. Theodore immediately returned to his father's house in London and by 30 October his condition was 'progressing favourably'.[12] Not so his companions, who were still dangerously ill.[13] When questioned by the press as to how Theodore had recovered so quickly, Lucy told them that she had promptly dosed him with ENO's liver salts, a fact that the manufacturers made great play of in advertising editorials over the next twelve months.

Their marriage seems to have started off well. Living at Newton in Cambridgeshire, not far from Newmarket, Theodore Brinckman enjoyed the social life typical of the eldest son of a member of the aristocracy, showing off his entrancing new wife at race meetings and the summer season in London, before taking her up to Scotland when 'society' decamped for grouse shooting and deer stalking. The family owned a shooting lodge on the shores of Loch Ericht in Invernesshire and Theodore was a renowned shot, being credited with many excellent stags. Some years later another journalist wrote that Lucy 'was no stranger to the Highlands ... she was there regularly in her youth when she was Mrs Brinckman. She was very popular; at the end of each season she gave a dance in the Newtownmore Hall.'[14] Lucy was financially independent and could indulge her passion for clothes and jewellery. She took up horse riding, and the society photographer Bassano took a portrait of her in formal riding apparel, mounted side-saddle in Hyde Park's Rotten Row.[15] She enjoyed simpler pleasures just as much: 'When I was first married and very much in love,' she later recalled, 'we used to take the steamer from Tower Pier down to Greenwich. There was sure to be a funny Cockney crowd on board, singing the songs I knew as a child, like "Ta-ra-ra-boom-de-ay". It was the cheapest enjoyment I ever had.'[16]

Cracks started to appear in their marriage when she became ill in 1889 and was ordered by her doctors to live abroad for a time. Theodore agreed to go with her but then changed his mind at the last minute. They tried living together again in 1893, this time in Kent, but after only six weeks Theodore announced he was going to stay with some friends in Scotland for a while. He never returned.[17] In December Lucy filed for divorce on the grounds of desertion, adultery and the denial of conjugal rights by her husband, though one suspects that the main reason for the break-up of their marriage was that Lucy had been unable to have children. (Might the explanation possibly be that Lucy had had an abortion when she was with Frederick Gretton in Paris? This is pure speculation.) Theodore, conscious of his pedigree and doubtless under pressure from his father, felt that it was essential for him to have an heir. He was only 31 and still rather immature, and when Lucy had told him of her intention, 'he went down on his knees and wept, begging me not to divorce him.'[18]

But then he did the 'gentlemanly thing'. He booked himself into a hotel in Hastings and, as things were arranged in those days, invited a local girl to join him for the night, the couple being duly discovered in bed together by the chambermaid and a prearranged witness the next morning. On 15 December it was noted that Lucy and her mother had checked in to the Alexandra Hotel, Hastings, for the first hearing of what would be an undefended case,[19] one that was concluded in the Chancery Division of the High Court of Justice in July with Lucy being granted a decree nisi, plus costs.[20] This decree would be made absolute the following January. There were no hard feelings on either side, and Lucy was given the hunting lodge in Scotland as a parting present. She returned there regularly over the years and in 1928, when Loch Ericht was dammed to make a reservoir, it was reported that the road to her shooting lodge would be flooded as a consequence.[21] That autumn, she had to rent Sir John Ramsden's lodge, Ben Alder, 'one of the most expensive deer forests'.[22]

Theodore had, it seems, already chosen his next bride, and within four weeks announced his engagement on 11 February to Miss Mary Frances Linton, daughter of the late Captain J. Wingfield-Linton and his first wife, who was now the Countess of Alyesford.[23] (Ten days earlier, his brother Claud had also become engaged, to a Miss Malthus.) When they were married, by special licence at the church in South Audley St, London, on April 27, there was a sensational interruption. At the moment when the priest asked the congregation if they knew 'any cause or just impediment' why the couple should not be married, a Father Black stood up and shouted out that the marriage was illegal because the bridegroom had been the guilty party in a divorce. A few other 'traditionalists' added their voice to the protest and, according to the press, a 'near riot ensued'.[24] Once Father Black had been evicted by the police on a charge of brawling, the priest in charge had to explain that this might have been correct if the marriage had been authorised by 'banns', but in this case dispensation had been granted by a licence from the Bishop of London and the ceremony was duly concluded. Two days later, the *Evening Telegraph* wrote that 'the Brinckman marriage controversy threatens to assume pretty formidable proportions'. It explained that under the Divorce Act of 1857, no clergyman in Holy Orders was compelled to celebrate the remarriage of a party whose previous marriage had been dissolved on the grounds of misconduct, but that he could not prevent his church being used by another priest whose conscience dictated otherwise, if the bishop had granted a marriage licence. This Act caused acute bitterness among the High Church element who, it was claimed, represented half the clergy and one third of the laity.

Theodore's second marriage was fruitful, the couple's first son being born in 1898 and christened T. Ernest Brinckman just before Theodore was posted with his regiment to the war in South Africa. In this conflict he served with distinction, was appointed a Commander of the Bath and then given command of the garrison on St Helena, which at the time acted as a prison camp for captured Boer soldiers. Here his wife joined him and, in 1904, gave birth to their second son, who was christened Roderick Napoleon – by historical association. Theodore inherited his father's title on the latter's death in 1905, and it is evident that he and Lucy continued to have affectionate regard for each other till the day he died; 'we were good friends ever afterwards,' she claimed. Furthermore, she got on very well with his second wife and seems to have considered their two children almost as her own. (When Theodore's first grandson was born in 1932, Lucy was invited to be a godmother and there is an amusing anecdote about this, but in order to appreciate the relevance it must wait until a later chapter in Lucy's remarkable story.) Unfortunately Theodore's second marriage also ran into trouble and the couple were divorced in 1913, whereupon the ever persevering but erring Theodore married for the third time on 30 April 1913, a French woman named Marie Bergeran. For her, Lucy nursed an unquenchable hatred.[25]

When in later life she reflected on her time with Theodore, she confessed that she had been devoted to him and that he, perhaps seeing her more as a mother substitute, had been equally devoted to her. 'Except at weekends. Then he stayed away and nearly broke my heart. Night after night I cried myself to sleep. I was a little fool then and I ought to have played him at his own game and popped off for the weekend myself, letting him think that I had a lover. There would have been plenty of volunteers! But I was far too good – and far too silly.'[26]

Five years after their final parting she set her sights on the man who was to become her second husband, a peer of the realm and a cousin, two generations removed, of the scandalous roué, adventurer and poet, Lord Byron. That is how he is remembered in England, though in the Balkans he is revered as a hero, a gallant warrior fighting for the cause of Greek independence from Ottoman rule. He had fought bravely in the defence of the town of Messolonghi, though he died in 1824, not in battle, but from septicaemia following inept medical treatment for a fever. He had been the 6th Baron Byron and the title passed first of all to his cousin George Anson Byron (1789–1868) and then, briefly, to the latter's only son who, confusingly for genealogists, bore precisely the same name and died in 1870. The title of 9th Baron thereupon descended on his young nephew, yet another George Byron, but a very different character indeed from his illustrious forebear. Historically he is a ghostlike figure, almost to the point of invisibility. There are no known portraits or photographs of him, nor is he mentioned in any dictionary of national biography. Out of the blue, Lucy was about to rescue him from total obscurity.

Chapter 4

Lady Byron, a Suffragist from Hampstead

Lord George Byron, 9th Baron Byron, had been born in 1855, obtained a Bachelor of Arts degree at Christ Church, Oxford, and was only 15 when he inherited the title from his uncle in 1870. He had at one time been commissioned as a lieutenant in the Essex regiment and perhaps Lucy first met him with Theodore at a regimental ball. Unlike Theodore however, 'Red-nose George' as he was known to his friends, had never even attempted to embark on marriage, but in 1901, at the age of 45, he succumbed to Lucy's charms. It seems that he had wasted away what money he had on gambling and alcohol and two years earlier had been declared bankrupt. So the match suited them both; he was about to marry a beautiful woman of independent means who could keep him in style, and she was going to take a major step up the social ladder. She was in 'delicate health', and their wedding at the church of All Souls, Marylebone on 1 March 1901 was reported as being 'a very quiet one'.[1] Lucy, described on the marriage certificate as 'single, unmarried' and living at 9 Wedderburn Road, Hampstead, the address of her younger sister Florence and her husband Arthur Wrey who attended as witnesses, had given her age as only 36, which they would have known to be a massive underestimate. She was in fact 44.

The couple spent their honeymoon abroad (did she take him to Paris to revisit some of the sites of her youthful adventures with Frederick Gretton?), but they were back in England by May, when they attended the Annual General Meeting of the Essex County Cycling and Athletics Association and 'were greeted with great applause'.[2] Shortly afterwards they went up to Nottingham to visit the Byron family home – Thrumpton Hall. [see PLATE C4] This massive Jacobean-style house, built in rose-coloured brick, had been completed around 1617 for the Pigot family before passing to the Westcombs in 1745. They also owned an estate at Langford near Maldon in Essex and in 1840 Thrumpton Hall, together with its 1,000 acres, four farms and fifteen cottages passed into the possession of 17-year-old Lucy Westcomb, the eldest of three strong-willed sisters. She married George Anson Byron, the 8th Baron and rector of Langford, in 1843, becoming Lady Byron when her husband inherited the title in 1868, and both estates now became Byron family property.

Meanwhile, her younger sister Mary Jane Westcomb had married George Anson Byron's younger brother Frederick Byron, a marriage that would be blessed with two sons and a number of daughters. George Anson Byron would only enjoy his title for two years, dying without issue at the age of 52 in 1870, whereupon the title of 9th Baron passed, not to his brother Frederick who had died at an even younger age in 1861, but to his eldest nephew, the 15-year-old George Byron. George now had his title but not Thrumpton Hall, since the entails of this fine estate gave his aunt, the Dowager Lady Byron, a lifetime tenancy and she would not die until 1912, aged 89. She lavished her attention on the magnificent gardens, particularly noted for their fine chrysanthemums, and opened them every year for a local fete. She was a formidable but popular character in the village, in spite of not agreeing to the opening of a pub, allowing the locals to walk in the park on Sunday afternoons and giving a Christmas party at the Hall for all the children. She remarried in 1878, to her cousin the Rev Philip Douglas, vicar of Thrumpton, and insisted on retaining her title rather than adopting the less glamorous 'Mrs Douglas'. 'She would sit bolt upright in the front pew of the church every Sunday morning with a plump lapdog under the hoops of her skirt and a gold watch in her hand. At midday precisely, even if her husband was in mid-sentence, she thumped the tiled floor with her ebony cane, whereupon the congregation rose for the last hymn while the rector crept back down the pulpit steps.'[3] There were now two Lady Byrons, and one suspects that they did not get on.

George Byron did own Langford Grove in Essex, though most of the land had been sold to pay off his debts, and the newly married couple divided their time between here and a London town house at 4 Clarges Street off Piccadilly, bought, very probably, by Lucy. They were among the nobles invited to the delayed coronation of King Edward VII at Westminster Abbey on 9 August 1902 and Lucy, in spite of her short stature, stood out as 'the most beautiful of all the peeresses in their coronets and ermine robes'. *The*

Times devoted virtually a whole page to the dresses worn at the coronation, noting that 'Lady Byron's kirtle front was draped with old duchess lace, and her jewels were superb. She wore her famous black pearls and the front of her bodice was festooned with rubies and diamonds.'[4] Doubtless the jewels had been bought for her in Paris by Frederick Gretton, and it is interesting that the black pearls were recognised as being special. She obviously had a fascination for these rare items, and, as we will see later, in 1924 she schemed her way into obtaining another string of black pearls that were even larger, even more glamorous and very, very expensive indeed. The Irish artist and court painter Henry Jones Thaddeus, whose wife Eva had known Lucy from her time in Paris and remained one of her closest friends,[5] was captivated by the sight of her and, although he never completed the portrait he planned, he sent Lucy his preliminary, mixed-media sketch two years after the event. [see PLATE C5]

Lucy, apparently on her own, was up in the Scottish Highlands in September as the guest of one of her greatest friends, the controversial novelist known to the public as Marie Corelli. Just two years older than Lucy, Marie had been born in Bayswater as the illegitimate daughter of the journalist Charles Mackay and a young widow called Mary Mills. The couple did later marry when Mackay's wife died, and the child, christened Mary after her mother, showed an early and precocious talent as a pianist. As a teenager, she was educated at a convent school in France, and in the 1880s launched herself onto the London and provincial stages as a singer and concert pianist under the name of Marie Corelli. However, the reviews of her performances were generally not very favourable, so by 1885 she had turned to journalism and the following year she published her first novel, *A Romance of Two Worlds*. Once again the critics did not like it, but its background of pseudo-science and mysticism appealed to the growing popular interest in spiritualism and the occult, and it sold well. This was a time when séances and the Ouija board were absorbing the interest of more adventurous members of the middle class. Oscar Wilde told her that she could 'certainly tell of marvellous things in marvellous ways'.[6] A series of novels followed and in 1893 her daring fictionalisation of the crucifixion story, *Barabbas: a Dream of the World's Tragedy*, became a best seller.

Captain Farqharson, the proprietor of Invercauld in the Highlands of Scotland, had invited Marie Corelli to bring a group of her friends to attend the annual Braemar Games as his guests in the Royal Enclosure. The society correspondent on the *Gentlewoman* magazine, reporting on the games the day the King and Queen attended, mentioned all the famous people in the Royal Enclosure, including Lucy and other titled ladies and gentlemen – but not Marie Corelli.[7] This snub caused Marie deep offence and she wrote to the editor in high dudgeon, pointing out that Lady Byron had only been there because of her personal invitation. The editor's published reply was to the effect that, as far as he could gather from the few of her books he had managed to read, 'Miss Corelli has gloried in the contempt she has expressed for the press and the snobs who seek notoriety thereby.'[8] It was hardly an apology.

Marie had bought the fine house, Mason Croft, in Stratford-upon-Avon in 1899, from where she masterminded her campaign to preserve William Shakespeare's heritage. At the time this was not universally popular in the business community, since she managed to prevent several buildings associated with the Bard from being pulled down for redevelopment. She also purchased Harvard House and had it restored as a meeting place for American visitors. In November 1902 it was noted that 'Lord and Lady Byron stayed on a brief visit'.[9] By then Marie's novels were making at least £10,000 a year from sales worldwide, on top of which she was earning high fees from her journalism. This was a real eye-opener for Lucy, not because of the money but the realisation that a woman, with a very similar background to her own, could have her radical opinions aired to a wide audience through newspapers and journals. Lucy was beginning to take a keen interest in support of the Women's Suffrage movement, the campaign for women to have the vote on equal terms to men. Such supporters, both male and female, were known as 'Suffragists'; the term 'Suffragette' only emerged later and was used, often in a derogatory sense, to apply to the militants who took the law into their own hands and campaigned through civil disobedience. It was, however, a subject on which the two friends took opposing stands, with Marie Corelli campaigning vehemently on behalf of the Anti-Suffrage League because she believed that any move by women in the direction of equality would undermine the authority of their men folk.[10]

Lucy, as we will see shortly, would be one of the foremost people to appreciate the future potential for radiotelegraphy, so perhaps this is an appropriate moment to mention a remarkable and visionary experiment of 1911, the precursor of the 'mobile phone'. One of the railways that served Marie Corelli's adopted home town at that time was the Stratford-upon-Avon & Midland Junction Railway, and the board of this company had invited an inventor called Hans von Kramer to demonstrate his 'Railophone' device which used 'wireless inductive telegraphy'. The equipment was duly set up in one of the company's railway carriages. The Mayor was then invited to join the short train and sit beside the apparatus and he was able to receive a telephone message on the move, one sent from the telegraph office in the centre of the town – by Marie Corelli.[11]

In December, George and Lucy attended the sumptuous ball given by the Earl and Countess of Warwick to celebrate the debut of their daughter and the return of their eldest son from South Africa.[12] But we know virtually nothing of their life together over the next few years until Lucy ran into a staff problem. 'Clement Norman, 37, butler to Lady Byron, pleaded guilty to stealing a champagne opener and other articles from his employer. He had been sacked in February when it was discovered that he had forged her signature on a cheque, pawned a silver picture-frame and sundry other articles.'[13] It was from the address in Clarges Street that the press recorded George and Lucy had left for a visit to Thrumpton in May 1908 to attend the funeral of his mother.[14] Lucy herself was getting more and more involved in women's charities as well as the burgeoning movement for female suffrage; she became a principal sponsor of a London and Paris dress exhibition and later an exhibition of Women's Work at Olympia.[15] In July 1909, the couple attended the 'brilliant spectacle' of a garden party given by King Edward's scandalous mistress Daisy, Countess of Warwick, at her family home of Easton Lodge, Great Dunmow in Essex.[16]

Compared to Mayfair, Hampstead, with its romantic Heath and its growing colony of artists and writers, was much more to Lucy's liking, so around 1909 she sold 4 Clarges Street and bought a charming Georgian house with a large garden, hidden in woodland that was not far from the famous Bull & Bush inn.[17] It was originally called Myrtle Lodge but Lucy renamed it Byron Cottage [see PLATE C1], and while she occupied the main part of the house, her husband was more or less banished to some small rooms at the back, behind the green baize door. He shared this part of the house with a butler and cook, Mr and Mrs Maclean, plus a parlourmaid.[18] Reminiscing about this period in her life to Wentworth Day, she described George as 'a nice man, my dear, quite harmless, but I think I terrified him.' And indeed she certainly did, but he retained a dog-like devotion to her throughout his life, while his clergyman brother Charles (later the 10th Baron Byron) 'had the greatest liking for his volcanic sister-in-law'.[19] Just after they moved into Byron Cottage, a new church for Hampstead, St Jude-on-the-Hill, was designed by Sir Edwin Lutyens and Lucy presented the silver trowel used in laying the foundation stone.[20]

The coronation of King George V in 1910 brought representatives from all the royal households of Europe and princes from all over the British Empire to partake in a celebration of imperial majesty the like of which would never be seen again. 'Among the proud aristocracy of Britain, ancient of line, blue of blood, resplendent in ermine, coronets and tiaras, none wore their robes with more dignity and none looked more beautiful than the 9th Lady Byron.'[21]

But behind her still youthful-looking beauty her body was not at all robust. As a friend from her Paris days described it, 'she could not lead a life of strenuous gaiety, and was happier in her home … where she received her friends, entertaining eminent personages, great actresses – like Réjane – poets, painters, musicians and her neighbour the ballet-dancer Pavlova.'[22] The guests at her soirées were captivated by Lucy's acute mind, her sharp wit and her down-to-earth, outspoken views on everything. She was an excellent listener and eager to catch up on her lack of any formal education in literature and the arts. The little girl from Kennington had used her charm to plan her way to the very pinnacle of the aristocracy without a touch of snobbery, and it was her force of character alone that now drew the famous and talented to enjoy her company. They in turn would be rewarded by the occasional gift of spontaneous generosity. She became a champion of her husband's notorious forebear, whose reputation she saw as being unjustly besmirched by Victorian prudery. One visitor whom she always welcomed was her former husband Theodore Brinckman. He would have been amused, had he ever found out, that Lucy had taken the opportunity of moving into the Hampstead artistic set to reduce her 'official' age by another considerable ratchet. According to the 1911 census, she admitted to being only 40 years old. She could certainly get away with this, as witnessed by the stunning portrait photographs taken of her around this time by Bassano. [see PLATES B6 & B7]

She began to take a serious interest in politics, and the seeds of her intense patriotism, which would later blossom into a forthright crusade, were sown and nurtured. She developed a great admiration for the men who had forged the British Empire in the previous century, soldiers like General Wolfe and Robert Clive, and those of her contemporaries who were carrying on the tradition, like Cecil Rhodes and General Kitchener. Lord 'Bobs' Roberts VC, who had finally rescued British pride from the ignominious blunders of the Boer War, sat and had tea with Lucy while telling her of his past exploits in Afghanistan, when he had redeemed to some extent the errors of ignorant politicians. She relished every work by the 'voice of the Empire', Rudyard Kipling, who, along with Lewis Carroll, became a frequent visitor.[23] Another of the men she met and greatly admired was the unconventional, frog-like Admiral 'Jackie' Fisher, who had had the vision to commission the 'Dreadnought' battleships, vessels that would revolutionise the Royal Navy and help ensure its domination of the oceans in the defence of the country she cherished with an increasingly patrician concern. Little did she suspect that she herself would play out a somewhat similar role thirty years later.

Lucy embraced the 'Votes for Women' campaign not only with financial support but with her own brand of fervent oratory, driving to Hampstead Heath on weekend afternoons, standing up in her carriage and haranguing the visitors with pleas that they should write to their MPs to demand 'justice'. She spoke firmly in short sentences and enjoyed brisk repartee with any man who disagreed with her. Hecklers quailed before her scorn. At the end of her speech, she would announce: 'Now I am going back to my house to enjoy a cup of tea. You go home and think seriously about what I have said.'[24]

George's formidable aunt, still calling herself Lady Byron, finally died in May 1912, leaving her estates not to George but to his younger brother, the shy, capricious, old-fashioned bachelor cleric 'Charlie' Byron, and the next stage in the history of Thrumpton almost dissolves into farce, as wittily recounted by the present (2016) owner, Miranda Seymour.[25] In spite of being nearly 60, 'Charlie' was quite a catch, and two women who set their cap at

him were Ismay FitzRoy, widow of the Rev Lord Charles FitzRoy, the fourth
son of the 7th Duke of Grafton, and her plain, awkward daughter Anna.

> Forced to decide whether flirtatious Ismay or bashful Anna would
> make the better chatelaine for his new home, he dithered and declined
> to commit himself to either. Ismay became imperious; Anna, seeing
> her last chance of marriage slipping away, grew tearful. Anna's elder
> brother decided to take the initiative. Escorting his nervous sister to
> Nottinghamshire, Charles FitzRoy [later the 10th Duke of Grafton]
> rang the bell at Thrumpton Hall, greeted his host, ordered him to take
> Anna into the billiard room – and locked the door. It was winter; the
> billiard room was chilly. Charlie Byron, growing a little shrill, demanded
> that he should be released. Charles FitzRoy sat still and waited. An
> hour later, Anna emerged an engaged woman.[26]

In September 1912, the *Daily Express* printed a letter from Lucy 'denouncing
the violent treatment of Suffragists by a Welsh mob', but she fell out with
the leaders of the aggressive arm of the movement, like the Pankhursts
and Mrs Pethick-Lawrence. In October she published an open letter to
Christabel Pankhurst under the heading 'A scolding for Christabel', urging
her to abandon the 'suicidal policy' of militant Suffragette methods.[27]

> As long as you adopted amusing methods, you advertised the cause and
> steadily gained support from all classes; but alas! you were not content
> when all was going so well. Some evil spirit whispered in your ear
> "Militancy", and what has been the result? Since that fatal day when
> everyone was horrified to hear of refined women descending to the level
> of hooligans by smashing the windows of innocent shopkeepers, the
> word 'Suffragette' became a synonym for a vulgar, violent virago. The
> cause you love is turned into a ribald jest for the mob to mock at and
> the refined to shrink from. Leave violence to the vulgar and try tactful
> tactics once more.

She then added a postscript, a challenge that became Lucy's best remembered
contribution to the cause.

If you will induce 670 of your friends each to buy a parrot and teach it to say 'Votes for Women!' by the 16th of next December, I will promise to supply the red, white and blue cages for them and send them to every Member of Parliament, wishing them a happy New Year – if women get the vote. Don't you think that this might prove as persuasive as setting fire to their houses?

It never happened, of course, and the following summer Emily Davidson committed suicide by throwing herself under the feet of the King's horse at the Epsom Derby. The police stepped in and sequestered the funds of the Women's Social and Political Union to pay for the damage the Suffagettes had caused generally, and in response to an appeal for new funds Lucy contributed £10.[28] But when Christabel Pankhurst's mother Emmeline was later thrown into prison and had severe personal financial problems, Lucy, even though she disapproved of her methods, was the first to contribute generously to a subscription for her benefit. The amount was never revealed but is believed to have been several thousand pounds.[29]

In January 1914 Lucy wrote a foreword to an interesting pamphlet written by an Indian psychology postgraduate, S. M. Mitra, including the following paragraphs:[30]

Every thoughtful English-woman must feel proud that the British educational system in our great Oriental Empire has produced such a careful student of the British constitution as Mr Mitra. The more one reflects upon psychological forces, the more one feels that woman's intuitive power is as mighty as man's much-emphasised material strength, and that a Parliament in which woman's voice is not sufficiently represented cannot be the microcosm of the nation.

The New Year of 1914 also kicked off with some concerns in the press about the impact of the latest import from Argentina – the 'Tango'. Few people believed that this erotic dance would ever find its way into the ballroom repertoire, the general feeling seeming to be that it was just a flash in the pan and that 'its lascivious delights will not last long'. The Argentine ambassador in Paris explained through the columns of the *Gentlewoman* magazine that in his country 'the Tango was confined to low-class establishments and that Society leaders never contemplated it, owing to its indelicate character.' There were some who called it the 'Dance of Moral Death', fearing that its increasing popularity would seriously undermine the morals of young ladies. The Duchess of Norfolk was quoted as saying that 'the dance was foreign to English nature and ideals'. Lady de Ramsey 'strongly disapproved and would never let it be danced in her house.' 'If it is anything like the horrible dances of negroid origin which have for the moment ruined English ballrooms,' wrote Lady Beatrice Wilkinson, 'then I strongly object to it,' while Lady Layland-Barratt considered it was 'an immoral and suggestive dance altogether, impossible for any girl of refinement and modesty.' Lucy, however, thought this was all the most dreadful humbug, writing to the same journal to say that the dance was merely 'a romp, the physical expression of the age, the result of undisciplined, unrestrained youthful exuberance. As to its being suggestive, "to the pure all things are pure".' She added a final dig against stuffiness with her opinion that it was far preferable to the game of bridge.[31]

Lucy continued to make generous contributions to charities, including £100 that she sent to the Hospital for Ladies of Limited Means in Osnaburgh Street, London, a nursing home that had been set up by a cousin of Theodore, the Rev Arthur Brinckman. She returned to the political arena in March 1914 when Spottiswoode and Co published a contribution from her in their quarterly journal *The 19th Century and After*. A review of the contents stated that there were 'several well-informed articles dealing with problems of national security, and the movement for fuller recognition of the claims of women in the State, including one by Mrs Archibald Colquhoun on "The Superfluous Woman; Her Cause and Cure". Also another by Lady Byron, proposing "A cabinet Minister for Women".'[32] But the cause she had espoused with such wit and vigour was forced to take a back seat when the whole world was thrown into turmoil that August by the outbreak of war, and Lucy turned her attention to finding practical ways of serving her country.

Chapter 5

The Angel of Mercy

In September 1914 Lucy was appointed President of the War Babies and Mother's League, an organisation set up 'to administer help, advice, assistance and care of the mothers of babies of men serving our country.' It was noted that Lord Kitchener and Lord Roberts VC had written to her wishing the scheme every success, while 'Mrs Winston Churchill had sent a box of baby clothes.'[1] The following month Lucy donated £100 to Princess Mary's Fund for Xmas Gifts for the Troops.[2] Friends returning from the Western Front had told Lucy that there was a shortage of any type of sports equipment behind the lines and the means of lighting cigarettes for the men in the trenches, so she bought and despatched a consignment of footballs, plus 100,000 wooden boxes of matches, each inscribed with the words 'A box of matches for our Matchless Troops from Lady Byron.'[3]

1915 saw Lucy turn her energy towards support for several new causes including the 'Great Britain to Poland and Galicia Fund'. This charity had been initiated by a letter to *The Times* from Baroness Bariatinski, pointing out that while public attention was focussed on the misery of the people of Belgium, there was an even greater humanitarian disaster in her home country, one that was many times larger.[4] 'Three times did the savage hordes of the Kaiser traverse Poland, pillaging everything they could take and burning what they could not. In Galicia, the retreating Austrian armies, even more merciless in their rage of defeat, did likewise. Cities and towns have been destroyed … all horses and cattle have been taken … no corn or potatoes left … millions of sufferers homeless and lacking food.'[5] The charity had been set up with Lucy as the chairman and its fundraising headquarters at Byron Cottage. Baroness Bariatinski expressed her especial gratitude for the involvement of 'Lady Byron, a name sacred to all Russians, and especially Poles, as that of a noble knight … who died fighting for the rights and liberty of small nations.'[6] By April, Lucy could report that a deputation from her committee was leaving for Russia, escorted by a representative of the Red Cross, 'with the first fruits of the fund, £3,000 and a considerable quantity of clothing'.[7]

The fund remained active throughout 1916, typified by advertising campaigns in the national press.[8] Lucy wrote:

The devastation of Poland is one of the greatest tragedies of the war. People who were once well-to-do stand in silent, anxious crowds waiting their turn as the soup-kitchens pass along. Thousands are living in trucks and sleeping on the stone floors of railway stations. Women with children in their arms have walked hundreds of miles to escape the horrors of German invasion. To all who feel compassion for the victims – broken men and women and starving children – an earnest appeal is made to send what help they can.

It was stressed that no contributions passed through German or Austrian hands, all money collected being sent to the Russo-Asiatic Bank in Petrograd (St Petersburg). She tapped her friends for funds, on one occasion taking a large party for lunch at Claridges, including the Consul General in London for Montenegro; also the eccentric Sir Squire Bancroft, the renowned actor-manager noted for his explanation that his fine health and fitness was the result of half an hour's skipping everyday – preferably backwards.[9] The chief commissioner of the fund from 1915 to 1919, operating largely on the ground under the auspices of the Russian Red Cross, was a man called John Pollock, the heir to Sir Frederick Pollock Bart.[10] He and Lucy got to know each other well through working together on the fund and many years in the future, as will be recounted in a later chapter, they would go into business together.

Like everyone else in Britain, Lucy was deeply moved by the sight of thousands of wounded men returning from the battlefields as ambulance trains disgorged their gruesome cargo at London's railway stations. The men were often attended by young nurses who had been treating their wounds in dressing stations behind the front lines in France. Matters were even worse on the eastern front. From a hospital in Serbia, Flora Sandes, an untrained nurse with the Serbian Red Cross, wrote in November 1914 that the wounded arrived by 'bullock wagon with only their first bloodstained field dressings on their wounds. Many of the worst wounded died on the way, and those that did arrive were in a terrible condition …' Three months later she arrived in Valjevo, Serbia, with Emily Simmons, a trained nurse. They found 'indescribable conditions … There was not nearly enough hospital accommodation, not nearly enough beds, and soldiers were lying in their dirty uniforms, straight as they came from the trenches, swarming with lice, all over the floors of the hospitals, on the floors of the hotels, in the shops, out in the streets, lying on the bare boards or a little filthy straw, with no blankets, in the depth of the rigorous Serbian winter …' In one hospital they discovered there was no surgeon to perform all the necessary operations, 'so as there was nothing else for it, we screwed up our courage and bit by bit we finally ended by doing the operations ourselves …'[11]

It was for these brave young women, often completely traumatised by what they had to endure, that Lucy felt particular sympathy and her heart went out to those who had no family at home to return to for recuperation from their haunting experiences. In 1915 she acquired another large house in Hampstead, 11 Tanza Road, just off Parliament Hill, which had a beautiful garden with access onto the Heath. [see PLATES C2 & C3] She paid for a cook-housekeeper and a Belgian maid. She furnished the house with comfortable beds, soft pillows and the finest linen sheets; she provided beautiful tableware and cutlery and had all the interior walls painted pale blue, to match a large blue porcelain bird in the sitting room that had been donated by Lady Bancroft. The property became known as the 'Bluebird's Nest', a haven of peace and comfort from the horrors of the war.[12]

Lucy maintained her campaigning interest in the Suffragists, and in July she was one of the women, among a list of famous names like the contralto Clara Butt, who led a march to present a petition to the Prime Minister Lloyd George, urging him to allow women to work in munitions factories if they wanted to, and recruit them to do other useful work for the war effort. Mrs Pankhurst told a correspondent from *The Times* that many thousands of women from across the whole country had said they wanted to partake, but had been frustrated by the lack of cooperation from the overstretched railway companies.

We want every woman in London to join in. It is only right that our Allies should know that we are willing, but we want the Germans to know also, and we have every reason to believe that every unexpected reserve we can bring against them must have a depressing effect on their morale. We want the Government to recognise us as just such a reserve and to train us so that we may be brought to our highest pitch of usefulness.[13]

The successful outcome did as much to give women a sense of enfranchisement as actually having the vote. Their sense of achievement in doing men's jobs would give them a yearning for greater independence and inform their attitudes to traditional social and political beliefs in the post-war years. However, the employment of women in the police force was a more contentious issue. Lucy was on the platform of a public meeting held by the Criminal Law Amendment committee at the Mansion House in March 1916 under the chairmanship of the Lord Mayor of London. He explained that the Metropolitan Police had successfully experimented with unofficial female patrols and that making their status official 'could be of great service in certain cases where women and children were concerned, and could release men, even if only a few, for the Army.' He urged the Government to look into the matter seriously, while admitting that the extent of any agreement would have to be determined 'by the qualified authority'.[14]

Lord Bryce, the former British Ambassador to Washington and author of the report into German atrocities to civilians in Belgium, made a speech that autumn in which he said that 'we must not hate the Germans, because to indulge in revenge would be to sow the seeds of future wars.' In the light of later events following the Treaty of Versailles, this was perhaps remarkably far-sighted though at the time it was branded as 'curious'. Lucy was outraged and flew into print. 'Germany has waxed rich and powerful on British Free Trade and has been able to pick up money to buy armaments to kill the British. If Lord Bryce met a mad dog, would he consider that killing it was an act of revenge?'[15] On a lighter note, she had also been infuriated to learn that the Poor Law trustees in the town of Thetford had decided that margarine was not good enough to serve in the local workhouse. 'I have eaten margarine myself for several months and many of my lady friends have done likewise since the war began.'[16]

In November Lucy wrote to the editor of *The Times* about another of her charitable campaigns:[17]

Sir – I receive letters every day from commanding officers of His Majesty's ships and Regiments telling me that the most insistent and never-satisfied need of the troops and sailors is for socks. To have to wear dirty socks, stiff with mud and slime, is a discomfort often felt to be the last straw of their misery. May I ask your readers to help me meet these demands, which I am so anxious not to refuse? When money is sent, orders for socks are given to schools for the blind, who knit beautifully and are grateful to be enabled to do their bit.

The campaign was certainly not restricted to schools for the blind; prep-school boys were also encouraged to knit scarves for the troops.[18] Byron Cottage was the headquarters for all her campaigns and the streams of visitors who came to give donations or attend committee meetings were doing her carpets no good at all. So when she found a product that helped solve the problem, she was happy to allow the manufacturers to quote her unsolicited testimonial in their advertisements: 'I have found that Chivers Soap has answered well in removing all grease from my carpets. Lady Byron.'[19]

George Byron's only sister, the Hon Margaret Alice Byron, had died in May 1916 and ten months later, at the age of only 62, amiable, dominated, 'Red-nose' George himself faded away on 30 March 1917, his title passing to his clergyman brother Charles. When, sometime later, unkind insinuations about Lucy's luxurious lifestyle were aired, she made it known that 'she had only bought two new dresses since the war began and then only because I had to attend two funerals.'[20] Lucy may have dutifully mourned the death of the man who had made her a peeress, though it is most unlikely that she was in any way broken-hearted. She donated £100 to the War Veteran's Association with the request that a bedroom be dedicated to the memory of Lord Byron – not her late husband but his valiant, poetic forebear.[21]

In fact she was considerably more upset by the news that the Russian Royal family had been deposed the previous month, and she became positively alarmed by the Bolshevik takeover in October. Then the following July came the shattering announcement that the entire Royal family had been murdered in cold blood at Ekaterinburg, and from this moment she vowed that she would campaign as vigorously against the spread of communism as she had championed the cause of her country against Germany. Russia signed a peace treaty at Brest-Litovsk with her one time sworn enemy in March 1918, allowing the Germans to transfer vast numbers of troops from the Eastern Front for their counter-offensive in France during April. It was largely through luck and some help from the fresh, but inexperienced, American forces being thrown into the front line that this last-gasp operation was resisted and contained. It was a close run thing. In October, it became known that the Germans had contacted President Wilson via neutral embassies with some sort of a peace proposal. Lucy, in her straightforward, down to earth manner sent the President a blunt telegram.[22]

> Dear President Wilson. I am only a woman, but if I were you I should return the document with one vulgar but forceful little word written across it – PIFFLE!

After that, largely due to the impact on the battlefield of mass formations of tanks – the 'land battleships' that Winston Churchill had advocated so strenuously – the Allies could return to the offensive and enforce the armistice of 11 November 1918. In a railway carriage parked on a siding in the Forest of Compiegne, the official document was put before the German delegation for signature. It was in effect an acknowledgement of conditional surrender. As the British people celebrated the end of hostilities and could, they hoped, look forward to a lasting peace and a return to normality and prosperity, Lucy was utterly exhausted but no doubt satisfied with what she had contributed to the Allied cause. And indeed the nation had recognised her efforts in a most striking way. In August 1917, King George V had decreed the formation of a new Order of Chivalry, the Most Noble Order of the British Empire. There were to be five levels of distinction, from Knight Commander through OBE to MBE. The second senior tier, Knights, included just five women who were to adopt the title of Dame of the British Empire, DBE. Headed by the Dowager Marchioness of Dufferin and Ava, the citations included

Mrs Alfred Lyttelton for her work on the War Refugees Committee, Mrs Charles Lee, member of the Education Committee and Mayor of Oldham, and the Marchioness of Londonderry for founding the Women's Legion. Fifth and last on the list was Lucy, the impish child and one-time chorus girl from Newgate Street, her contributions being too many to enumerate individually. [see PLATE C6]

Chapter 6

A Swing to the Right and
Seducing the 'Robber Baron'

Even before the end of the war, there were rumblings of discontent among supporters of the Conservative party who believed that Britain's prestige in the world was open to serious threats, not only from outside and but more particularly from within the country itself. So the British Empire Union had been founded on 1916 on the basis of the earlier Anti-German League, with the stated objectives of consolidating the British Empire by stimulating trade within its members and reversing the free trade doctrine, altering the naturalisation laws effectively to outlaw or intern all persons considered as 'aliens', and to promote a programme of educational propaganda throughout the country in support of a more vigorous prosecution of the war. These fears were enhanced by the Bolshevik revolution in Russia in 1917. When the 'Great War' finally ended, the British Empire Union turned its attention to the increasing economic influence of America with its anti-imperialist attitudes, and the consequences of extending the voting franchise that would inevitably increase support for the Labour party. Therefore those on the right of the political spectrum felt there was a need for more radical solutions to Britain's future social and economic problems than those offered by traditional, some would say old-fashioned, Conservative politicians. In 1919, the British Empire Union effectively merged with the Economic League, founded by the MP William Hall (director of Naval Intelligence 1914–19) with the aims of promoting free enterprise and the points of view of businessmen and industrialists, while keeping track on communist and left-wing organisations and individuals. It was noted that Lucy was an active supporter of the British Empire Union, because it was 'an organisation for the promotion of peace and prosperity'.[1] The same article argued that it might be necessary to form a paramilitary unit to combat mass strike action in the country in case the effectiveness of the police, and the loyalty of the army, was undermined.

Some of the British Empire Union's worst fears came to a head in August 1920 when the Labour Party announced that it would call a general strike if Britain gave active support for the 'White' Russians in their civil war against the Bolshevik 'Reds'. Then, in September, another form of union, the Miners' Trade Union, announced that they were calling their members out on strike, causing the Government to form an emergency committee under the chairmanship of Sir Eric Geddes MP, the first Minister of Transport and previously the First Lord of the Admiralty. He warned the public that, if the strike was prolonged, it might be necessary to introduce food rationing.[2]

The Suffragist movement swung into action. On 22 September a conference was convened in Westminster Central Hall by the National Political League, the new name of the Women's Freedom League that had originally been founded in 1911 to further social and political reforms on an all-party basis. 'Women are to take the field against the miners,' stated a newspaper headline, adding that, paradoxically as it might seem, 'miners' wives will form the biggest battalion of the fighting forces.'[3] The article went on to say that 'Lady Byron is lending the full weight of her influence … and has called on every woman to refuse to cook, clean and cater for the strikers.' 'I feel,' Lucy is quoted as saying to a reporter, 'that the time has come for women of all classes to unite solidly and to demand that the Government brings in a law making all strikes illegal. The intolerable tyranny of the comparative few over the many has become unbearable, and no self-respecting nation should tolerate it any longer. The impertinence of the whole thing is that Mr Smillie, the strike dictator, has been beaten seven times in seeking election to parliament.' Her disdain for the tactics of militant Suffragettes was confirmed when, on the day the strike actually started, 16 October, Sylvia Pankhurst was charged with sedition after calling on workers to loot the London Docks. Sylvia had been a great admirer, and possible lover, of the original leader of the Labour Party, Keir Hardy, and had been a supporter of the Russian Revolution, visiting the country and meeting Lenin. She had also been one of the leading supporters at the formation of the British Communist Party in July 1920, an organisation secretly funded with a donation of £50,000 by Lenin himself.

By 25 October, the threat to law and order had reached the point when the Government moved a second reading of the Emergency Powers Bill, but fortunately enactment became unnecessary when the strike was called off on 3 November after only a small minority of Trades Union members voted for its continuation. The strike had threatened to bring the country to its knees and it undermined many people's trust in the effectiveness of the whole democratic process. The golden vision of a return to peace and prosperity was seriously tarnished, but in the short term Lucy had other, personal matters to occupy her. She was still a wealthy woman from Frederick Gretton's will trust but she needed more money for the next stage of her political adventures, and so, as she turned 64, she was on the lookout for another husband.

By all accounts Sir Robert Houston was a most unpleasant character. He was known as the 'Robber Baron' or 'Black Bob', a reference to his blue-black hair and beard and his dark, piercing eyes. [see PLATE B8] He had a reputation for being a ruthless businessman and was tainted by allegations that he had made his fortune by running a fleet of 'coffin ships' out to South Africa on behalf of the Government during the Boer War, ships that sailed overloaded with troops in conditions more reminiscent of the slave trade. He was a confirmed bachelor, even a misogynist, believing that women, if they had any opinions whatsoever, should keep them strictly to themselves. On the other hand, he must have also had some hidden merits because he could inspire devoted loyalty in a few male friends and the men who captained his ships.

He had been born in Liverpool in 1853, the son of a marine engineer from Renfrewshire, and worked his way up in the shipping industry from a shipyard apprentice, via hands-on roles in ship construction to the stage where he was appointed as superintendent engineer of an Atlantic steamship company at the age of 21. On the death of his father in 1877, he invested his inheritance in a packet steamer and in 1880 he founded R.P. Houston Company, chartering ships for trade with the East Indies. A shift of emphasis to South America in 1884 saw him construct the first refrigerated ship to bring beef to England from Argentina, while passenger services to New York were added the following year. In 1898 he formed the British & South American Steam Navigation company with a fleet of six ships. He also speculated on the Stock Exchange, not always successfully; after his death, a journalist wrote that 'he had talked to a man who knew the late Sir Robert Houston all his life, and remembers a time when he sat up with him all night because he believed he had been ruined by his investment in a South African goldmine and it was thought he might shoot himself.'[4] It was the start of the Boer War that completely restored, and later increased, his fortune. He alone among shipowners anticipated that the conflict would go on far longer than originally envisaged and that there would be a huge demand for the transport of men and animals, so he took up a massive position in forward freightage which he could unwind on to the military authorities at a huge profit when freight rates duly went sky high. His first move had been to supply fodder for the cavalry, buying up all available supplies of hay and oats in the UK and then shipping them out to Cape Town, where he sold them to the army at what one paper described as 'famine rates'.

Houston became well known in the law courts, never hesitating to resort to litigation when he thought his business rivals were trying to do him down. His frequent briefings of the brilliant young barrister F.E. Smith during the 1890s led to a close friendship that was much commented on at the time, in spite of or perhaps because of the twenty-year age gap. Indeed, when Houston died in 1926 and there was speculation as to who would benefit from his will, Lord Birkenhead (as he was by then) was the first name on many people's lips.[5]

It was politics that became his consuming passion and he managed to get himself elected as the Member of Parliament for the Liverpool West Toxteth constituency in 1892. He was an ardent, outspoken Tory and a scourge of the emerging Labour party. Whether his party was in power or opposition he would prove to be an aggressive thorn in the side of the Admiralty when it came to matters concerning the Government's handling of maritime matters. 'He regarded every official of that department as an ignorant, incompetent ass.'[6] Typical was an outburst in 1916: 'In a remarkable speech, the Rt Hon Robert Houston severely criticised the Admiralty for their misuse of requisitioned merchant vessels, adding that a night or two previously the Department had threatened him in the House.'[7] He followed this up with a letter to Lord Charles Beresford, a retired admiral – once expected to be appointed as Admiral of the Fleet until a fall-out with Admiral Beatty – and

MP for Portsmouth on the threat from German U-boats and the Admiralty's failure to put adequate armament on merchant ships to defend themselves.[8]

> Dear Topmate, I look to you and my old shipmate Tommy Bowles to bear a hand in waking up the people to the deadly danger that threatens them and to rouse them to action, for nothing short of high-explosive shells well planted in Downing Street, Whitehall and Westminster will rouse this Coalition Government from their 'twilight sleep'.
>
> If this country is not to be brought to the verge of starvation in a few months, we must arm our merchantmen, for the best kind of defence is attack, and *start out to hunt the submarine*.
>
> PS. There will be no happier man in England than myself when I have paid the last £2,000 for the fiftieth German submarine sunk by a British merchant vessel.

Another practical example of his contribution during the Great War was his financial support in raising and equipping a second battalion for King Edward's Horse regiment, a cavalry unit originally founded in 1910 as the 4th County of London Imperial Yeomanry.[9]

Houston claimed his own particular seat on the front row of the House of Commons – like Lord Randolph Churchill and Sir Charles Dilke before him and Dennis Skinner in later years – and woe betide any other member who had the presumption to try and sit there. His three particular cronies, whom he lavishly entertained to lunch every day when the House was sitting, held political views that could not be further from his own. Two of them were Liberals: 'Jim' Hogge, who sat for Edinburgh East and was a supporter of the Women's Suffrage movement, and William Mather Rutherford, who had originally been elected as the Member for Lancashire North-West and later became 'one of the most intransigent and pertinacious of the anti-Lloyd-George Liberals'. The third member of the coterie was the rabble-rousing journalist and Irish Nationalist MP T.P. O'Connor, who held the only Irish Home-Rule seat in England, representing Liverpool Scotland from 1885, a neighbouring constituency to Houston's with a very large Irish population. Houston's 'protegé' F.E. Smith controversially, and perhaps unwisely, contested the Liverpool Scotland seat in 1905 on an Irish Unionist ticket, and although he was not successful it caused a furore on the streets and rattled their friendship.

Houston was a workaholic, and 'in spite of his great wealth he worked like a galley slave, sometimes ten, twelve or fourteen hours a day.'[10] This arduous regime started to undermine his health and by the end of the Great War his appearances in the House of Commons became less frequent. He was a keen yachtsman and owned a succession of fine yachts over the years, but his ultimate pride and delight was the luxury steam yacht *Liberty* that he bought in 1919 after it was released from service as a Royal Navy hospital ship.[11] [see PLATE B10] At 1,600 tons and 304 feet long it was the largest steam-yacht of its day in private hands and had originally been built in 1908 by the Ramage & Ferguson shipyard at Leith in 1908 for Joseph Pulitzer, the American congressman and newspaper magnate. By that time Pulitzer was nearly blind and ultra-sensitive to noise, so every cabin on the yacht had special soundproofing insulation and all the furniture was designed with smooth, rounded edges.[12] After 1919, Houston spent the next three summers cruising in the company of other wealthy yacht owners, like the witty whiskey baron Sir Thomas Dewar and Sir Thomas Lipton of tea fame. Lipton is best remembered in sporting circles for his five attempts, over three decades, and all unsuccessful, to wrest the America's Cup from the USA with his yachts *Shamrock* and *Shamrock II*.[13] He was a personal friend of King George V, though his background in trade prevented him from being elected to the Royal Yacht Squadron until shortly before his death in 1930.

In 1921, aboard Lipton's luxury yacht *Erin*, the two elderly bachelors hatched a plot.[14] Dewar, who was fascinated by Lucy, told Lipton, who was terrified of her: 'We must marry her off, Tommy. It's not safe to have her about loose!' 'Not to me, God forbid!' replied Lipton. 'Who on earth could master her?' The name they came up with was Robert Houston, so the two men agreed that one of them should invite Lucy as his guest and the other would invite 'Black Bob'. 'I guarantee she'll sink him on sight,' was Dewar's parting shot – which is how the unlikely couple came to be introduced the following summer. Years later Lucy recounted to Wentworth Day her impressions of that first meeting. 'I determined to marry him the moment I set eyes on him; he was a real man – never wasted time or money.' In return, Houston admitted that he had been captivated by the petite woman with the melting manner and the sharp tongue, who looked twenty years younger than her true age. He had never in his life before encountered a woman like her and she both charmed and frightened him. To his skipper, Captain Goodwin, he remarked: 'Mark my words, Goodie, she's after my bloody money!' And there was more than a grain of truth in this, because Lucy was beginning to plan a political crusade that she knew would be very expensive if it was to have the impact she envisaged. Houston's abrasive hostility to the Government during the War meant that he had been passed over when honours were freely distributed by Lloyd George after the armistice, but he achieved elevation to the baronetage in 1922 – it was rumoured that he had paid handsomely for the privilege.

Over the next two years, Lucy was a frequent guest on *Liberty*, at Cowes and on cruises in the Mediterranean to Cannes and Monte Carlo. Other guests included the great and famous of the day, including Russian grand dukes and duchesses, like Grand Duke Cyril who had married a great-granddaughter of Queen Victoria, Princess Victoria Melita, and would have been the heir presumptive to the Imperial throne of Russia; and Grand Duke Michael Mikhailovich and his wife Countess Torby – from their lips Lucy heard first-hand accounts of the butcheries and tortures of Russia and the orgy of slaughter that had been the Bolshevik revolution. It was accounts like these that strengthened Lucy's determination to fight the threat of communism spreading into Europe with the same determination that she had shown in her campaign for female suffrage. On this political battleground she and Robert thought along very similar lines and it would give a common purpose to their unconventional courtship. Robert also began to appreciate Lucy's business acumen when, against his own instincts and the advice of his business partners, she persuaded him to sell his entire shipping fleet. She could sense that an economic slump was coming and in fact her timing was immaculate; Houston sold out at the peak of the market and doubled his cash fortune.

Houston resigned from Parliament in April 1924 by applying for the stewardship of the Chiltern Hundreds. He only had a majority of 139 from the general election of December 1923 and, in the by-election that followed, the seat was lost to the Labour party candidate, Joseph Gibbins.

For Lucy's birthday earlier that month, he had ordered a Bond Street jeweller to send round a tray of gems for Lucy to choose a present. The selection included a pearl necklace priced at £1,200 and a diamond bracelet for which the asking price was £15,000. Lucy had disdainfully rejected the lot, which Houston found rather hurtful. 'Surely you don't think I'm going to wear any of that rubbish!' she told him, and when he offered the opinion that 'any woman would be proud to wear it,' she positively exploded. 'I am not *any* woman!! If you want to give them to *any* woman, go and find her and give them to her!' Lucy then took herself down to Bond Street where, in another shop, she found a string of exquisite black pearls. The jeweller told her that they were absolutely unique and so expensive that he believed no individual, except perhaps an Indian Prince, would be able to buy them. The price was £50,000.

That evening a somewhat crestfallen Houston telephoned her to ask if she had found anything that appealed to her. She told him about the black pearls and heard him gasp at the other end of the line. 'If you knew anything about jewels at all, you would know that they are the finest investment we could possibly have. Your ships may sink and your shares go down, but those pearls will always go up.' Then she taunted him. 'However, I don't expect you to buy them – they are much more than you can afford.' His vanity pricked, the pearls were duly delivered to her the following day and she wore them every day for many years.[15] [see PLATE B14] [*Author's note*. There is some mystery as to what happened to these priceless gems. Wentworth Day (pp. 42–44) recounted how, in 1933 or '34 he had been ordered to take them back to England in a plain brown envelope; Lucy had stopped paying the insurance premium on them and claimed she was being hounded by the insurance company. He was to give them for safe keeping to Lucy's elder sister Sophia Martha, Mrs Catty, who had been born in 1846 and had married a bookseller of German extraction, whose name had originally been 'Cathy'. Wentworth Day claimed that he could not deliver them because 'Mrs Catty had gone away for a long weekend and the servants did not know her address.' But Sophia Martha had in fact died in 1922, followed by her husband the following year. Wentworth Day had spent that weekend shooting on Lord Mandeville's estate, with the pearls still in his pocket, but who did he give them to afterwards? An answer to this enigma is suggested in Chapter 10 and the saga completed in the final chapter.]

One of the many people who tried to dissuade Houston from getting more deeply involved with Lucy was his long-time friend F.E. Smith, now Lord Birkenhead and Lord Chancellor of England. He was also a guest on board *Liberty* when the subject of conversation turned to the fact that Houston, unlike all his contemporaries, did not seem to have a grey hair in his striking blue-black beard, 'which shone in the sunlight like a raven's wing'. Birkenhead quipped that it was because he dyed it with Stephens' ink, the subject of a popular advertisement on railway stations at the time. Houston's brittle pride was hurt to such an extent that there and then he determined to strike his old friend out of any will he might make.

He was now over 70 and in ever declining health, leading to the first of a number of strokes in the autumn of 1924. It was probably Lucy's promise that she would personally supervise his nursing that finally broke down any last resistance to her blandishments and this 'odd couple' were duly married in Paris in December 1924. The engagement ring he had given her was an enormous emerald set in platinum, a ring which we will hear more about later. To avoid what he considered to be the penal tax regime in England he decided they should take up residence in the Channel Islands, buying a quite modest Victorian villa, 'Beaufield', in the parish of St Saviour on Jersey. [See PLATE C7] They were however in Harrogate, taking the spa waters, in December 1925 when he suffered another stroke. To get back to Jersey as quickly as possible and avoid the possibility that he might die in England, Lucy chartered a special train to take them to Southampton where they boarded a Great Western Railway ferry, also hired just for their personal use (in the summer, it normally carried 1,000 passengers).[16]

  Back in Jersey, Houston wrote a draft will and showed it to Lucy, probably expecting her gratitude, with the remark that 'he had left her quite a lot of money, one million pounds.' Lucy tore it up and threw it on the floor. 'If I am only worth a million pounds, then you had better go away and remake your will and leave it all to someone who deserves it better than I do!'[17] Lucy's tactics had outwitted him yet again and he slunk away like a whipped dog. A few days later, on 19 January 1926, he drew up his final will and testament, signed in the presence of two Jersey solicitors. It would become a cause célèbre and, according to Lucy, the source of a very sinister plot.

Chapter 7

Plots and Persecution

Cynics might argue that it was now in Lucy's best interests not to prolong her husband's life, but it seems that in fact she did everything she could to try and keep him alive. And the truth may be that she had actually fallen in love with her bold, bad buccaneer. He in return had learnt to respect her judgement and positively relish her combative company, so, unlikely as it might have seemed at first, he may have fully reciprocated her devotion. Now he needed her constant nursing care more than ever. He had made many enemies during his life and in the spring of 1926 events began to take on a sinister aspect. Lucy became obsessed with the idea that someone was out to murder him.

As she later recounted to Wentworth Day,[1] 'His tongue was black one day and he was white and gasping. So I gave him an emetic and made him sick on the spot. Castor oil, my dear! The finest cure for everything.' She could not resist then adding a political twist: 'I would like to dose Ramsay MacDonald and all his damned socialists with it.' After this incident, she insisted on tasting his food herself. 'If they were trying to poison him, they could poison me as well; then there would be a hell of a scandal and someone would have to answer for it.'

Sir Robert Houston eventually died in their Jersey house at 9.20 on the morning of Wednesday, 14 April 1926, and his distraught widow collapsed in a state of complete mental anguish and turmoil. The private funeral took place two days later at St Saviour's parish church. Lucy was too ill to attend in person but had sent 'a magnificent cross of arum lilies that rested on the coffin.'[2] The only family mourners were Lucy's elder brother, Arthur Clifford Radmall (1850–1927), a stockbroker, plus a man the reporter from the *Jersey Evening Post* called 'Mr T. Radmall, nephew', Arthur's son.[3] A Mr G. Squire represented the board of R.P Houston & Co, and there were two partners from the London solicitors Fiske & Gedge. Robert Houston's only close friend at the funeral was G.H. Appleton, a business associate and the chairman of the Liverpool West Toxteth Conservative Association, accompanied by three of his five sons. Among the floral tributes were wreaths sent by Lucy's younger sister, Florence, and her husband Arthur Henry Wrey.

The two main topics of conversation at the wake that followed the funeral were the cause and extent of Lucy's illness and the likely content of Sir Robert's will. In Lucy's absence, G.H. Appleton as joint executor was responsible for seeing that the will was proved by due legal process, a fact that was made public the following Monday, 19 April. By Jersey law, unlike that in England, the total value of his estate was never given. Estimates in the press suggested a figure of around £7 million. 'I give and bequeath to my beloved wife, whose self-sacrifice, devotion, care and wonderful intuition on two occasions saved my life, when doctors despaired of it, £100,000 to be paid at once; also my steam yacht *Liberty*, with her equipment, my house 'Beaufield' and my furniture, pictures, silver plate and other personal effects. To George Appleton £50,000, to be paid at once.' Three further cash payments amounting to £30,000 were specified, together with a sum of £50,000 for distribution, at the trustees' discretion, to 'such persons as were in the service of R.P. Houston and the British & South American Steam Navigation Company before 1918.' (Two years later, journalists asked Lucy the meaning of the phrase 'wonderful intuition'. She said: 'I have a magic touch; one or two people have it in every generation. It is something in my fingers – nervous disorders respond to it. Twice the doctors gave him up for dead and twice my magic touch saved him.')[4] Then came the meat of the will, which left one-fifth of the residual estate to George Appleton and four-fifths to Lucy absolutely. This would eventually amount to about £4½ million and make her the richest woman in England. (Later that year, the sizeable but unquantified collection of Robert Houston's £5 War Bonds, signed by Earls Jellicoe, Beatty and Hague, were auctioned on Lucy's instructions for the benefit of the King George's Fund for Sailors.)[5]

On the same day that the will was published, two doctors examined Lucy and signed the following declaration:

> We certify that, in our opinion, Lady Houston D.B.E. is not in a fit condition, physically or mentally, to prove her late husband's will or to perform the duties of an executor. [see PLATE B9]

The insinuation was that Lucy was mad, and doctors and nurses were appointed to look after her and in effect become her warders. This position was formalised the following week when the Jersey Royal Court was convened 'to depose as to her state of mind'.[6] The Court concluded that 'she was suffering from delusions of persecution' and His Majesty's Attorney General for Jersey 'asked the Court to pronounce interdiction' by way of the appointment of a curator to manage all her affairs. Later Lucy would describe the ensuing months as like being under house arrest – her persecution mania that someone was trying to kill her was merely enhanced. When the nurses came to change her pillows, she cried out, 'If you murder me, you will surely be hanged. You're going to murder me. I know it.' The *Daily Express* reported, 'We understand that Lady Houston is lying dangerously ill in Jersey.'[7] The *Daily Graphic*'s 'Mr London' wrote in his column, 'I believe there are hopes that she will recover. The energy with which she, as Lady Byron, threw herself into politics and social affairs left their mark on her. She wore herself out with worry, frequently about things that did not matter much.'

Liberty had arrived in the Jersey roads the day before the funeral and the Curator appointed by the Court now took charge of the vessel and ordered the crew ashore. This was probably for the perfectly innocuous reason of establishing the value of the vessel and its contents, but to Lucy it was a deliberate provocation to her freedom and an attempt to make certain that she could not escape from her captivity. Via the help of a friendly nurse she managed to send out telegrams to a number of eminent psychiatrists and doctors in England, which had the result that Sir William Arbuthnot, Sir Maurice Craig, Sir Thomas Horder and Dr Farquilar Buzzard duly arrived on the island over the weekend of 22 June. They came to the conclusion that she had had a severe attack of jaundice, which had temporarily affected her mind, but that she was now perfectly sane. They wrote a unanimous report to this effect and submitted it to the Jersey Court when they departed late on the Monday morning. But the Court ruled that it had not been submitted according to the correct procedure, namely before noon, and furthermore they could only accept the evidence if it was given to the Court by all the witnesses in person. Lucy's application for the annulment of 'the curatorship over her person and property' was refused and the Jersey Attorney General even added the condition that the curatorship should apply for a full year. Lucy collapsed in utter despair.

Ten days later, in response to further pleading telegrams, the expert witnesses returned to Jersey to testify in person before the reconvened Court. Three additional doctors gave further evidence, including Dr John Macdonald who was the doctor at Newtownmore, the nearest town to her hunting lodge in the Highlands. Dr Joseph Babinski, from Paris, declared that 'her illness had temporarily weakened her intellect, but this weakness had now completely disappeared.' Dr Pierre Janet, also of Paris, stated that he had known Lady Houston for twenty-four years, and that he had seen her the previous day and had 'found no trace of mental confusion.' The Curator, Mr Cyril Crill, admitted that he himself, though only a layman, could see no reason why his role should not be terminated; and the Chief Magistrate concluded that it would be 'unjust to keep Lady Houston under restraint any longer' and that her civil rights should be restored forthwith. A major battle had been won at last, but there were other conflicts looming.

Sir Robert's will was finally proved in 1928, showing that his assets in England only amounted to £6,843.[8] Soon afterwards the Government's legal advisers, under pressure from Labour MPs in the House of Commons, were examining the question of whether a part of his estate, such as his shareholdings in several shipping companies and his 'great holdings' of gilt-edged stock, should be liable to English death duties, despite his declaration that he had been domiciled in Jersey for two years, 'at the end of his somewhat adventurous life.'[9] The Treasury could not ignore the possibility of a windfall of about £1 million and there were demands for the Channel Islands to be brought within the UK tax system.[10] By August, Lucy had still not been paid the cash sum from the will and on the 20th she wrote a stinging letter to the Vicomte de Jersey demanding to know why, when the doctors who declared her insane had been paid their fees, those she produced to prove her sanity had not been paid theirs also? And why had she not received the £100,000 yet?[11] For the time being at least, she wished to get away from the island that she felt had persecuted her so unjustly, but before she left she gave instructions to the undertakers regarding the memorial to be erected over her husband's grave in the churchyard of St Saviour. [see PLATES C8 & C9] This was to be a magnificent Celtic cross, on the base of which she insisted that the following contentious words should be written in bold letters:

THIS CROSS IS ERECTED BY HIS SORROWING WIFE TO THE MEMORY OF ROBERT PATERSON HOUSTON, BARONET, WHO DIED MOST MYSTERIOUSLY ON THE 14th OF APRIL 1926. 'MY ROBERT, MY DEAR, DEAR ROBERT'

She was aboard the *Liberty* on 26 August when it arrived in Torbay for her to watch the yacht racing, before moving on to Weymouth the following day. She had left behind another simmering court case, brought against her by a man called Cecil Houston Skinner, who contested the contents of Sir Robert's will on the basis that he was a grandson of Robert Houston's elder sister Ellen, and therefore his family were 'heirs-in-law' to the fortune. Through her lawyer, Lucy announced to journalists on 28 September that 'she had decided to treat the Skinner family with great generosity.' Cecil Skinner was aged 33 and had served during the war in the King's Liverpool Rifles, but after the armistice he had struggled to find employment. His wife had worked at the munitions factory in Aintree and had been injured in the traumatic explosion that had killed thirteen fellow workers. When tracked down by reporters to his corporation dwelling in Wallasey, Cecil Skinner, who had recently managed to get taken on by a Liverpool printer, told reporters, 'Less than twelve months ago, I was practically penniless and having a daily fight against want, so you can therefore tell what Lady Houston's words mean to me.'[12]

Settlement of Lucy's good intentions would have to wait a while however, because she had still not received any money herself – she had had to arrange for jewellery worth £150,000 to be smuggled over to her in the bottom of a basket of fruit so that she could pawn it and pay the fees of the various doctors who had helped in her 'release'. On 2 November, Cecil Skinner intimated to the press that Lucy's offer of £50,000 had been accompanied by conditions (unspecified) 'that made acceptance impossible', but on the 27th newspapers reported that a final settlement had been agreed. Not only would Cecil Skinner and his family receive £50,000, but a like amount would also be paid by Lucy to four of his married aunts – Mrs Silk and Mrs Roberts, who lived in Vancouver, Mrs Wade of Mouldsworth in Cheshire and Mrs Walker of Brighton.[13] And with all the conditions of the will finally wrapped up by March 1927, Lucy stated that she was once again going to return to Jersey to take up residence at Beaufield. Not for long though.

Both of Lucy's biographers devoted considerable space to what she claimed was the miraculous, semi-mystical revelation that she underwent during her so-called madness;[14] how, like a novitiate nun, she had prayed to God that if he spared her she would devote herself to a new life of service, that she would renounce her enjoyment of the luxuries of life and suppress her selfish pleasure in frivolities like gems and jewellery. This is an over-romanticised interpretation of what turned out to be the creed that would drive her future ambitions, ambitions that were indeed totally unselfish but highly political. And to understand the driving force behind her new philosophy we need to backtrack to the legacy of the Great War and its untidy settlement at the Treaty of Versailles.

Chapter 8

The Legacy of Versailles and the Fascination of Fascism

Democracy substitutes election by the incompetent many for the appointment by the corrupt few ... (it is) the last refuge of cheap government.

George Bernard Shaw

The Versailles Conference had been convened on 18 January 1919 with the laudable intention of establishing a framework for a lasting peace, based on President Wilson's 'Fourteen Principles' and the establishment of the League of Nations. His hope was that the conflict of 1914–18 would be consigned to a repulsive memory of a war so terrible that nations would never again start another. But the most pressing objective was for the victorious allied powers – originally the USA, Britain, France, Italy and Japan, though the latter soon lost interest, thus reducing the main participants to four – to draw up a proposed settlement with Germany, converting the armistice of November 1918 into a peace treaty. This would then, according to accepted principals of diplomacy, be presented to Germany for further discussion before any attempt at signing and ratification. These good intentions soon foundered when it became clear that the objectives of the 'Big 4' were largely incompatible, each country pursuing a completely different agenda. A speedy agreement was not going to happen.

France, led by Georges Clémenceau who was all too mindful that 1914 had not been the first time his country had been invaded by its eastern neighbour, wanted Germany to be militarily castrated and preferably broken up into its former constituent states. At the same time, France demanded control over the coal and steel resources of the Ruhr to compensate for the plant and mines that the Germans had destroyed during their occupation of the north of the country, plus the return of the regions of Alsace & Lorraine. Lloyd George, leading the British delegation, was hell-bent on extracting enormous cash reparations to refill the exhausted coffers of the Treasury, reparations that would in effect cripple Germany financially for an entire generation. President Wilson for the USA, which had suffered little in terms of human sacrifice and had prospered financially during the four years of conflict, wanted the whole thing to be over as quickly as possible, so that his country could forget about the tiresome Europeans and get back to driving forward the limitless wealth-creating possibilities at home. And he needed to get back to canvass votes for his re-election. Italy was almost exclusively interested in territorial gain, expanding its borders into the Tyrol and along the northern borders of the Adriatic Sea around Trieste. When Prime Minister Orlando realised that he was being treated as a minor partner in the Allied quartet he temporarily withdrew his delegation in a huff.

President Wilson had set 7 May as an arbitrary deadline for the completion and conclusion of this part of the conference, a target that was only achieved by the leaders of the four powers going into closed sessions in what Wilson described as a 'race between peace and anarchy'. The German delegation was then summoned, not for any consultation but to be presented with a *fait accompli* – agree and sign. The German team was headed by the foreign minister Count Ulrich von Brockdorff. He did their cause no favours by adopting an attitude of bombastic arrogance and insisting on making speeches of self-justification; Lloyd-George later admitted that he had wanted to box his ears. The delegation turned on their heels and left. Under threat of an immediate resumption of hostilities and a tightening of the naval blockade, the German government, faced with the growing threat of starvation, Communist inspired strikes and internal revolution, sent a new delegation and on 28 June 1919, in the same Hall of Mirrors where the unified German Empire had been proclaimed at the conclusion of the Franco-Prussian War in 1871, the deed was done and the Treaty signed. Marshal Foch, who had been the supreme Allied commander during the closing months of the Great War, was sceptical about its lasting impact and with great prescience stated that 'this is not peace; it is an armistice for twenty years.' Over the next few months, separate treaties were negotiated and signed with the other belligerents like Austria, Hungary and Turkey. German overseas colonies in Africa and the Far East, together with countries formerly under Turkish rule in the Middle East, were put under League of Nations mandates with administration assigned to Britain and France, another point that upset the Italians.

The concept of the League of Nations as the means to achieve the main objective of the conference had been universally applauded at the time, but it lacked committed leadership. The League had been President Wilson's great idea, but he failed to get the consent of the United States Senate and Congress for his country to be a member at all. (Over the years that followed, some original members, like Japan, Italy and Spain, left the organisation, while others, such as Germany and Soviet Russia, were allowed to join.) How could a lasting peace be guaranteed? The simplistic answer was by universal disarmament, but who, without the participation of the richest nation in the world, had the authority, and power, to see that decisions reached at sundry conferences were implemented and enforced?

Lucy Houston was one of the more outspoken people to recognise this fallacy and deplore the United States' withdrawal into isolationism, blaming President Wilson for conceding to the armistice too soon and then not being strong enough to persuade the politicians to support the League. She condensed her feelings into a poem that she submitted, without success at the time, to various newspapers; it was eventually printed in the *Saturday Review* of 6 January 1934, when the weakness of the League was becoming all too apparent. Verse one of three went as follows:

Who ran to help them when they fell
And did some pretty story tell,
Of Armistice and League as well
Instead of sending them to ……… (Berlin)? Mr Wilson!

France decided to put its faith in the mediaeval concept of fixed fortifications along its border with Germany, constructing at vast expense the ultimately impotent Maginot Line. And Germany? They could be made 'to play the game' as long as Allied Forces occupied the demilitarised zone of the Rhineland, but the Treaty of Versailles itself limited the duration of this policing role to fifteen years only. Britain, economically weak, embraced disarmament as a seemingly attractive way of saving money, a policy that was adopted by all the mainstream political parties. The size of the armed forces was reduced, the warship building programme was drastically curtailed and servicemen's pay was cut. Hardest hit of all the services was the fledgling Royal Air Force, whose funding was decimated. Lucy never believed in the League of Nations, and when some years later – August 1936 to be precise – it was reported that Winston Churchill might be joining the Executive Council, she wrote him an open letter saying: 'Don't be silly! For only the silliest of the sillies still believe in the League of Nations … [the one] you belong to, Mr Churchill, is the British Empire, the finest League of Nations the world has ever known!'[1]

In Germany, after the final conclusion of the Versailles Treaty in 1921, the democratically elected government of the Weimar Republic had to struggle with the punitive terms of the reparations demanded by the allies and boiling resentment within all sections of the German population. The restitution of Poland as a nation state, with the 'Danzig Corridor' to the Baltic Sea physically separating East Prussia from the rest of Germany, was a particular thorn. Hyperinflation of the currency, food shortages and unemployment had taken the country to the brink of revolution, and in April 1924 the world first began to read about a man called Adolf Hitler, who had attempted – unsuccessfully – to overthrow the government by a putsch. He had been sent to prison for his role, but at elections in May his nascent political party, the National Socialist German Workers' Party (NAZI) gained their first seats in the Reichstag. Then the allies had stepped in with a new financial plan under the US banker Charles Dawes, and the currency had been rejigged with the support of a loan of 800 million gold marks. Stability and economic growth began to return to the country. On the diplomatic front, Germany was to some extent 'brought in from the cold' through a series of treaties negotiated at Locarno, Switzerland in 1925. The most important of these, known as the Rhineland Pact, reconfirmed Germany's western borders while Germany, France and Belgium signed an agreement that they would not attack one another – with Britain and Italy acting as 'guarantors'. The question of Germany's eastern borders was left much more fluid, with Britain particularly hoping that further negotiations might resolve the problem of the Danzig Corridor and the difficulty of German communities living in the Sudetenland within the newly created state of Czechoslovakia. These hopes were somewhat dashed by the French signing unilateral agreements with both Poland and Czechoslovakia, pledging mutual assistance in the event of conflict with Germany. In 1926, in confirmation of the 'spirit of Locarno', Germany was admitted to a seat at the League of Nations.

Italy meanwhile had managed to stem the rise of communism, often with brutal force. The newspaper editor Benito Mussolini had formed a new political party in 1919, the 'Fasci Italiani di Combattinento' which had a strong paramilitary arm, the *squadristi*, better known as the Blackshirts. The government of the day found it convenient to use the Blackshirts to break a communist-inspired strike at the Alpha-Romeo factory in 1920 and Mussolini's party had won thirty-six seats in the parliamentary elections of May 1921. By the following year he had reconstituted his nascent political party as the National Fascist Party with over 700,000 members and felt in a strong enough position, covertly encouraged by the American ambassador, to mount the game-changing 'March on Rome' in October 1922. The Prime Minister put the city into a state of siege, but King Victor Emmanuel III, fearing a civil war, refused to back him and instead invited Mussolini to form a cabinet. Mussolini had therefore achieved power within the terms of the constitution, a position that was confirmed at a general election in April 1924 which the Fascists won by a large majority. But in July Mussolini tore up the constitution, dissolved parliament and declared himself dictator – under the King. This too, undemocratic though it was, restored the country to stability and a popular sense of patriotic pride. A massive programme of infrastructure projects, such as new road and railway construction, hydro-electric generating schemes and the draining of the Pontine Marshes, brought employment to the national workforce – at least in the north and central regions of the country, though the south, and the island of Sicily in particular, were left to their own devices. Communist inspired strikes were ruthlessly repressed.

The period of Lucy's marriage to Robert Houston had been a turbulent time in British, as well as continental, politics. In 1922, the coalition government of David Lloyd George had been dissolved and the Conservatives returned to power, first under the invalid Andrew Bonar-Law and then 'the safe pair of hands' of Stanley Baldwin. A general election in December 1923 confirmed the Tories as the largest single party, but they lost a vote of confidence in the

House of Commons in January 1924 on the question of tariffs, protectionism and free trade, leading to the first, brief, Labour-controlled, but minority, government in British history, led by Ramsay MacDonald. (Appendix III is included to help readers with a concise summary of the shifting sands of British parliamentary governance in the interwar years.) Lucy had been appalled by MacDonald's first move, to give formal recognition to Russia as the Union of Soviet Socialist Republics (USSR), which she saw as condoning the savagery of the Bolshevik Revolution and taking the next steps to encouraging the spread of communism. In May 1917 MacDonald had been one of the signatories to a 'Great Labour, Socialist and Democratic Convention to hail the Russian Revolution' to be held in Leeds. Addressed particularly to members of trades unions, the invitation to attend stated that 'Russia has called to us to follow her. You must not refuse to answer that appeal.' (In a later chapter we will see how Lucy reminded Ramsay MacDonald of this event, and from this time on he became her 'hate figure number one'.)

He had called another general election in October 1924 hoping to secure a working Labour majority, hopes that were dashed by the publication of the controversial Zinoviev letter. This seemed to imply active Russian encouragement for MacDonald's party and policies and rattled the British electorate to such an extent that traditional Liberals, and many grassroots Labour supporters, swung to the Conservatives, giving them a landslide victory, gaining 154 seats, with forty-seven per cent of the votes cast. The Labour party lost 40 seats while the Liberals lost 118 out of their previous 158, condemning them to a minority role for the rest of the century and polarising British politics into a two-party contest.

Away from British politics, Lucy was intrigued by the goings-on in Italy and to understand her political epiphany, how and why she came to embrace the less conventional aspects of right-wing politics and become a fervent admirer of Benito Mussolini, it is of some interest to explore the origins of the relationship between Britain and Fascism.

It is particularly difficult for readers in the twenty-first century, whose historical education may have been largely influenced by the evils of Fascism as witnessed in the Second World War, by the Nazi Gestapo and the horrors of 'the Holocaust', to appreciate the widespread support in Britain for its aims in the 1920s and '30s. This was particularly true among the aristocracy and the officer classes, whose sons had been sacrificed doing their duty on the battlefields of the Western Front, thereby almost eliminating an entire generation educated in the traditional mould of British leadership. And for what purpose? Nations that should have been natural allies, whose monarchies had been tied by kinship as descendants of Queen Victoria, had blundered into a conflict in 1914, sparked by – yet another – local difficulty in the Balkans. This spark had ignited the tinder of paper alliances originally drawn up with the best of motives but without due consideration of the consequences, particularly the Treaty of Europe in 1839 whereby Britain had guaranteed Belgian neutrality and assistance if she was ever invaded. Then, after millions of people had been killed and maimed, short-sighted diplomats at Versailles had delegated the responsibility for a long-term solution to teams of bureaucrats, men who had to draw somewhat arbitrary lines on maps of Europe and the Middle East defining new nation states, irrespective of age-old ethnic groupings bonded by language and 'tribal' traditions. (Exactly the same mistakes would be made in the partition of India, and the separation of Burma, in 1947.) Military commanders were used to exercising authority and they lamented what they saw as a lack of moral discipline in the next generation, typified by the 'bright young things'. They were sickened by the weak leadership of elected Members of Parliament and the dilution of the House of Lords by men who had bought their way into the peerage.

The widespread interest in Fascism, the concept of government by an autocracy rather than democracy, which emerged in Britain between the two world wars was not a phenomenon purely of the period. Its roots went back well into the nineteenth century when it formed the basis for the administration of British Imperial and Colonial governance, with the prime example being seen in India. Here the Viceroy and his civil servants, distanced from Whitehall by time and distance, exercised virtually unfettered power, power that was paralleled by the feudal authority of the neighbouring Princely States. Projects were initiated and undertaken for the promotion of efficiency and the effective use of resources, whilst maintaining law and order under the mantle of impartial British justice. The railways in particular improved trade and the movement of resources and people, including the military, as well as providing opportunities for employment in construction, in engineering, in the operation of trains and track and in the vast clerical bureaucracy that oiled the wheels behind the scenes. All the latter functions required a certain degree of literacy, as encouraged and promoted by the railway training schools. Education for selected members of the local population was a practical demand of business efficiency, not a moral or philosophical experiment in universal enlightenment. Such were also the motives for the railway companies to set up hospitals and clinics; a healthy workforce was a more effective one. The Government of the Raj was essentially concerned with practicalities, not with wishing to change historical cultures or religious convictions. In this respect, missionaries were deemed to be sometimes unhelpful, and the influx of British wives, the *memsahibs*, was found to be a disturbing influence.

When overseas government officials returned or retired to the UK, many of them were acutely dismayed by the ineffectiveness and sheer inefficiency of the democratic process, the tardiness of decision-taking and the fact that government policy could be completely reversed as the result of a general election. Typical of such men was the Conservative politician and statesman Lord Curzon of Kedleston who had been the Viceroy of India from 1899 to 1905. He had served with some distinction in Lloyd George's war cabinet and was widely tipped to become leader of the Conservative party, a role that in fact went to the far less charismatic Stanley Baldwin. Curzon could see all too clearly the potential dangers to the future of his party from any expansion in the franchise, those eligible to vote in elections, and had become the leader of the Anti-Suffrage League. The Parliament Bill of 1918 was passed by the House of Commons in November that year, whereby constituency boundaries were redrawn to give greater emphasis to the cities and the right to vote was given to the majority of all men over the age of 21.

The realistic proportion was approximately sixty per cent, and there was still an emphasis on property ownership and employment, those benefiting from the provisions of the Poor Laws being specifically excluded. The efforts of the Suffragists, aided and abetted and sometimes hindered by the militant Suffragettes, were also going to be rewarded, and for the first time women would be allowed the vote as well. But when the numbers were calculated, Parliament received a shock. If women's suffrage was made comparable to men, the former would outnumber the latter because of the slaughter of the war. This was seen as a step far too far, and so the registration age for women was set at 30 years, combined with a number of other restrictions. When the Bill came up for debate in the House of Lords, Lord Curzon led the opposition to its implementation, but was overruled by a majority vote and the Act received the Royal Assent early in 1919. In May the following year his daughter Cynthia (Cimmie) married the handsome Lothario and dynamic young Tory MP Sir Oswald Mosley, who had described his policy in his election manifesto of 1918 as 'Socialistic Imperialism'.[2] In 1922 he was elected to Parliament as an Independent, before crossing the floor and joining the Labour Party later that year. He will re-emerge later as a major character in Lucy's story.

The total pre-war – all male – electorate had numbered 8 million; the passing of the Act increased this by an extra 5 million men and no less than 8.4 million women. Stanley Baldwin observed at the time that 'democracy has arrived in England at the gallop,' and then asked the question, 'can we educate them before the crash comes?'[3] A cartoon in *Punch* magazine satirised the misconceptions of a vote for Socialism. Two women in domestic service are depicted chatting in the street, the one saying to the other: 'I intend to vote Labour at the next election, and then we will all be equal and I can have a maid.' Critics of the Act feared that millions of younger people, politically ignorant and susceptible to socialist, utopian propaganda, would effectively hold the balance of power.

For those on the right of British politics, the situation was made even worse by the Representation of the People's Act of 1928, championed by Baldwin and introduced by the Home Secretary Sir William Joynson-Hicks, the pompous, verbose abstainer known to colleagues and cartoonists alike as 'Jix'. This act reduced the voting age for women from 30 to 21, introducing what became known as the 'flapper vote'. Lord Rothermere, owner of the *Daily Mail* and *Daily Mirror* along with several other provincial newspapers, was so convinced that this would inevitably swell the Labour party's share of the vote that he challenged Joynson-Hicks to accept a £100 bet at odds of ten to one on that the Conservatives would lose the general election in 1929. Lucy now waded in, implying that Rothermere was a wimp and offering to take on the bet if he would up the stakes to thousands of pounds. Rothermere replied that he did not know Lady Houston personally and 'never made bets with strangers'.[4] Another person who saw the disadvantages of universal suffrage was Winston Churchill – 'The franchise, having been given to all, is despised by all.' He resuscitated an idea first put forward by Benjamin Disraeli of a 'weighted franchise' that would award extra votes to those with certified qualifications of education, leadership and manual or technical skill.[5]

This politico-historical digression has taken the time frame of our story several years ahead of the period of Lucy's marriage to Robert Houston – which is where this chapter started – and so now we must return to its immediate aftermath and pick up the threads of her life in 1927 and her first, somewhat flirtatious encounter with Winston Churchill.

Chapter 9

Winston Churchill and Lady Bountiful

Lucy compared what she saw as the successful developments in Italy with what she witnessed happening in her beloved England, where all she could see was economic stagnation, the rise in power of the trades unions and a complete lack of firm political leadership. However, she had been encouraged by the return to power of the Conservatives at the general election of October 1924, and she had initiated a charm offensive, the first of two, aimed at the Prime Minister Stanley Baldwin, who replaced her *bête noire* Ramsay MacDonald. She particularly applauded Baldwin's appointment of Winston Churchill, one of her wartime heroes, as his Chancellor of the Exchequer. During her brief return to English waters during the winter of 1926, she could not avoid hearing the gossip and unkind insinuations that she was guilty of tax avoidance at the best and tax evasion at worst. On 27 July 1927 she sent a telegram to the Treasury for the personal attention of Winston Churchill:[1]

> Lady Houston begs to inform the Chancellor that as an act of grace on her part she desires to present the British Government with her share of the English death duties on her late husband's estate, which would have been due had he been domiciled in England; but it is her duty to remind the Chancellor, that 'to say that he made all his money in England' is a great mistake. Most of his money was made in South America ... and there is no denying the fact that Sir Robert WAS domiciled in Jersey.

The Treasury replied the following day to say that they were grateful for Lady Houston's offer, coupled to the expectation that G. Appleton, her co-beneficiary and executor, would be prepared to do the same. However, if this was not the case, then 'the Chancellor will be obliged to reserve the right to continue the judicial proceedings which have been instituted.' Lucy, then staying in Invernesshire, replied that she could in no way be responsible for Mr Appleton's actions but was glad to understand that her own, completely spontaneous, offer had been accepted.[2] This prompted a further letter from the Chancellor's office enquiring whether they could be informed of the precise details of Sir Robert's entire estate so that they could calculate the duty owed. Lucy telegrammed to say that, after her holiday, she would give the matter her attention.[3] Her legal advisers said that their fees for undertaking such a calculation would be a minimum of £20,000 which she thought was a ridiculous waste of money and so she decided to take the initiative herself.

She requested a private meeting with the Chancellor and on Saturday, 29 October 1927, the Treasury was kept open especially for this purpose.[4] She was escorted by an official into Winston Churchill's office where she was very cross to find that he was not alone, but had the Attorney General Sir Douglas Hogg at his elbow. 'You coward! You dare not face me without a lawyer to back you up, and I, a poor defenceless woman, have come to face you all alone.'[5] Winston Churchill would later, during his 'wilderness' years, be a frequent visitor to Byron Cottage and he gave his own description of the event in conversation with Wentworth Day. 'The doors were thrown open and in swept the British Boadicea riding on an invisible chariot, with unseen scythe-blades mowing down hordes of un-guessed enemies.'[6] It seems that a certain amount of haggling then took place but the matter was not concluded. A few days later, Winston Churchill agreed to her demand for a completely private meeting, at which she sat down, drew out her chequebook and started to write out a cheque. 'Tell me, how many noughts are there in a million? Don't you think you should come round and guide my hand?' Winston Churchill recalled that her flirtatious archness had been compelling and when she finally signed the cheque for £1½ million, with the pen she had borrowed from him, she had leant back in her chair and said: 'Now, haven't I been a good girl? Don't you think I deserve a kiss?' 'You do,' he had replied, 'but you won't get one. I will give you a cup of tea instead.' She had then chattered away about all her schemes and plans for bettering the country, which made a deep impression on him. 'She was a grand old lady – the greatest gentleman adventurer alive,' he recalled.[7] Lucy's gift was announced in the House of Commons on 15 November.[8]

Another outspoken woman for whom Winston Churchill had expressed some admiration in 1920 was the controversial writer and historical analyst Nesta Helen Webster.[9] She had been born as Nesta Bevan at a stately home in 1876, educated at Westfield College and at the age of 21 had travelled to the Far East, absorbing the religious philosophies of its various peoples. She married Captain Arthur Webster, a superintendent of police in British India in 1914. On her return to England she wrote a critical reassessment of the causes of the French Revolution, exploring and expanding the theory that the monarchy had been subverted by a Judeo-Masonic conspiracy. She was invited to give lectures on her theories about these age-old conspiracies to undermine civilisation to officers in the army and the Secret Service, laying the blame very largely on the German Freemasons and the self-proclaimed 'Illuminati'. In his pamphlet entitled *Zionism versus Bolshevism; A Struggle for the Soul of the Jewish People* Winston Churchill wrote that 'this movement among the Jews is not new. From the days of Spartacus-Weishaupt to Karl Marx ... this world-wide conspiracy for the overthrow of civilisation on the basis of arrested development, of envious malevolence and impossible equality has been steadily growing. It played, as Mrs Webster has so ably demonstrated, a definitely recognisable part in the tragedy of the French Revolution.' She went on to expand her theories in later works, such as *Secret Societies and Subversive Movements; the Need for Fascism in Great Britain* and the *The Menace of Communism*. Lucy became an avid reader.

Around this time Lucy was approached by the Admiralty with a request to charter her prized yacht *Liberty* for the purpose of conducting some top secret experiments on underwater sound detection. These experiments were part of the development of ASDIC, the important technique for detecting enemy submarines, and *Liberty*'s unique sound insulation would be of great assistance in progressing this work. Lucy readily agreed because she planned to use the ship only in the summer. A large amount of equipment was loaded on board and teams of scientists started work. Not for long though. News about Lucy's voluntary settlement with the Treasury and her generous settlement on the Skinner family opened the floodgates to streams of pleading letters that arrived with every mail delivery, letters from people who were mostly fraudsters or professional beggars. She now realised that if she resided in England, or Jersey for that matter, she would be plagued by such correspondence, so she decided that the only answer was to live on her yacht, preferably abroad. Therefore in November she ordered the Admiralty to get everything and everybody off the ship so that she could reinstate her own crew and set sail for France. For much of the following year *Liberty* cruised along the River Seine and the Loire while she looked for the perfect spot for her self-imposed exile. An enterprising American journalist managed to track her down and published an article about Lucy and her life with Robert Houston, including a provocative photomontage of the pair.[10] [see PLATE B11]

She still donated generously to causes that aroused her sympathy, such as £2,000 she sent to assist the relief work following an earthquake in Greece in May 1928.[11] Nor was she idle during these months. She kept abreast of political developments in Europe, had all the newspapers sent to her and she compiled biographical sketches of every Member of Parliament in the Labour Party. She knew that many had been conscientious objectors during the war, to her mind a sign of unpatriotic treason, and now believed that many were latent communists. The General Strike of 1926 had been a warning shot of a potential revolution. To Lucy's thinking, all British politicians, with few exceptions, were weak and those on the left were potentially dangerous. The economy was being mishandled, though she probably found it hard to admit that one of the major causes had been Winston Churchill's disastrous decision to return Britain to the gold standard in 1924. As Chancellor of the Exchequer he had tried to balance his own natural scepticism against the opinions of several economists, treasury officials and the board of the Bank of England before taking the plunge. He admitted later that it had been the worst decision of his whole career. The result had been a sharp rise in the value of sterling, which in turn led to a flood of cheap imports while British exports were priced out of the market. Industry went into decline, unemployment rose and wages had to be cut to try and maintain competitiveness. Such a contrast to what seemed to be happening in the re-emerging economies in Germany and Italy and the palpable sense of their growing national self-confidence.

Lucy decided that she had to go back to her homeland and use her money to shake up the British political establishment. She returned to take up residence in Byron Cottage, though she maintained domicile in Jersey, and immediately the begging letters started to arrive again, including some that contained 'photographs of fascinating gentlemen offering themselves in marriage – many from Germany'.[12] Most of the requests for money she forwarded to the Charity Organisation Society. This was on the advice of a Miss Hoare, a lady who was a close neighbour and who became a great personal friend, one for whose judgement Lucy had the greatest regard and unbounded faith. Miss Hoare was the aunt of Sir Samuel Hoare (1880–1959), a senior Conservative politician who had been Secretary of State for Air during most of the 1920s and one of the politicians who would play an important role in Lucy's later political adventures. During the Great War he had acted as a recruiting officer for the Secret Service, then called MI1(c) and later MI6, learnt Russian and became the liaison officer with Russian Intelligence in St Petersburg, before being transferred to Italy in 1917 with the brief of persuading them to stay in the conflict on the Allies' side. The Italian army had been suffering bruising defeats in mountain warfare against the Austro-Hungarian forces and morale in the country had slumped. In Rome, one of the agents Hoare recruited was the editor of a left-wing newspaper, *Il Popolo d'Italia*, the 34-year-old Benito Mussolini, and it was Hoare who persuaded his masters in London to pay Mussolini regular, and considerable, sums of money to keep up his flow of propaganda (this revelation only came to light in 2009). Hoare and Mussolini remained friends, a friendship that would have major political implications a few years later.

About this time Lucy herself recruited a secretary, the loyal, devoted but put-upon Miss Bessie Ritchie, a 'practical, hard-working, God-fearing Scotswoman, full of common-sense and womanly charm.'[13] She became Lucy's dearest friend and companion, right up to the day of her death. While Miss Hoare advised Lucy on her larger charitable donations, Miss Ritchie dealt with the daily correspondence and the posting off of smaller gifts to people who for one reason or another had caught Lucy's attention. On one occasion a cutting in a local paper described how a burglar had come before the Marylebone magistrates and had got rather more than he bargained for. He had shouted from the dock at the woman whose house he had broken into: 'You gave me a punch on the jaw!' 'I gave you a clout somewhere,' 65-year-old Mrs Eleanor Bower had replied, 'though I don't know where.'

Lucy had clapped her hands with delight and ordered Miss Ritchie to find her address, take her photograph and give her a five pound note. The photograph duly appeared in the *Saturday Review* weekly journal with the caption: 'One of the bulldog breed!'[14] It typified one of Lucy's favourite and often recited expressions, a quote from her most respected author, Rudyard Kipling: 'The female of the species is more deadly than the male.'

Another story that caught Lucy's imagination was the death of a pioneer aviator, Captain Hinchcliffe, who had been killed trying to fly from the UK to America with Lord Inchcape's daughter as passenger. £100 was posted off to the pilot's widow who replied saying that the gift had been an absolute godsend, one that would 'make life a little brighter for my two babies and myself.'[15]

Examples of her simple sense of humanity were legion. 'Sometimes I would put on an old coat and sit on Hampstead Heath at 6.00 in the morning and talk to the tramps. They think I am one of them and we have some very interesting talks.'[16] After she had left, the tramp might be amazed to find that she had slipped a fiver into his pocket.[17] Another purely altruistic example of her patriotic generosity occurred in 1928 when she read that the important medical archives of Sir Ronald Ross were to be auctioned. Ross was an outstanding British scientist who had devoted his life to studying the causes of malaria, the single greatest cause of death both in Africa and Asia. For his work in isolating the *anopheles* mosquito as the culprit he had been awarded the Nobel Prize for medicine in 1902, but had failed to receive any grant from the British Government to fund the Centre for Tropical Medicine that he had established at Putney. The sale of his archives was the only way he could see to enable him to carry on this work and there was wide concern that his notebooks and papers would now be sold piecemeal and lost to the nation. Lucy agreed to pay £2,000 and presented the entire collection to the British Museum, which then passed them on to what became the London School of Hygiene and Tropical Medicine, where they are still preserved.[18]

But sometimes her generosity had more political implications and, also in 1928, she became involved in a cause that went back to the General Strike two years earlier. This strike had been initiated by the Trades Union Congress in support of the Miners' Federation, who had called their members out in protest at the mine owners' threats of introducing lower wages and longer hours. The coal industry had exhausted its most productive seams during the wartime emergency and was now suffering competition from cheap imports coming in from Germany and the United States. The price of coal had come down but the costs of extraction had increased sharply, and the mine owners saw no other alternatives for keeping the UK industry competitive. When the Miners' Federation rejected these terms, the owners had carried out their threat of a total lockout. The almost universal support by workers for the General Strike had taken both the TUC and the Government by surprise and both sides became alarmed by the possible implications for civil unrest and a breakdown of law and order, even a threat of revolution. Fortunately the tactful mediation of Sir Herbert Samuel allowed both sides to step back from the brink without loss of face and the General Strike had been called off after nine days. But the Miners' Federation held out and the mine owners refused to change their demands, while the Government stood back from any involvement, knowing that the stockpiles they had prudently accumulated would last for many months. Mining communities across the country suffered destitution and soon the workforce started drifting back to work, forced to settle for the harsh terms originally offered. They had gained nothing by the strike, while the TUC, blamed in many quarters for having brought the situation about, fragmented and lost over one million members.

One man who caught the national mood of sympathy for the wives and children of the miners, some of which were on the verge of starvation, was Edward Prince of Wales who visited some of the communities and famously remarked to a journalist that 'something must be done'. What he did was to set up the Prince of Wales's Miners Distress Fund, appealing through the Lord Mayor of London for contributions from the public, and Lucy was one of the most generous donors, sending off a cheque for £30,000. A few days later, she circulated an open letter to the miners in which she encouraged them to 'send all Trades Unions to the place where all bad people go,' adding the suggestion that in future they should 'vote for the party which will give you Tariff Reform and no nonsense about it.' Labour MPs, like Hugh Dalton, were highly indignant and raised the matter in the House of Commons, to which Lucy replied through the press that she had merely 'sent a message that came from my heart, advising them as I would have advised my best friend.'[19] The vice president of the Miner's Federation in Lancashire, a Mr McGurck, recommended that Lucy's gift should not be accepted because 'the miners and their wives were too self-respecting to accept relief that carried with it such an insulting condition.' Lucy responded by inviting a journalist to her Jersey home and showing him 'the hundreds of letters she had received from miners and their wives, congratulating me and telling me that what I had said about their leaders was absolutely true.'[20]

There was another fallout from the General Strike that engaged Lucy's sympathy. In 1929, Hull City Council had been won by the Labour Party and in an act that looked to many people like purely political revenge they had threatened to sack 115 tramway drivers and other men who had defied their union in 1926 and volunteered to continue working. This had caused public outrage and was seen as an act of vindictive discrimination, particularly since the Prime Minister at the time, Stanley Baldwin, had pledged that volunteers would enjoy Government protection. Lucy went public in saying that she would pay all the costs of the defence and issued a 24-hour ultimatum to the Council saying that unless the notices of dismissal were withdrawn she was prepared to take the matter to whatever higher court of appeal was necessary.[21] 'I am doing this because I wish to give the Council time to reconsider their illegal action.' She sent a cheque for £1,000 to pay the tram-workers' wages over Christmas and the New Year while the matter was pending.[22] At the same time she wrote a typically feisty letter to Miss Margaret Bondfield, the newly appointed Minister of Labour and the first woman to hold a cabinet post, who had said that it was not in her power to intervene in the matter, stating, 'If you cannot insist on justice being done to the working classes, then your title should be Minister of Injustice to Labour!'[23]

One of the first things Lucy had done on her return to London in 1928 was to visit the Boswell Printing and Publishing Co Ltd at its offices in Essex Street, just off the Strand, the company that published the works of Nesta Webster. They agreed to print Lucy's researches into the background of Labour party MPs and it was published – anonymously – under the title *Potted Biographies: A Dictionary of anti-National Biography*. 'It was an invaluable publication, for it gave chapter and verse of the anti-war activities and inflammatory doctrines of every member of the Labour party who had ever preached the gospel of belittling Britain.'[24] At the same time, Lucy agreed to donate a large, but unknown, amount of money towards Boswell's finances.[25] Apart from publishing books by authors sympathetic to the far right of British politics, Boswell would go on to publish monthly journals such as *The Patriot*, and *Action!*, the mouthpiece of the British Union of Fascists founded by Sir Oswald Mosley in the 1930s. Lucy had firmly hitched her colours to the mast of those like the press barons Max Aitken (Lord Beaverbrook) and Lord Rothermere, along with the Duke of Hamilton, Viscount Lymington MP, Lord Lloyd and Admiral Domvile, who believed that threats to undermine British society by communism had to be combated by a necessarily exaggerated stance by the right wing of the political spectrum. They were impressed by what Mussolini was achieving in Italy and the initial results of the fascist experiment in Germany and believed that it might be in Britain's best interests to extend to that country the hand of friendship and understanding.

The fear of Bolshevism was the best recruiting officer for the cause of fascism. As the redoubtable Queen Marie of Romania, another granddaughter of Queen Victoria, put it, 'Fascism, although also a tyranny, leaves scope for progress, beauty, art, literature, home, and social life, manners, cleanliness, whilst Bolshevism is the levelling of everything.'[26] Winston Churchill visited Italy in 1927 and was impressed. 'Externally Mussolini's movement has rendered service to the whole world … Italy has shown that there is a way of fighting the subversive forces … She has provided the necessary antidote to the Russian poison. Hereafter no great nation will be un-provided with an ultimate means against the cancerous growth of Bolshevism.'[27] Lucy herself was suffering from increasing bouts of ill health brought on by an abnormally low blood pressure, and at the end of December 1929 the press reported that Lord Dawson of Penn, personal physician to King George V, had arrived in Jersey to treat her.[28] Her recovery was slow and she was still very ill as the winter dragged on.

Chapter 10

A Whisper of Mortality

As Lucy approached her 73rd birthday she still looked like a woman in her early fifties or even younger. [see PLATE B15] Her eyes were as bright and impish as ever, and the artfully arranged kiss-curl on her forehead gave her the appearance more of a 'flapper' than a dowager. It is doubtful, however, if she thought about celebrating her birthday, because in spite of her youthful looks she was increasingly worried that her body was ageing and letting her down while she still had so much that she wished to achieve. She was recuperating aboard *Liberty*, moored in Poole harbour, in March 1930 when she had another serious attack of illness and this time sent for Sir Thomas Jeeves Horder, another personal physician to the King – his other patients had included the former Prime Minister Andrew Bonar-Law and, ironically, Ramsay MacDonald. Born the son of a draper in Shaftesbury in 1871, he had made his name by performing a crucial, possibly life-saving diagnosis on King Edward VII, an event that would associate his services with the royal family for three generations. He was knighted in 1918, appointed a baronet in 1923 and finally, in 1933, two years after his call from Lucy, he was created Lord Horder of Ashford.

He was still on board *Liberty* after seeing Lucy through her latest crisis when she summoned him in the middle of the night to complain that she could not sleep, ordering him to give her some sort of sleeping pill. Taking the pillbox in one hand, he shook out a tablet onto the palm of the other and gave it to her. Lucy had recovered enough to give him a severe reprimand. 'What do you mean by handling the stuff you're giving me? For a doctor, you should know better! Throw it over the side immediately!' Somewhat shamefacedly, Horder complied; he put another tablet onto a teaspoon and invited Lucy to open her mouth. 'Now what do you think you're doing!' she snapped, 'feeding the sea lions at the zoo?' Horder slunk back to his cabin like a naughty schoolboy. A few days later Lucy received a bill for £500. In a typical example of her wry sense of humour, she sent him a cheque with a note enclosed which started: 'To my dear doctor, my *very dear* doctor.' She then added: 'You have now become one of the luxuries I can no longer afford and so I fear I shall have to dispense with your services.'[1] Horder replied a couple of days later that he would be extremely sad to lose her from his list of distinguished clients and felt sure that he could offer her one or two free consultations. 'The Booby!' Lucy exclaimed with a girlish laugh, and proceeded to call him out at her slightest whim – and never paid him another penny.

It was during this bout of illness, one which invoked a whisper of her own mortality, that she drew up a will. Dated 30 March 1930, and witnessed by Miss Ritchie and her nurse Grace Bicknell, it was an extremely short and simple document scrawled onto a sheet of her yacht's writing paper. In it she left everything, her entire fortune, to her loyal companion and long-standing friend Miss Hoare, to be 'disposed of at her discretion'. [see FIG 1]

This would seem to beg the question why she made no mention of any legacy whatsoever to any member of her own family. Her parents, Thomas

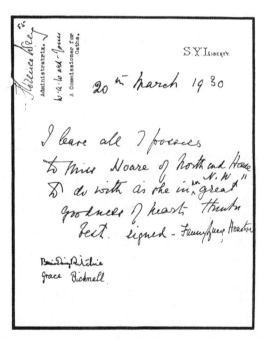

Figure 1. Lucy's hasty will written on board her yacht Liberty, 30 March 1930. The note at top left was added after Lucy's death in 1936 by the administrators of her estate. *(HM Probate Office)*

and Maria Radmall, had both followed a trade and doubtless had aspirations not only for themselves but also for the status of their family, so the fact of Lucy, the pet of the family, running off to Paris in 1873 with a man rumoured to be already married, would have shocked their bourgeois sensitivities. As the neighbours tittle-tattled, the family probably closed ranks and tried to forget the shame that Lucy had brought upon them. It seems on the face of it that Lucy's decision in 1930 might have been some sort of payback. We have already seen one example of Lucy's distance from her family in chapter 6, when, if Wentworth Day is correct, she was unaware that her elder sister Sophia had died. In fact in 1930 only one of her siblings was still alive anyway, her younger sister Florence who had been born five years after her in 1862 – when their mother was 44 years old. Florence's first experience of marriage at the age of 22 had been a disaster; her husband, a corn-merchant named Harold Wood, had been married before and was a serial wife-beater. Florence managed to obtain a divorce from him in 1895 on grounds of physical cruelty and two years later she married a stockbroker and occasional author called Arthur Henry Wrey, a younger son of Sir Henry Bourchier Toke Wrey, Bart. This union proved to be childless, but Lucy did have a large number of nephews, nieces and great nieces alive in 1930. She also had a favourite step-son, 'Naps' Brinckman of whom we will hear more shortly, so perhaps the simplest explanation for the brevity of her will was that she truly had been on the brink of death and had been persuaded to at least commit something to paper in case the worst happened.

Was Lucy ever close to any of her relations? We have seen in an earlier chapter that her mother was at her side during the divorce procedures from Theodore Brinckman in 1895. But the only anecdote which survives, and a somewhat mercenary one at that, relates to 1931, when Lucy tried to involve her niece Cicely Radmall (then aged 20) and her great-niece Violet 'Boo' Catty (18, and probably only on a visit from America) in the general election that year. She hired a private plane to fly them up to Lossiemouth in Scotland with instructions that one of them should somehow arrange to stand at the last minute as an Independent candidate against Ramsay MacDonald in his own home town.[2] Lucy had enormous political savoir faire but this incident also exposes her naivety about the details of the election process. Firstly, any candidate has to be nominated some time in advance of an election, the nomination supported by a defined number of signatories. Secondly, Ramsay MacDonald's constituency was in fact Seaham in County Durham, one that he had taken over in 1927 from Sidney Webb, the leading Fabian who had been very largely responsible for writing the first Labour party manifesto. The small fishing community at Lossiemouth actually came within the Moray constituency, which in the event returned a National Conservative candidate unopposed. (At Seaham, Ramsay MacDonald, standing on a National Government ticket, had a tough fight against the Labour party candidate, his majority being reduced to 5,600.)

The somewhat terrified girls opted to return by train and pleaded with Lucy to be allowed to go back to the far less adventurous but more comforting routine of living with their mothers. Soon afterwards, Miss Ritchie suggested that Lucy might give away some of the clothes in her wardrobe that she never wore, such as a sumptuous evening coat made from ermine fur. Lucy had it wrapped up and posted to her niece Cicely with a brief note saying 'don't leave on the Tube!' (which was precisely what she did, though it was returned to her via the lost property office).[3]

Finally there is the mystery of what happened to Lucy's famous black pearls, as recounted in Chapter 6. I believe it is likely that Wentworth Day managed to give them to Florence May Catty, the spinster daughter of Lucy's deceased sister Sophia Catty, and the evidence for this may lie in the fact that when she died in 1944 she was a rich woman, her will showing that she could leave a total of £63,858. But that may not be the end of the trail as we will see later in chapter 20.

Lucy had fully recovered by the summer of 1930 and in June she donated £11,000 to the Christian Protest Movement, a campaign against religious persecution in Russia. The *Daily Herald* published an article attacking her for being one of the 'Tory plotters against Russia', which induced her, against all legal advice, to sue the newspaper for libel. In an out-of-court settlement, they agreed to pay £500 to any charity of her choosing and Lucy had the added pleasure of requiring them to make the cheque out to the very same Christian Protest Movement. She had never had a good opinion of lawyers, and this incident convinced her that she could rely on her own judgement as to how far she could taunt political hypocrisy and get away with it. As we will see in later chapters she would soon test this mantra to its limits.

Chapter 11

Wings Over the Water – the Schneider Trophy

Of all the actions taken by the Labour Government after its election in 1929, the one that upset Lucy most was the further reduction in funding for the Royal Air Force. Lucy's acute political intuition and foresight saw this as nothing short of a treacherous dereliction of responsibility, and so she embarked on a one-woman crusade to do something about it. Her body might be growing increasingly fragile but her mind had never been more active. Her eyes sparkled and her skin retained a remarkably youthful glow. Boadicea's chariot was about to take flight – with quite extraordinary and far-reaching results.

By the end of 1930 Lucy became involved in her most ambitious, patriotic project of all, one that would bring her to the notice of the general public in a truly dramatic fashion. To understand the significance of this and how it came about we have to go back to 1912 and a rich young Frenchman called Jacques Schneider, born the son of an armaments manufacturer in 1879. He himself was a keen aviator and believed that an international air race would do more than anything else to stimulate the development and improvement of aeroplanes and aircraft engines. His initiative led to the founding of the annual Schneider Trophy Race by the International Sporting Club of France in 1912. [see PLATE C12] The rules stipulated that the competitors had to be able to take off from and land on water and fly a triangular course of not less than 150 miles. The winning country would host the next event and a country that won on three successive years could keep the trophy in perpetuity.

Three years after the Wright brothers had made their first historic, but largely unwitnessed flight in a heavier-than-air flying machine, the major attention to this new era of aviation had shifted from the USA to France. In a field near the Bois de Boulogne, Paris, on the cold afternoon of 23 October 1906, a thousand spectators stood to watch Alberto Santos-Dumont take off and make a short, tentative flight of only a few seconds. In front of official photographers, he established the world's first air speed record – of 24.7 mph. But it was not until Wilbur Wright had visited France in 1908 and demonstrated sustained flights of over two hours duration, with smooth take-offs, graceful turns and steady landings, that French aviation really began to develop momentum. What the Wright brothers had worked out, partly by mathematics and partly by persistent trial and error, was the secret of how to control motion around each axis of flight; pitch by the use of fore and aft elevators, yaw by vertical rudders, and banking by changing the shape of the wings themselves ('warping') so that one wing could be induced to provide more lift than the other. Power, and hence speed, would come from advances in the design of internal-combustion engines, where the motorcar industry was leading the way. France was already the most prominent country in organising car racing, both on circuits and long-distance endurance affairs, but the engines used were massive and heavy. The essential requirement for aircraft was minimum weight combined with the maximum ratio of power to weight. Automobile engines were cooled by circulating water around the cylinders through extensions to the cast-iron cylinder blocks (extra weight) before being passed through radiators. These themselves would exert considerable 'drag' when fitted to aircraft. It was the invention – also French – of the air-cooled rotary engine that provided a quantum leap in solving the power-to-weight ratio problem. At least for a time.

Given the large number of French pioneer aviators and the enthusiasm of the French public for speed racing, it was probably natural that the first major international air race, organised by the International Sporting Club, should be promoted by a Frenchman and take place in the French enclave of Monaco. Jacques Schneider himself was actually a balloonist, but a crash in 1910, in which he broke both arms very badly, prevented him from becoming a pilot of heavier-than-air machines. It was he who became the driving force behind the competition, believing that it would enhance his country's prestige.

The primary requirement for competitors was that the planes had to take off and land on water. The long-term thinking behind this was that since seven-tenths of the world's surface was covered by water, eventual long-distance flights would be made by 'hydro-aeroplanes', thereby avoiding the need for specially prepared, level runways on land. Furthermore, it was thought that in the event of an emergency landing, the sea would be a more yielding medium to receive the aircraft. Competitors had to prove that they could not only take off from calm water but also do the same from a 'broken' or choppy surface before flying around a triangular course. This requirement made totally different demands on aircraft designers, because the drag from driving the aeroplane, inevitably partially submerged at rest, through the water would be much greater than that of wheels on a solid surface, even grassy turf.

Over the years, designs for such seaplanes would divide between two distinct categories: 'flying boats' where the fuselage rested in the water (the wings supported on separate floats near the wing-tips) and 'floatplanes', where the fuselage was above the water and supported on a pair of large floats capable of providing sufficient buoyancy. The first type required fundamentally new design parameters while the second could potentially be achieved more easily by taking a standard 'land' aircraft and substituting the wheels with floats (or keeping both, thereby producing an 'amphibian').

The winner of this first race, out of seven entrants, was a biplane/floatplane with a Gnome rotary engine designed by Henri Farman; second place was taken by his brother Maurice's entry, in this case powered by a Renault engine. In this precursor competition of 1912, marks were also awarded according to how many passengers accompanied the pilot and it may come as a surprise that the Maurice Farman complied with the rules while having five passengers on board.[1] Later that year, rules for an annual competition, the Schneider Trophy, were formally codified. These included the following: a) the contest must take place over open sea; b) the distance must be at least 150 nautical miles around a triangular course; c) entrants must prove themselves to be seaworthy; d) no country could enter more than three aircraft; and e) the winning country would host the next event. The rule about 'passengers' was dropped. A final clause stated that a country winning in three successive years would retain the trophy in perpetuity.

The first race under these rules again took place at Monaco on a sunny, calm April day in 1913. Three French entries were eliminated in preliminary trials and the remaining four starters consisted of another three Frenchmen and one lone American. Two of these never completed the course and France emerged the winner at an average speed of 45 mph. So it was France that organised the next race the following April, once again at Monaco, a site that not only offered a sheltered harbour but also a fine amphitheatre for thousands of spectators. This time there were twelve entries, five from France, one German and two each from Switzerland, the USA and Great Britain. It was a British entry, a Sopwith 'Tabloid' floatplane piloted by Howard Pixton that was judged the winner, nearly doubling the previous speed record to 86.8 mph.

The competition had to be suspended during the Great War and it next took place at Bournemouth on 10 September 1919, attracting six entries; from Britain (3), France (2) and Italy (1). One of the French entries had to ditch in the English Channel during delivery and the other crash-landed on arrival at Cowes, both pilots ending up wet but luckily unharmed. The day of the race dawned in thick fog but this was judged to have cleared sufficiently for the race to start at 2.30, though soon afterwards the sea-mist began to thicken again. All three British contenders retired on lap one, which left just the Italian Savoia S.13 flying, and Sergeant Guido Janello duly landed after completing the full eleven laps. Then the bombshell. In the poor visibility he had mistaken the turning beacon at Swanage and therefore flown the wrong course, so the result was declared null and void. The angry Italians appealed and there was much debate about poor organisation and officious inefficiency by the regulators, with the result that the somewhat crestfallen Royal Aero Club, the organisation responsible for all air sport in the UK since 1910, recommended to the Fédération Aeronautique Internationale (FIA) that the trophy should be awarded to Italy. This, to the increased fury of the Italians, was rejected by the FIA, though they did award a consolation prize – Italy would have the honour of hosting the competition in 1920.

Italy won both the races held at Venice in 1920 and 1921, the first – a 'fly-over' because both the other (Italian) competitors withdrew – at an average speed of 107.2 mph, the second the following year at 117.2 mph. A win in 1922 would hand the trophy over to Italy for keeping, a prospect that stirred both the French and the British to patriotic action. The race, now to be held in the Bay of Naples, was scheduled for 12 August, though the two French entries were forced to withdraw before the preliminary trials had even taken place. This left three Italians and one British, and for the first time all participants were flying boats rather than floatplanes and they all completed the course in what turned out to be a very close and thrilling finish. The winner for Britain was Henri Biard flying a Supermarine 'Sea Lion Mk. II' at an average speed of 145.7 mph, just beating the Italian Savoia S.51 by a mere 2.5 mph, in spite of the fact that the Supermarine's Napier Lion engine was rated at 450hp against the Savoia's 300hp Hispano-Suiza. Sleek, light-weight aerodynamic design had nearly triumphed over brute power mounted on a heavy, cumbersome airframe that suddenly looked very old fashioned.

This should have been a wake-up call to the British aircraft industry in advance of the contest to be held at Cowes on 28 September 1923, but in the event the only home-grown contestant that survived the preliminary trials was the slightly updated Supermarine 'Sea Lion' now fitted with an even beefier Napier engine. (Blackburn had entered a rather pretty-looking flying boat called the 'Pellet', very much in the 'Italian' style but this had crashed before the start, the pilot being successfully rescued after an agonising sixty seconds trapped in the sinking cockpit. The Sopwith/ Hawker 'Rainbow' had also crashed during early trials, this time on a golf course.) The Supermarine entry was privately financed by two directors of the company – the RAF having claimed poverty as a result of the war – and the modifications in the new version were designed by R.J. Mitchell, who had recently been appointed head of the design office at the age of only 27. The 'Sea Lion III' was sleeker than its predecessors but still a biplane with ungainly struts and bracing wires between the wings, and Mitchell knew that this was nothing like the graceful, gull-form monoplane that he was already beginning to make sketches of in his spare moments.

In the event this aeroplane completed the course and came third (out of only three) at an average speed of 157.2 mph; it was completely outclassed by the two Curtiss CR-3s from America that came first and second at average speeds of 177.4 mph and 173.5 mph respectively. These floatplanes were still biplanes, but the water-cooled, in-line Curtiss engines of only 465 horsepower allowed a sleek, streamlined fuselage that looked absolutely 'fit-for-purpose'. The most important innovation was the clever design of the radiator cooling system, one which offered very little drag on the air-flow.

Baltimore was chosen by the National Aeronautical Association (NAA) for the 1924 contest, but the distance from Europe, shortening the time for development and trans-shipment, resulted in no competitors from that continent being entered. By the rules, the Americans could have claimed victory by a mere 'fly-over', but the NAA, in a most sporting gesture, agreed to declare that year's contest void and so attention turned to October1925.

This race attracted eight entries, three from the USA navy (all upgraded Curtiss CR-3s) – two from Italy (the new Macchi M.33 monoplane flying boats) – and three from Britain, two of which were Gloster III biplane floatplanes incorporating the promising new Napier Lion water-cooled engine capable of delivering 700 horsepower. Completely radical in layout was R.J. Mitchell's S.4 floatplane for Supermarine, which incorporated the same Napier engine. The revolutionary feature was the slim monoplane wing configuration, tapering to delicate tips, and without a single supporting strut or bracing wire in sight. It looked futuristic and early trials suggested that it would be capable of previously unheard-of speeds. The British teams arrived early in the month and started familiarisation tests when fate intervened. One night, in fierce gales, a flag pole blew down and damaged the S.4's tailplane. Then the pilot, Henri Biard, was struck down with flu, though he insisted on being at the controls for the preliminary trials at the start of the race itself. Screaming across Chesapeake Bay, he entered a steep turn at full throttle and 'blacked out', only regaining consciousness just before the plane nosedived into the water.[2] He survived, with broken ribs, but any real hopes of a British victory had been smashed. The winner was a young American pilot soon to be world famous, Jim Doolittle, with a speed of 232.6 mph. A surprise second was the British reserve entry, one of the Gloster IIIs, 33 mph slower. Most disappointing perhaps was the small but sleek Italian entry. Hampered by large radiators on its relatively low-powered engine (435 horsepower), the sole qualifying Macchi III managed only 168.4 mph, slower than the winners two years previously.

The only foreign entries in 1927, when the competition was moved across Chesapeake Bay to the US Navy facilities at Norfolk, were three from Italy. The British – and the French – tried to argue that the weather in the middle of November was unsuitable, demanding a postponement to the following summer and then refusing to enter when this was refused. Benito Mussolini however, appreciating the prestige and propaganda value of the contest, arranged for unlimited funds to be put at the disposal of Macchi to develop a new airframe, one that turned out to be very similar to Mitchell's S.4, and Fiat to produce a new 882 horsepower engine. He also ordered the Italian air force, the Regia Aeronautica, to select and train a special cadre of 'high-speed' pilots. On the day, both teams were dogged with bad luck, but the eventual winner was Major Mario de Barnardi in one of the two Macchi M.39s that completed the course, raising the winning speed to 246.5 mph. Mussolini sent a verbose congratulatory telegram to the team and then bragged to the world that the contest at Venice the following year would be the grandest and most impressive yet, a dazzling showcase for the supremacy of Italian aviation.

He had not taken into account the provocation stirred up in British patriotism. On the one hand the Royal Air Force set up their own 'high-speed' flight, while on the other the firm of Vickers, who had taken over Supermarine, gave R.J. Mitchell positive encouragement and funds to improve on his earlier design and produce the S.5, now powered by an even more mighty version of the Napier 'Lion' engine. Two of these aircraft came first and second (at speeds of 281.7 mph and 273.0 mph) while all three Italian entries were forced to retire during the race due to mechanical failures. The third British entry had been a private venture aircraft, the Short/Bristow 'Crusader'. It was unique in using a supercharged Bristol air-cooled radial engine rated at 650 horsepower, and its larger frontal area was a hindrance to streamlining – and the view from the pilot's cockpit.[3] Never a serious contender, it crashed on take-off during preliminary trials, though luckily its wooden construction allowed the fuselage to break up so quickly that the pilot was thrown clear, unharmed. Under the circumstances, the Italians took their defeat with surprisingly good grace, the spirit of sportsmanship championing over the rhetoric of politics. So the next venue would be Calshot in the Solent, but it would not take place in 1928 after the FAI, under pressure from all participating countries, agreed at a meeting attended by Jacques Schneider himself that it was better if the race for the trophy became a biennial event.

France now decided to enter the fray again and ordered four planes from two manufacturers, but the death of one of their pilots and problems with the development of power plants meant they withdrew their entries a month before the contest date of 7 September 1929. Italy initially took six aircraft to Calshot including a revolutionary design by Savoia, their S.65, which had a short central fuselage with one engine in front of the pilot and another behind driving a 'pusher' propeller, the tail assembly being carried on two narrow booms. In this way, 2,000 horsepower could be delivered from two proven power plants while avoiding the extra drag from a conventional twin-engine layout. Yet another, even more radical concept, was that from Piaggio. This did away with traditional floats altogether, but neither was it a conventional flying boat though at rest the fuselage did sit in the water. Beneath it were two submerged water skis on angled 'stalks', while underneath the tail unit was a standard marine propeller connected to the main engine by a separate, clutched driveshaft. The idea was to gain sufficient speed from the marine propeller so that, like a speedboat, the fuselage would rise up out of the water on the skis, whereupon the airscrew would take over and the machine would fly. On calm, lake water at home it did; on the choppy water of the Solent it didn't. Reliability problems with the Savoia forced the Italians to make their final choice of three from the Macchi stable, two of type M.67 with new 1,400 horsepower engines from Isotta-Fraschini and one type M.52R with the 'old' Fiat 1,000 horsepower unit.

The first British entry consisted of a Supermarine S.5 with the proven Napier 'Lion' engine but at the limits of its design capabilities. R.J. Mitchell had designed a new, slimmer airframe, the S.6, but needed a completely new engine, and it had taken all the diplomatic negotiating skills of the Vickers board to persuade their opposite numbers at Rolls-Royce to become involved. Deeply concerned about their reputation for quality and long-term reliability, they considered racing, whether in cars or aeroplanes, to be somewhat vulgar, with the risk that hot-headed young men would literally blow this reputation to pieces while seeking transient glory. It was representations from the Air Ministry that finally provided the tipping point, suggesting that there was a far more noble glory at stake, one of patriotic pride.

The secret to increasing the power of an engine of given weight was to compress the fuel/air mixture before induction into the cylinders. This could be achieved by the addition of a 'supercharger', a concept already well proven in racing automobile engines. Rolls-Royce had recently applied the technique to their prototype 'Kestrel' engine which by 1927 was capable of sustained output of nearly 500 horsepower from a unit weighing only 760lbs. In parallel, they had the huge 'Condor' engine, developed in the Great War for the large Handley-Page bombers, which had evolved into the 'Buzzard'. This far from satisfactory engine was now completely redesigned as the 'R' Type, capable of producing just under 1,000 horsepower. Mitchell reckoned that he needed a minimum of 1,500 horsepower for his S.6 but without any increase to the frontal area. It is to the eternal credit of Rolls-Royce that they managed to achieve this, and more, while at the same time, in conjunction with Mitchell, designing an aerodynamic cooling system that could handle the extra heat generated.

In front of a vast crowd of spectators lining the cliffs along the Solent on 6 September 1929, Flying Officer H.R. Waghorn managed to pilot his S.6 around the course at a staggering average speed of 328.6 mph. The other S.6 of the RAF High Speed flight would have been in contention as well, had the pilot not been disqualified for missing one of the turn pylons, so it was an Italian Macchi M.25R that chalked up second place, though a full 40 mph slower, just beating the 'low-powered' S.5 into third place.

There were now two years before the next competition, again at Calshot, and if Britain could win, the trophy would remain in this country. And on this cliff-hanger, it may be worth reflecting on what the competition for the Schneider Trophy had achieved in terms of world aviation generally. 'Racing improves the breed' is a well-worn adage and there is no doubt that the contests inspired major progress in many aspects of aircraft design, though the exclusivity rule about seaplanes proved to be a somewhat trying restriction. As far as airframes were concerned, the sheer speed advantages of smooth, streamlined fuselage shapes, monoplane wings and the elimination of drag from superfluous struts etc was proven. Manoeuvrability in a combat situation was quite another matter though, which is why many countries, like Britain, persisted for a few years with biplane fighters. Load carrying was confined solely to a single pilot and a minimum amount of fuel, so nothing was learnt about the ability to incorporate weaponry. Maximum engine power for a given weight was critical, hence the accent on superchargers and cooling systems once the streamline advantages of in-line water-cooled engines was proven. Alongside all these developments, very important progress was made in the efficiency of propellers/airscrews, with easily-shaped wood giving way to complex, machined metal. But the Schneider Trophy was not the only air-racing event in the world. The Royal Aero Club sponsored several race meetings in the UK, of which the King's Cup was the most famous. In the USA, the Pulitzer, Thompson and Bendix races achieved their own fame and produced new heroes, while many countries contested the FIA-sponsored 'World Speed Record', the fastest straight dash over a measured distance. Jacques Schneider had died on 1 May 1928, having lived to see the winning speed for his trophy rise from 45 mph to 281 mph and the power of aero-engines lifted from 200 to 1,000 horsepower. But he regretted that his dream, his original intention, of motivating the development of long-range passenger-carrying airliners had been completely perverted.

At the celebration banquet to celebrate Britain's victory in 1929, Ramsay MacDonald, extremely well wined and dined, had proclaimed, 'we are going to do our level best to win again.' Yet only a few months later it was announced that neither the Government nor the Air Council, responsible for the finances of the Royal Air Force, would provide a single penny towards the costs of competing. The shocked reaction of the general public, and the aircraft industry, was summed up in an excoriating article in the *Aeroplane* magazine. 'A government that will give £80,000 to subsidise a lot of squalling foreigners at the Covent Garden Opera and will refuse £80,000 to win the World's greatest advertisement for British aviation is unworthy of the Nation.' The *Daily Mail* echoed the theme on 23 January 1931 with a banner headline: 'If we let the Schneider Trophy go, aeroplane trade will go too. Government blunder. Public astounded.'

The Italians could not believe their luck. General Balbo, Mussolini's Air Minister, gave his government's full backing for the Macchi company to design a revolutionary new airframe, the MC.72, that would incorporate Fiat's even more radical new power pack, one that promised an output of 2,500–3,000 horsepower. This consisted of two engines – as originally tried in the Savoia of 1929 – though now mounted one behind the other in front of the pilot, driving two shafts geared to a pair of contra-rotating propellers on a single, shared hub. This would eliminate the dangerous sideways 'torque' experienced with single propellers on take-off, potentially allowing smaller,

Plate B1. Lucy Radmall as a teenager. (*Bassano*)

Plate B2. Lucy in Paris as 'Mrs Gretton.' (*Bassano*)

Plate B3. Frederick Gretton's thoroughbred 'Isonomy', rated as one of the finest British racehorses of its century. (*Image by courtesy of the National Horseracing Museum*)

Plate B4. Lucy, Mrs Brinckman.

Plate B5. The handsome, athletic Theodore Brinckman, Lucy's first husband. (© *National Portrait Gallery, London*)

Plates B6 & 7. Lucy photographed by Bassano in 1909 when she was Lady Byron and aged 52. These portraits capture both her youthful beauty and her steely determination. (© *National Portrait Gallery*)

Plate B8. 'Black Bob', Robert Houston MP, 1903. (© *National Portrait Gallery, London*)

BEAUFIELD,
ST. SAVIOUR'S,
JERSEY, C.I.

Monday April 19th
1926

We certify that, in our opinion,
Lady Houston D.B.E. is not in a
fit condition, physically or
mentally, to prove her late
husband's will or to perform
the duties of an Executor.

Plate B9. Document certifying that Lucy was effectively mad. (*Courtesy of Jersey Court archives*)

Plate B10. Lucy's luxury steam yacht *Liberty*, 'dressed overall' for the birthday of Edward Prince of Wales, 1935. It was left to her in Sir Robert Houston's will, 1926. (*Courtesy of Solent Sky Museum, Southampton*)

The Late Sir Robert Houston, Who, Lady Houston Claims, Was Murdered.

Plate B11. Illustration from an article in the Milwaukee Sentinel, 10 November 1928, quoting Lucy's opinion that her husband had been murdered.

Plate B12. Maggie Meller, the French courtesan and dominatrix, with whom the young Edward, Prince of Wales, fell passionately in love in Paris, 1917. Not only would the affair have a permanent effect on his sexuality, but the letters he wrote her would prove to be an embarrassment to the Royal family when she was tried for murder in London in 1923.

Plate B13. Lucy on board *Liberty* with members of the successful RAF High-Speed Flight, 1931. Back row from right; R J Mitchell, Flt/Lt Dry (Engineer Officer), Flt/Lt Hope, Sq/Ldr Orlebar, F/O Day. Front row from right: F/O Snaith, Flt/Lt Stainforth, Lucy, Flt/Lt Bootham, Flt/Lt Long. (*Courtesy of Solent Sky Museum*)

Plate B14. Lucy wearing her famous 'black pearls' – the upper string – circa 1927. Compare with plate C22.

Plate B15. Lucy circa 1931. Amazingly, she is now over 70 and about to enter the most intensely active period of her whole life. (*Keystone*)

Plate B16. The 'Houston–Westland' aircraft, piloted by Lord Clydesdale, approaching the summit of Mount Everest, 3 April 1933. (© *The Times photo archive*)

Plate B17. Jubilant advertisement by Westland Aircraft and Bristol Aero Engines. (*Author's collection*)

Plate B18. Members of the successful Houston–Mount Everest expedition at their base in Purnea in northern India, in front of the 'Houston–Westland' aircraft. The men seated (from the left) are: Barkas, Etherton, Lord Clydesdale, Fellowes, Blacker, McIntyre, Bonnett, Ellison and Fisher. (© *The Times photo archive*)

Plate B19. James Wentworth-Day – in the bowler hat, left – with the men he recruited to sell the *Saturday Review* on the streets of London when the usual distributors refused to handle editions that they considered to be potentially libellous.

Plate B20. Lucy 'mourning the truth' on the cover of the *Saturday Review*, March 1935. She may have hoped that readers would think the photograph was contemporary but it had probably been taken at the funeral of her second husband, Lord Byron, in 1917.

Plate B21. Captain George Lloyd – right of the picture – then an officer with the Warwickshire Yeomanry, working with Colonel T.E. Lawrence on a sabotage raid in Palestine, 1917.

Plate B22. Wallis, Duchess of Windsor, wearing the engagement ring given to her by Edward VIII. The large emerald was probably sent as a present from Lucy in the summer of 1936. (*Illustrated London News*, © *Mary Evans photo library*)

Plate B23. One that got away. The grain clipper *Herzogin Cecilie* stranded on a rock off Bolt Head, South Devon, April 1936. Lucy offered to pay the salvage costs and donate the vessel to the Admiralty as a training ship but her offer was refused. (*Author's collection*)

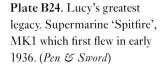

Plate B24. Lucy's greatest legacy. Supermarine 'Spitfire', MK1 which first flew in early 1936. (*Pen & Sword*)

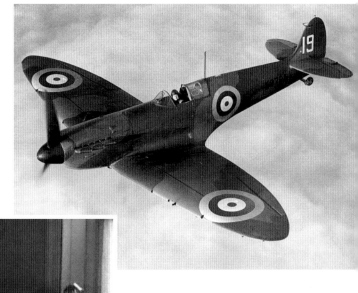

B25. The last known photograph of Lucy, taken from her filmed interview with Lord Clydesdale at Byron Cottage 1932.

lighter floats to be used. France intended to partake as well, with powerful new engines promised from both Lorraine and Renault.

It looked as though Britain would now merely host an event to glorify the achievements of foreigners. That is until Lucy's friend and noted aviator Colonel Sempill approached her with the idea of possibly financing a British entry and the 'eccentric, ebullient, generous-hearted and patriotic'[4] Lucy immediately wrote out a cheque for £100,000 in favour of the Air Ministry and gave it to The Royal Aero Club. At the same time she sent a telegram to the Minister for Air saying that she was doing this because the Government had been 'spoil-sports' and that their penny-pinching had 'made her blood boil'. Her cheque was received with ill grace and the Exchequer demanded that her bank provided a guarantee that she had the funds to back it up. Then the socialist Under-Secretary for Air added insult to injury by making a speech in the House of Commons in which he said that he was not interested 'in the thermal state of her blood' and that she had 'the bad taste to exhibit the worst sides of her political and class prejudice, in supporting what she regards as her country's best interests.'[5] But the cheque was cashed.

Now, and only now, could Vickers/Supermarine press ahead with a new version of the S.6, the S.6B, and Rolls-Royce accelerate their development of the 'R' engine to produce a remarkable 2,350 horsepower and sustain it for over one hour. [see PLATES C15–C17] The secrets behind this increase were manifold: higher engine revolutions; a major increase in the super-charger boost pressure; new bearing metals and connecting rods forged from a special aluminium alloy; novel designs of piston rings that reduced oil consumption. Also a special 'high-octane' fuel mixture was devised, a fearsome cocktail of methanol, benzol, acetone and tetra-ethyl lead.

In the final event, the French never turned up, one of their pilots having been killed during trials. A similar tragic fate struck the Italians, just after one of the Macchi MC.72s had proved it could achieve 375 mph; and when it became impossible to extract consistent performance from the new Fiat engines because of acute overheating, the Italian team also withdrew leaving Britain with the option of winning by a 'fly-over'. The fact that the Royal Aero Club refused to contemplate requests for a postponement by twelve months, as the Americans had sportingly done in 1924, would leave a somewhat sour note in some people's minds for a long time.

Then the British weather took a hand. Conditions were so bad on Saturday, 12 September, that the race was postponed to the following day, somewhat to the disappointment of the thousands of spectators that had turned up from all over the country. Team tactics suggested that no risks should be taken and that Flight Lieutenant Boothman should concentrate on completing the course in compliance with all the rules rather than at a maximum speed, a mission he accomplished at an average of 340.1 mph. [see PLATE C10] What might have been achieved under the spur of competition was demonstrated later in the afternoon when Flight Lieutenant Stainforth made four timed runs over the course to establish a new world speed record of 370.1 mph. (Eighteen months later, the Italian Macchi MC72 achieved a new air speed record of 424 mph – using standard aviation fuel.)

Lucy had been watching the event from *Liberty* moored in the harbour at Cowes. She had invited her favourite stepson, 'Naps' Brinckman, to be with her, plus two of his friends, though she had stipulated that 'they had to be good-looking'.[6] (He chose his cousin John Combe and 'Boy' Browning, who would later become General Sir Frederick Browning, husband of the novelist Daphne du Maurier and controversial mastermind of the airborne raid on Arnhem in September 1944 – though he claimed he always believed it was 'a bridge too far'.)

When Lucy came ashore to accept an invitation to join the victorious Schneider Cup team and officials who were coming over from Calshot for tea in the club house of the Royal Yacht Squadron, there was a moment's embarrassment for the steward. Ladies were not allowed into the building, and even Queen Mary, when she accompanied King George V, always stayed on the terrace outside. Fortunately a very senior member of the club put protocol aside and Lucy was welcomed as the true heroine of the day by the assembled throng. Immediately afterwards, Lucy invited the team on board *Liberty*, and the event was recorded in a historic photograph. [see PLATE B13] Looking her most glamorous, and remarkably youthful for 73 years old, she had every right to look happy and pleased with herself. Soon afterwards, the Royal Aero Club hosted a dinner at Claridges for all the participants and representatives from the entire British aviation industry, chaired by the Duke of Atholl. To great cheers, Sir Philip Sassoon read out a telegram from Lucy: 'To a company of gallant gentlemen, Lady Houston sends her heartiest greeting.' The company drank her health with equal heartiness. (The whole story of the 1931 Schneider Trophy race, Lucy's contribution, the development of the Spitfire and R.J. Mitchell's tragic death was incorporated in the 1942 film *The First of the Few* – starring Leslie Howard and David Niven.)

Lucy had become an overnight headline heroine, but she had already sailed away on *Liberty* to her mooring on the Seine to escape from the mailbags of congratulations that poured into Byron Cottage. She wrote to her friend Oscar Pulvermacher, the editor of the *Daily Mail*, 'You have been doing me proud in your newspaper. So dear and nice of you. I am *prostrate* with popularity! I am told all the young men *adore me* for what I have done. Now, after a little breathing space, my next move must be to get this Government out and it's going to happen.'[7] And she meant it.

But before we plunge into the next phase of Lucy's political crusade, it is worth standing back to reflect on the true legacy of Lucy's support for the British entry into that contest of 1931, as a result of which the Schneider Trophy can now be seen and admired in the Science Museum, South Kensington, displayed in front of the iconic Supermarine S.6B itself.[8] Securing the trophy was the immediate impact. Much longer lasting and of more crucial importance was the timely boost her donation gave to the accelerated development of the Rolls-Royce engine and to Mitchell's airframe design which would become the prototype of his iconic Spitfire fighter. The country's air defences were only barely adequate to fight off the German aerial assault of 1940, when radar, the careful planning of Air Marshall Dowding and, above all, the bravery of young airmen enabled us to win the Battle of Britain. Rolls-Royce took the lessons learnt from the development of the 'R' engine and applied them to the smaller 'Kestrel' design, resulting in the magnificent Merlin engine that powered every single British fighter engaged in the dogfights of summer 1940.

It must never be forgotten that although the Spitfire, with its unique wing-plan and sleek lines, is remembered as the hero of the hour, most of the aerial combat was undertaken by far greater numbers of the Hawker 'Hurricane'. Never so sleek and elegant looking, never so fast, this tough aircraft could absorb more combat damage and could mount the same armament load, because of the Merlin engine it shared with its more famous partner. The Battle of Britain was a very close run thing. If mass production of the Spitfire and the Merlin had been delayed by even a few weeks because of uncompleted development, the outcome might have been very different. It was the impetus that Lucy gave to this process that is surely her greatest legacy and one for which the whole nation should be eternally grateful.

[Postscript. There is an amusing file buried in the Treasury papers at the National Archives, Kew.[9] 'We have had a most unexpected intimation from Lady Houston that she regards the Schneider Trophy aircraft and engines as her own property.' Had she let slip in conversation with some friend in Parliament that wouldn't it be fun to have the planes on display on the lawn of Byron Cottage? On 9 February 1932, the Treasury solicitor was asked for his opinion on the legal position if Lucy seriously pressed the point, and the following day the Minister for Air received the advice that there seemed to be no prior conditions attached to her 'donation' and therefore there was no 'contract of ownership'.]

Chapter 12

The National Government, Squadrons of Planes for London and an Eccentric Clergyman

'Let him who desires peace prepare for war.'

Vegetius (4th century BC)

'To be prepared for war is one of the most effective ways of preserving peace.'
George Washington.

By the autumn of 1931, Britain was in crisis. The Wall Street crash of 1929 had triggered a slump in the United States that reverberated in markets around the world and caused a slowdown in economic activity everywhere. The worst effects, in terms of mass unemployment, may have been felt in America but the situation in Britain became dire. With the currency linked to the gold standard, the pound was overvalued and British exports, vital to industrial output, employment and income for the Treasury, were uncompetitive, at the same time that the costs of providing unemployment benefits were soaring. The Budget went into deficit and there was a massive run on the pound, which the Government initially tried to support at its unrealistic value. Funds drained away at an alarming rate. The cabinet of the then Labour Government was undecided as to what to do; raise taxes and import duties, or cut employment benefits and expenditure on the armed forces still further.

On 24 August the Government resigned and, as the sense of emergency heightened, King George V summoned the leaders of the three main political parties to agree to the formation of a National Government – still under Ramsay MacDonald. Its first move was to take Britain off the gold standard, allowing the pound to be devalued but at least stopping the drain on the limited Treasury reserves. Then, on 15 September, units of the Royal Navy at Invergordon mutinied as a result of their pay cuts, a flash point that forced the politicians to seek a popular mandate by calling a general election for 27 October. Both the Labour and Liberal parties were split by internal divisions, while the Conservatives managed to present a more united front in support of Stanley Baldwin and a National coalition and his promises to balance the budget by introducing protectionist trade policies if necessary rather than cut expenditure.

The outcome was a massive swing to the National Conservatives who won 470 seats of the 615 contested (gaining 210) on 55% of the vote. National Liberal MPs won 68 seats, National Labour MPs 13 and 4 National Independents were elected, giving the National Government a total of 554 seats. Its opponents had fielded a total of 599 candidates of which 'traditional' Labour represented the largest number. Fifty-two of their 516 candidates were elected, while 213 seats were lost. The next largest number of candidates had been the British Communist Party who put up 26, none of whom gained a seat and achieved a mere 0.3% of the votes. The Independent Liberals put up 7 candidates of which 4 retained their seats.

Lurking within the tables of statistics is the fate of Sir Oswald Mosley's 'New Party' which he had formed earlier in the year. Twenty-four candidates had stood for election but none had succeeded. Mosley had risen quickly in the Labour party and was sitting on their front bench by 1930, the year he published his proposals for tackling the economic depression and dealing with the unemployment problem in what became known as the Mosley Memorandum. His radical, 'National Socialist' proposals involved tariffs on all imports from outside the British Empire, government control of the banks and agricultural planning, together with large road-building programmes. Following the doctrine of Maynard Keynes, he advocated borrowing to finance a massive programme of house building and improving the standards of existing housing as a further route to solving unemployment, echoing the strategy of Mussolini in Italy and anticipating to some extent F.D. Roosevelt's 'New Deal'. Although supported by seventeen Labour MPS, including Aneurin Bevan, John Strachey and Oliver Baldwin (Stanley's son) together with A.J. Cook, general secretary of the Miners' Federation, Mosley's proposals were spurned by the shadow cabinet, and so, in disgust at his rejection, he resigned from the party and set up his own 'New Party' in 1931.

Mosley's manifesto was based on the concept of a small number of Government ministers who would exercise supreme power over decision taking – like the war cabinet during the Great War – and an emasculation of the role of parliament. Two Labour MPs defected with him together with the Liberal MP Cecil Dudgeon but only one Unionist Conservative, Bill Allen. Harold Macmillan, later to be Tory Prime Minister, confessed that 'his heart was entirely with the New Party, but his head told him to stay loyal to the Conservatives.'[1] Mosley himself told Harold Nicholson that the main response to the formation of his party came from 'the younger conservative group … and is distinctly fascist in character.' It was initially funded by Lord Nuffield (Morris Motors) with a donation of £50,000 and it published a weekly magazine called *Action!*, the editor being the diplomat and writer Harold Nicholson, perhaps better known for his unconventional marriage to Vita Sackville-West. A sudden by-election in April 1931 at Ashton-under-Lyne, a town suffering forty-six per cent unemployment, gave the first opportunity for the New Party to contest for a parliamentary seat and 7,000 people turned out to hear Mosley speak on behalf of the candidate Allen Young. In the event, Young secured only sixteen per cent of the vote, but his intervention split the Labour vote to such an extent that the seat was won by the Conservatives.

At the general election in October 1931, they had four sitting members following their defections, and the party fielded another twenty candidates, but in the event they only attracted 36,377 votes in total (0.2%). Mosley and his three companions lost their seats and Mosley was the only one not to lose his deposit.

Mosley blamed the failure of the New Party on being 'too democratic', and after visiting Italy and Germany in 1932 he united the various ultra-right wing factions in the UK to form the British Union of Fascists (BUF). The New Party had already recruited men into a private militia caricatured as the 'Biff Boys', and one of Mosley's first actions was to extend this into platoons of 'stewards' to eject hecklers from his public meetings, which were becoming extremely popular because he was an excellent and forceful orator. But wider public awareness of the role of these 'stewards' was thrust into prominence when they were employed to keep protestors at bay during his marches and demonstrations. Mosley encouraged the wearing of a distinctive uniform and these strong-arm supporters, and their female associates, were soon known as the 'Blackshirts'.

Lucy viewed the new National Government with disdain. A coalition would mean compromise and excuses for procrastination; the large majority in Parliament would surely lead to complacency. The 'old guard' were still running the cabinet and there was no role in government for her hero Winston Churchill, who was making himself particularly unpopular in official circles by opposing moves to grant India independence. He shared Lucy's view that this would throw away the brightest jewel in the Imperial crown while the Government saw it as another way of saving money, by extricating themselves from an increasingly expensive law-and-order issue as Mahatma Ghandi fanned the flames of Indian nationalism. Back in 1919, Parliament had passed the Government of India Act which proposed a review of India's constitutional arrangements through a new form of federation, though progress had stalled. Now the Government was proposing a revised 'White Paper', one that would form a major plank of policy.

After Stanley Baldwin led the National Conservatives to the landslide victory in the 1931 general election, Lucy initially believed that he could, and should, take the country back to more traditional Conservative values. Some would argue that these tenets of deference to authority, strong military defences and pride in the British Empire were merely 'old-fashioned', and both inappropriate for the social conditions of the time and uneconomical in the deteriorating financial climate. Baldwin was a pragmatist. He had campaigned strongly in support of a National Government, a concept that he described in a Mansion House speech as a 'great ideal'. He sincerely believed that the country's most urgent need was greater political cohesion, which is why he had agreed that the ailing Ramsay MacDonald, Lucy's 'Lossiemouth Loon', should remain as titular Prime Minister while he assumed most of that office's responsibilities in the role of Lord President of the Council.

For several months Lucy went on a charm offensive, sending Miss Ritchie and her chauffeur Foster off at dawn to buy flowers at Covent Garden. Week after week bunches of roses, sheaves of carnations and armfuls of lily-of-the-valley, each with a note attached saying 'with Lady Houston's love', were dropped into Downing Street, to be followed up later in the day by six-page letters written in violet ink.[2] In these she exhorted Baldwin to fight socialism and preserve the Empire, warning him about the weakness of the armed forces and her increasing conviction that Germany would soon be planning a new European war. In one letter she invited him to come and see her for a chat over a cup of tea.

A reply of acceptance came from his private office and a date was fixed, but in the event, because of some new crisis arising, it was 'homely, solid and dowdy'[3] Mrs Baldwin who turned up one afternoon at Byron Cottage. The two ladies chatted for a short time about the weather before Lucy launched into her attack. 'I think it is high time your husband woke up to the danger of having that traitor MacDonald in his confidence. Mr Baldwin is quite capable of running the country and a Conservative Prime Minister should run it without having all that Socialist rabble round him.' 'Oh! but Stanley thinks it is very necessary to have a working arrangement with the Labour Party,' the loyal wife countered, 'so that all shades of opinion can be represented for the general good of the country.' 'Stanley's wrong!' came the instant riposte, 'and I'll tell you where he's wrong and why he's wrong!' And over the next half hour that is precisely what Lucy did. When a somewhat bruised Mrs Baldwin made her excuses to leave, Lucy fired her parting shot. 'Give my love to Stanley and tell him I hope he'll alter his views. He *must* if he is going to do any good at all.' Miss Ritchie showed Mrs Baldwin out and later gave her verdict that 'the poor lady looked as though she had been pulled through a hedge backwards.'

It is easy to dismiss Lucy Houston as a political dinosaur, an old-fashioned Imperialist living in an unrealistic dream-world of Great Britain's past, unable to accept the realities of life in the early 1930s. But there is no doubt that she also had an uncanny 'sixth sense' about the future and her political antennae were tuning in to lurking dangers of cataclysmic proportions that gave her sleepless nights. By 1932 she had begun to take notice of Adolf Hitler's rise to power in Germany, because, like her hero Benito Mussolini, he was a 'strong man' standing up against the threats of communism. German industry was forging ahead, aircraft factories (some in Switzerland – to get round Versailles Treaty restrictions) were building large, advanced airliners to German designs, the shipyards were busy with new passenger liners and men were being employed to make new roads and modernise the railways. Her lurking worry was whether this industrial muscle might be turned towards armaments in defiance of the Treaty of Versailles, because she knew that the League of Nations would be impotent to do anything about it. There was talk of new German battleships being planned, but it was not this aspect that kept Lucy awake at night – the Royal Navy was still the dominant force in the world. Lucy's involvement with the Schneider Trophy had made her appreciate that with the right amount of money and the right engineering skills, remarkable advances in aircraft design could now be achieved very quickly indeed. Both Germany and Russia had flown giant, lumbering bombers before the end of the Great War; what might they be capable of now? And this was where Britain's defences were weakest. Surely Britain would never get involved ever again in a continental land war, but what if some country decided to launch an attack against her? The English Channel and the Royal Navy might protect her from invasion, but how about an all-out aerial assault, particularly by night? She had lived through the terrifying Zeppelin raids on London in 1917 and her dreams now became nightmares as she envisaged London ablaze, with buildings falling in flames and children running screaming through the streets. Unable to get back to sleep, she would wake Miss Ritchie and spend the hours until dawn telling her in graphic detail about her premonitions and her fears for the future.[4]

Lucy was no armchair critic or futuristic fiction writer. If it was in her power to do something, she would act. First of all, to reconfirm her patriotic credentials, she sent a cheque to the Treasury for £65,000 in settlement of the tax that she believed would have been due from her if she had been domiciled in England. This was cashed. Then one morning in the spring of 1932, when she was on Jersey, she wrote a cheque for £200,000 and a letter to the Chancellor of the Exchequer, at that time Neville Chamberlain, stating that she wished him to spend the money on buying squadrons of the most modern fighters to be on standby for the defence of London. Her money would have been enough to buy about seventy aircraft.[5] (In this she was anticipating by several years the formation of the Royal Air Force Auxiliary Reserve.) She summoned Miss Ritchie and asked her to take *Liberty* to Southampton, travel to London and hand her letter personally to the Chancellor and await his reply. Arriving at the offices in Eaton Square,

Miss Ritchie was told that the Chancellor was very busy and, if she still insisted that the envelope could not be given to anybody else, she would have to wait. Eventually Neville Chamberlain appeared, took the letter and opened it in her presence. As she recounted, 'he glanced at the cheque and then looked thoroughly pleased. Then he asked me to thank Lady Houston very much indeed and tell her that he would reply when he had considered the matter – with his other colleagues in the Cabinet.'[6]

When Lucy had received no reply three weeks later, she wrote a stinging letter to the Chancellor. 'A cheque of mine for £200,000 has been kicking around your office for the last month and I have not even had the courtesy of an acknowledgment!' This did induce a reply, a bald statement that 'the Cabinet could not accept the money because of the conditions on how it was to be spent.' Lucy took up her pen and spat back. 'If I pay the money, I have a right to say how it is spent! It's the poor people of London I'm thinking of, not the Cabinet or its dignity!'

That same month provided another example of the muddled thinking within the Air Ministry concerning aircraft procurement – not for the first time, and certainly not the last. In 1929, the German firm of Dornier had achieved the first flight of a vast flying boat airliner on behalf of Lufthansa, the national airline. This monster, the Dornier X, had no less than twelve engines and had accommodation for up to seventy passengers arranged over three decks which provided for comfortable lounges and even a restaurant. Admittedly its performance never matched its mighty appearance, though it did manage to make one, very sluggish transatlantic crossing in 1930, in several stages via Lisbon, Las Palmas, Portuguese Guinea, the Cape Verde Islands, the islands of Fernando de Noronha and finally Rio de Janeiro.[7] The British Air Ministry in 1929 decided to invite tenders for something similar, finally awarding the contract worth £86,585, not to Short Bros who had built up considerable experience with large civil flying boats, but to Supermarine, who only specialised in military aircraft. The massive 104-foot hull of the aircraft, designated the 'Giant' or more prosaically 'Type 179', was nearing completion when the whole contract was cancelled.[8]

A few days after the rebuff of her far-sighted offer to fund new fighter aircraft, Lucy ordered *Liberty* to anchor off Portsmouth. The ship's electrician spent a frantic day wiring up a series of lights from the rigging and as darkness fell the sailors and shipwrights in the dockyard were amazed to see the ship suddenly lit up.[9] In letters three feet high, it proclaimed Lucy's slogan:

DOWN WITH THE TRAITOR MACDONALD

It was not long before a pinnace drew up alongside with a group of very angry Admiralty officials who demanded that Lucy had the lights turned off. A ferocious argument finally ended with Lucy agreeing to weigh anchor and depart. Not far though. More hasty rewiring, more festoons of light bulbs and an hour later crowds of holiday-makers strolling along the sea-front at Southsea saw Lucy's modified message blaze out again, now in letters eight foot tall:

TO HELL WITH THE TRAITOR MACDONALD

Without staying long enough for the authorities to catch up with her again, she ordered her captain to head for Poole Harbour, where a day or so later she turned the illuminations back on again. She was delighted when told that her message could be seen from a mile away and that crowds were packing the coastline to gawp at her audacity.

Lucy kept the £200,000 she had earmarked for her 'defence of London' campaign in a separate bank account and on 4 December 1933 she renewed her offer via a long telegram to the Chancellor of the Exchequer, saying that she had the backing of Lord Londonderry, the Duke of Sutherland and Lord Lloyd among others. When, twelve days later, she had received no reply, either of acceptance or rejection, she wrote a 'Manifesto to the Citizens of London', headed,

WHICH IS MORE IMPORTANT,
THE SAFETY OF LONDON or the
IMAGINARY
Dignity of the Prime Minister?[10]

In it she pointed out that London, 'the city we love and are so proud of', was the only one she knew of that was without any defence against invasion from the sky. 'Are you content,' she asked, 'in order to please the Prime Minister, to remain in this deadly peril? I will gladly give £200,000 to save London and its inhabitants from this terrible danger, as a Christmas present to this country. The Government will do nothing unless YOU tell them THEY MUST accept my offer.' She signed herself off as 'your true friend.' Once again the official reply was an outright rejection.

Politics and politicians have dominated this chapter and will occupy much in those that follow, so perhaps for a little light relief we might turn to Lucy's passing involvement with the bizarre story of an eccentric clergyman who turned up on her doorstep one day pleading for financial assistance.

Lucy was still dispensing money generously to charitable causes that she considered worthy, and as rewards for particular individuals that caught her attention. One example was prompted by John Gordon, the editor of the *Sunday Express*, who enjoyed something of a journalistic coup when he initiated a competition to try and find the one single person who had done the most to bring the Great War to an end. This produced a welter of correspondence and interesting suggestions and finally the newspaper decided that the winner should be Lieutenant R.J. Rollings MC. This young officer had led a daring armoured car raid that had captured the secret plans of the final German defences, the Hindenburg Line. It was judged that this single action had finally broken the backbone of German resistance. Lucy immediately sent Rollings a cheque for £5,000 with 'her love and admiration'. The story of the Reverend Harold Davidson would, however, end rather differently.

Harold Davidson was the rector of the parish of Stiffkey (pronounced 'Stewky'), a village on the north coast of Norfolk.[11] He had been born in 1875. His father had also been a clergyman though Harold's career ambitions after he left school, where he had been a poor and inattentive student, had taken him in a completely different direction. Although he had neglected his studies, he had shown some talent as an actor and soon after leaving Whitgift School he appeared on the London stage in a 'comic routine', following this up by touring the country playing the leading role in a production of the popular farce *Charley's Aunt*. He was a strict teetotaller and gave bible readings to the elderly residents in the towns where he was performing. At the age of 22 he finally agreed to read for Holy Orders and friends of his father managed to get him accepted into Exeter College, Oxford, in spite of his lacking the necessary academic qualifications. Here his behaviour became increasingly bizarre; he neglected his studies, failed every exam and was forced to leave. Finally though, after two years at a crammer, he was ordained in 1903 and in 1905 he was the curate at St Martin-in-the-Fields, London.

One day he officiated at the marriage of John Townshend, the 6th Marquess Townshend, to a failed actress by the name of Gladys Sutherst. Neither family approved of the match but somehow Harold Davidson had poured sufficient oil onto the troubled waters to resolve the difficulties, and in gratitude for his efforts the Marquess gifted him the valuable living at the joint parishes of Stiffkey and Morston. This came with a fine Georgian rectory, sixty acres of glebe land and a very respectable stipend of £800 per annum. The following year he married an actress he had known from his touring days called Molly Saurin who bore him a succession of children. But he soon adopted the habit of spending every weekday in London, where he became involved in charitable work for the Docklands Mission and the Actors' Church Union. He spent his evenings backstage at various London theatres, 'ministering to the needs of the showgirls – sometimes with an unwelcome persistence.' He particularly enjoyed 'chaperoning' dancers to Paris on behalf of the Folies Bergère, while he would often return to Stiffkey at weekends with as many as twenty out-of-work actresses whom he invited to stay at the rectory. He had served as a Royal Navy chaplain during the war and had got to know a shadowy character called Mr Gordon. In 1924 he had been persuaded by Gordon to lend money for a new theatrical venture, but Gordon turned out to be a fraudster and Davidson was declared bankrupt, his stipend being reduced by half to pay off his debts.

Unlike the former Prime Minister William Gladstone, who took prostitutes back to his home for the purpose of trying to persuade them to give up their trade, Davidson wanted to offer his very personal help to save teenage girls from the temptations of this profession before they sinned. This approach gave him almost endless scope, though he believed that it was 'tweenies', young waitresses in tearooms such as Lyons Corner Houses, who were potentially the most vulnerable. The sight of chubby, potentially strokeable, thighs under short black skirts sent him into ecstasies. He adored their clear cheeky eyes and small firm breasts and had a particular fetish for strong, healthy teeth. At night he invited them back to the Mission house. 'He spoke to them, smiled at them, kissed them and kept them, but muddled himself up so cosily between adoring them and saving them that the difference soon escaped him.' Then, possibly out of jealousy, his favourite convert, a girl called Rose Ellis, began to make allegations of sexual impropriety against him, and Davidson, perhaps unwisely, leapt to his own defence through letters to the newspapers. Suddenly a few details of his unusual lifestyle became public knowledge. It was a sensation. On Sunday, 7 February 1932, over 500 people turned up for evensong at Stiffkey to hear Davidson preach, some by bicycle from Norwich and others even on specially hired buses from as far afield as Bournemouth. Encouraged by what he interpreted as his 'Sermon on the Mount' moment, and against the advice of friends and the bishop's legal advisors, he contracted to write a series of articles for the *Empire News*. He became a celebrity.

The church authorities decided to take a stand, summoning Davidson to a consistory court to face charges under the Clergy Discipline Act of 1892. The hearing was convened for 29 March in the Great Hall of Church House, Westminster. To the initial disappointment of spectators, the charges read out seemed petty: that he had made improper suggestions to a waitress in Walbrook, that he had kissed a girl in a Chinese restaurant, and that he had generally been guilty of immoral conduct over a period of ten years. If the Chancellor of Norwich had assumed that matters would be concluded within a day and that Davidson would plead guilty and merely receive a stiff reprimand, he was soon disillusioned. Davidson, with a smile on his lips, denied all and every one of the charges. This meant that the Bishop's Counsel, Roland Oliver KC, supported by Walter Monkton KC, would have to present the prosecution case in detail and the press suddenly realised that here was a honey pot of sensational sweetness. When further articles by Davidson appeared in the press, the Bishop of Norwich sued the *Daily Herald*, the *Empire News* and Davidson himself for contempt of court. Over the ensuing weeks, streams of witnesses were called by both sides and in April Davidson's counsel, the cheapest he could find, asked for an extension of time because the defence funds had run out. The prosecution, desperate to bring matters to some conclusion, generously offered to contribute £250 merely to speed things up, but Davidson haughtily declined, saying that he had never in his life accepted charity and did not mean to start now.

It was probably at this stage that Davidson turned up on Lucy's doorstep, claiming that he needed to see her 'on a matter of life or death'.[12] (He certainly did visit Byron Cottage several times, though Wentworth Day is imprecise about the exact dates.) Miss Ritchie turned him away on every occasion, so he tried sending his daughter, 'a charming young girl with an educated voice and tragic eyes', who pleaded that her family desperately needed £500.[13] Miss Ritchie remained adamant that the rector's scandalous cause would not be one that Lady Houston would ever consider. She might dispense charity to tramps but not to a man of the cloth whose own actions had brought about his fall from grace.

On 6 June the court was adjourned for the Chancellor to work on his summing up while Davidson headed for Birmingham where he had been invited to give 'dramatic recitations' to audiences of up to 2,000 people. When the day of judgement arrived on 8 July, Davidson was found guilty on all five charges against him, whereupon he ran out of the Great Hall and across the road to present his pre-written appeal at the offices of the Privy Council. After this was rejected, he lodged a private bill of petition to the Privy Council and was told that this could not be considered before October. This was followed by an order from the Bishop of Norwich that he was forbidden to hold services at Stiffkey after 25 August, whereupon he headed to the seafront at Blackpool and proceeded to set himself up as a sideshow, living in a barrel like the cynic Diogenes several centuries earlier. His pitch was next door to a flea circus and 3,000 people paid to see this freak exhibit. As chilly autumn winds started to blow in from the Atlantic, he received the equally chilling news that his final appeal had been rejected, though his spirits were lifted by the fact that he, and the long-drawn-out trial with its enormous legal expenses and titillating publicity, was the subject of the leading article in *The Times* for 14 October. Under the banner headline 'The Stiffkey Scandal' the editor questioned whether the authorities of the Church of England had been wise to resort to such a public route to resolve what was essentially an internal, ecclesiastical matter, and, although justice needed to be seen to be done, should they not review their procedures? Was it really in the public interest, let alone that of the Church of England, that so much dirty linen should be laundered in such a public fashion? The editor sincerely hoped that this would be the last that the world would hear of the Rev Davidson.

Little chance. A week later Davidson was summoned to Norwich cathedral at 12.15 for the solemn ceremony at which he would be defrocked. At the appointed hour, the dignified procession of the Bishop, the Chancellor, the Dean, the Archdeacons and the Canons started up the aisle, when the Registrar dashed in to read out a telegram from Davidson in which he sent his apologies that he was delayed and would be a little late, but hoped that they would not mind waiting a while. The procession reversed its way back to the vestry. When Davidson finally did turn up in his muddy little car to cheers from the crowds outside, he leapt out and ran into the cathedral to take a seat immediately facing the Bishop's throne. The dignitaries returned and, after a few short prayers, the Bishop stood up and started to pronounce the sentence. He had got no further than 'In the name of God ...' when Davidson leapt to his feet and shouted 'may I not be allowed to say anything before sentence is passed?' After a hasty word with the church solicitors, the Bishop wearily agreed that he could – but only very briefly. Davidson, encouraged by *The Times* article, launched into the attack. 'I am entirely innocent ... there is not one single deed which I have done which I shall not do again with the help of God ... it is the church authorities that are put on trial, not myself ...' Then, at last, the exasperated Bishop, summoning every ounce of gravitas for the awesome occasion, declared the sentence. 'We, Bertram, by divine permission Bishop of Norwich, pronounce, decree and declare that the Reverend Harold Francis Davidson ought to be deprived, and we do deprive him thereof by this our definite sentence ...'

The Bishop then signed the document and headed for the high altar to deliver the final, solemn proclamation, only to find himself beaten to his objective by Davidson who had sprinted ahead of him. They both knelt in fervent prayer before the bishop stood up, mitre aloft, crozier in hand, and declaimed, 'We, Bertram, by divine permission do hereby declare that the said Reverend Harold Francis Davidson ought to be entirely removed, deposed and degraded ... and we hereby, by the authority of Almighty God ... do so remove, depose and degrade him.' The Bishop crumpled to his knees muttering prayers about human frailty, while Davidson cried out, in a high, imperious voice that could be heard at the back of the cathedral, that he knew his rights under the Clergy Discipline Act and that he intended to appeal to the Archbishop of Canterbury in person.

Over the next five years, Davidson reverted to his role as an entertainer, living hand-to-mouth in increasingly bizarre locations at seaside resorts where the public might pay to listen to lectures from the one-time Sunday newspaper sensation. The summer of 1937 found him advertised as preaching from inside a lion's cage on the front at Skegness and a large crowd assembled to watch the amazing phenomenon. The lion-tamer opened the grill and Davidson slipped inside to introduce himself to the huge male lion called Freddy. Freddy, however, had apparently not read the script, and, after a few moments of playful pawing, grabbed him by the throat and shook him almost to death. The final irony was that the lion-tamer, who very bravely dashed in to rescue the limp, bleeding body of the Christian martyr, was a pretty, 16-year-old girl with strong thighs and gleaming white teeth called Irene Somner. The 'troublesome priest' died in hospital two days later.

Figure 2. The Rev Harold Davidson's initial, playful encounter with 'Freddy', Skegness 1937.

Chapter 13

Oswald Mosley Rejected and Lucy Gets her New Man

The daily routine at Byron Cottage began with Miss Ritchie bringing Lucy breakfast in bed – bacon and eggs if she was feeling well – along with copies of all the London daily newspapers. Lucy always started with the *Daily Herald*; 'such good articles,' she declared, 'if it wasn't Socialist, it would be a very good newspaper.'[1] It was at the time the world's best-selling daily, with a circulation of around two million. Once the official organ of the Trades Union Congress, it had been sold in 1930 to Odhams Press who also owned *The People*, published on Sundays. Close on its heels in terms of popularity was Lord Beaverbrook's *Daily Express*, a paper of a very different political hue and one whose editor, Arthur Christianson, was extremely adept at gauging what its readers wanted to read, such as introducing the Rupert Bear strip cartoon. Lucy had a great admiration for tough little Lord Beaverbrook – 'I adore him, so full of fire and go' – and he was a frequent visitor at Byron Cottage.

Next on her reading list was the *Daily Mail*, then owned by Lord Rothermere who had founded the United Empire political party and been responsible for publishing the crucial Zinoviev letter that had undermined the Labour Party election campaign in 1924. (This was subsequently shown to have been a forgery, but by then it had served its purpose.) Rothermere also owned the *Daily Mirror* which he had bought from his brother Lord Harmsworth. Harmsworth had originally founded it in 1913 as 'a paper for women, run by women' but this formula had proved to be a disaster. It had been revived by introducing a large pictorial content which lifted its circulation in the 1920s to over a million, but it was on the decline in the early 1930s. Another newspaper in decline, but one that Lucy admired, was the Tory *Morning Post*, once the preferred reading of the retired officer class. Then there was *The Telegraph*, dating back to 1855 and now under the ownership of William Berry, Lord Camrose. Lucy applauded the style of its editor Arthur Watson, who later took a strong stand against the policy of appeasement with Germany. Last on Lucy's reading list was *The Times*, which had been bought by Lord Astor from Lord Northcliffe in 1922. 'Stuffy, pompous and full of its own importance. In my youth they called it the "Thunderer",' she proclaimed, 'now it is just a Government mouth-organ.'[2] She disliked it even more when it became an ardent supporter of the League of Nations. It was the only newspaper whose offices she never visited.

Lucy was becoming increasingly fascinated by the whole newspaper industry and she wanted to be part of it. She enjoyed nothing more than accepting an invitation to drive down to Fleet Street and witness the process of 'putting a newspaper to bed', seeing the final frantic adjustments to the typesetting before watching the great printing presses starting to roll out the first editions. On every such occasion she experienced a rush of adrenalin. These visits also forged personal friendships with some of the great, practical newspaper men, particularly Colin Brooks, Ralph (R.D.) Blumenfeld and Oscar Pulvermacher, the night editor of the *Daily Mail*. He had printed a number of articles that she submitted to the newspaper over the years, for the first of which she had received a cheque for £8 8 shillings. She thanked him in a letter of girlish delight:

> Dear Editor, I feel *very important* having earned eight guineas with my pen! – but I am returning the cheque – perhaps you would like to give it to your printers' fund? I am becoming quite a big shareholder in the *Daily Mail*. Congratulations are still coming in to me for my articles – I am having extracts from them collected and nearly *all* blame Baldwin. I shall send them to him just to prove that it is not only the *Daily Mail* that wants him out.

She realised that newspapers were the best medium for influencing public opinion, as a potential avenue of propagating her own political convictions. In truth, however, newspapers were the only route for reaching a mass audience. Radio, the 'wireless', was becoming more popular, but the wavelengths were controlled by the British Broadcasting Corporation and its programme output was dictated by the formidable, God-fearing educationalist Lord Reith. There were just two ways in which listeners could break through this monopoly, both of which required more sophisticated receiving sets. The first of these was a commercial radio station broadcasting in English from the continent under the name of Radio Luxemburg, offering popular music between the advertisements. It would remain a source of secret pleasure to many for several decades to come.

The second was a lesser-known wireless station on the continent aiming its transmissions at Britain under the title of Radio Normandie, the brainchild of Captain Leonard Plugge (born 1889). He was a wireless enthusiast and, touring around France in the 1920s in a large car with a powerful transmitter, had been gratified to discover that his fellow 'radio hams' could receive his signals back home. In 1931 he formed the International Broadcasting Company and set up his first commercial transmitter in the Normandy town of Fécamp. It was the first of a number of his commercial stations on the continent from which he made a large fortune, and in 1935 he was elected as Conservative MP for Chatham, incidentally beating the future leader of the Labour party, Hugh Gaitskell. One place within easy range of Radio Normandie was Jersey and Lucy was an interested listener. She tucked the concept away at the back of her mind and, as we will see later, revived it in 1934. She was not alone in recognising the potential of wireless for political propaganda; so was Dr Joseph Goebbels in Germany.

We have already seen how Lucy became a great admirer of Benito Mussolini and, to her mind, his very effective style of government. In Germany it seemed to her that another man, Adolf Hitler, might have to be taken seriously. She wrote personal letters to both of them, applauding the fact that they were both 'strong men' exercising patriotic leadership and battling against communism.[3]

It is impossible for readers in the twenty-first century to view Adolph Hitler as anyone other than a mad tyrant, a crazed megalomaniac who precipitated all the miseries of the Second World War and the 'Holocaust', a dictator determined to undermine the very foundations of Western civilisation. So it needs a leap of imagination to try to understand the image he presented to the world when he first began to gain political power in Germany in the early 1930s – via the democratic process of the ballot box. Through his powerful oratory he seemed to offer Germans a solution to unemployment and the economic depression. Most important of all, he inspired a vision of a New Germany that would restore the nation's self-esteem, recalling the legends and heroes of the country's Teutonic past while denouncing the restrictions imposed by the Versailles Treaty. He exhorted younger listeners to be healthy, to build up their own strength and vitality through physical exercise, and their sense of community by joining disciplined youth organisations. His creed, reflected in the title of his political party, was one of Nationalistic Socialism that viewed communism as a virulent plague. His political manifesto, *Mein Kampf*, written in prison during the 1920s, was available for every citizen to read. However, the translations of this work available outside Germany were only condensed, watered-down versions of the original, completely ignoring the chapters on how Hitler planned to achieve Germany's goal of *lebensraum* ('space for the people') via overt military conquest beyond its eastern borders. Also expunged were damning references to other international movements that might subvert and undermine the cohesion of German society – particularly the Jews. So if one can adjust one's mindset back to the early 1930s it is easier to understand why Lucy, and many other people in Britain on the right of the political spectrum, saw Hitler in the early days as another version of Mussolini, one to be admired rather than vilified.

Where, Lucy asked herself, were the good, strong, patriotic Englishmen with political conviction? 'The plight this government is bringing England to,' she had written to the Conservative peer Lord Lloyd in November 1930, 'should be enough to make you see how imperative it is that a strong man should take power into his own hands and out of the hands of these betrayers and scoundrels. Of course Baldwin ought to do it, but Baldwin *cannot* be strong, he hasn't got it in him!'[4] As recounted later in our story, in three years' time she would return to this theme, trying to persuade Lloyd to form his own, new political party.

One man, however, who had already done precisely that was Oswald Mosley, as we saw in the previous chapter. Having changed the name of the New Party to the British Union of Fascists (BUF), he and his glamorous wife Cimmie, daughter of Lord Curzon, started on a nationwide series of public speaking engagements that drew enormous crowds due to what *The Times* grudgingly described as 'the astonishing power of his platform appeal'. He certainly had great sexual appeal for women, who made up a high proportion of his audiences, and he reciprocated by positively encouraging their recruitment to membership. Many were former Suffragettes. He modelled his party's fascism on that of Benito Mussolini, with whom he got on very well when he visited Italy on a number of occasions. Initially his main financial sponsor was Lord Rothemere's *Daily Mail* which produced headlines such as 'Hurrah for the Blackshirts!' and helped the number of paid-up party members to peak at around 50,000 in 1934. Then Mosley made a serious tactical mistake. Instead of promoting the BUF as an alternative, mainstream political party advocating populist policies (like Nigel Farage and the UKIP party in the 2010s), one that would put forward hundreds of candidates to contest seats at the next general election, he began to take much more notice of Adolf Hitler's version of fascism in Germany. He completely misread its startling popular success, linking this to its perverted anti-Semitic priorities. When he made these a cornerstone of his own activists' marches into the East End of London, he lost not only the goodwill of middle class supporters but also upset the advertisers in the *Daily Mail* to such an extent that Lord Rothermere was forced to withdraw his financial backing.

Mosley's mistake was his failure to understand the demographic differences between the Jewish populations of the two countries. In England this could be counted in tens of thousands, most families being well established since the previous century and well integrated into communities spread widely across the country. Many had fought patriotically for Britain during the Great War and the working classes particularly applauded them for their sporting prowess in national teams. In Germany, however, the number was over 600,000 and recently swollen by emigration, the 'diaspora', from Russia following their series of pogroms in the 1920s. Simplistically, there just were not enough 'unpopular' Jews in England to make their presence any kind of social issue. Nor were Mosley's visits to Germany and his meetings with Adolf Hitler very successful, though he did manage to persuade the Nazi party to donate £50,000 towards his funding. Hitler thought he was too much of a dilettante and not a serious enough politician, though he did recognise that a well-connected, like-minded fascist in England might serve his purposes at some later date. He even recommended that Mosley might be more successful if he changed the name of his supporters from 'blackshirts' to 'ironsides', echoing the winning side in the English civil war of the seventeenth century.

Lucy, like so many other disillusioned people on the right wing of British politics, had originally thought that Mosley might be her 'man of destiny', but his methods appeared to be too crude, too unsophisticated and too un-British. His increasing anti-Semitism might have touched an underlying nerve in a small part of the national psyche but she found it very distasteful – and said so. A grateful Jewish girl, signing herself Miriam, wrote her a poem of gratitude of which the first lines were as follows:[5]

> O lady of the Bannered Muse
> Wrapped in Red, White and Blue,
> May a mere daughter of the Jews
> Endorse her thanks to you?

Worst of all, in her eyes, was that Mosley lacked a sense of humour. So Lucy had to look elsewhere for her 'strong man', but first she needed to recruit another man, a trustworthy personal assistant who would do her political leg-work for her – and much, much more.

One of the great British newspaper editors of the early twentieth century was Ralph (R.D.) Blumenfeld, a journalist born in America in 1864 who had spent two years as business editor of the *Daily Mail* before being bribed away by Arthur Pearson to join the newly founded *Daily Express* in 1902. He was a wealthy man in his own right and had been made a director in 1908 and editor the following year, a post that he held until 1929. Max Aitken, Lord Beaverbrook, was by now the owner and exerting increasing editorial influence, leading to Blumenfeld's resignation that year. But in 1932 he was invited back as chairman of the board of directors, a position he would hold until his death in 1948. He was an old-style Conservative who in 1908 had founded the Anti-Socialist Union. Lucy held him in the highest esteem and so she went to seek his help for her latest project. She was now aged 75, yet amazingly enough was about to launch herself into the most active period of her life.

'I want you to find me a young man. Not too young – not too old,' she told him. 'He must be a true Blue Tory and he must hate Ramsay MacDonald and Stanley Baldwin just as much as I do. In fact he must be prepared to go to gaol for his principles if need be. I am going to have my own newspaper and I am going to print in it exactly what I think of all these people. Never mind your silly libel laws! This young man will have to edit it for me … if he is sent to gaol, I shall go with him.' She added, 'he must also be able to make a good political speech, stand up to hecklers and preach my doctrine at every by-election there is. I am going to attack every National Government candidate who puts up, unless he promises to vote for a bigger Army, Navy and Air Force … and for no more throwing away the Empire.'[6]

Blumenfeld suggested that it sounded as if such a man would be kept pretty busy. Lucy chuckled: 'Of course he will! I'm always busy – why shouldn't he be? I'd do it all myself only I am just a poor weak woman.' It was now Blumenfeld's turn to smile. 'If I was only half as weak as you are, I'd give up editing this newspaper and go out and conquer a few Empires of my own. And I think that I have the man for you – he's on my staff.'

Unbeknownst to Blumenfeld, Lucy had also given the same job description to another great friend, the controversial pioneer aviator Colonel (later Lord) Sempill, the man who had canvassed her support for the Schneider Trophy. He had served in the Royal Naval Air Service at the end of the First World War, after which he led a delegation to Japan to help them establish a new naval air base. Perhaps he became too involved in this programme and he was suspected of selling advanced British aircraft plans to the Japanese. This never became public knowledge because the Air Ministry had gleaned their intelligence from breaking the secret Japanese naval codes, which put them in the same dilemma as Winston Churchill in the Second World War regarding some of the intelligence gleaned from the Enigma programme at Bletchley Park. To have warned in advance about the blitz on Coventry would have alerted the Germans to the fact that their 'unbreakable' codes had indeed been penetrated. Sempill confessed to having broken the Official Secrets Act and was let off with a caution – for one thing, the Japanese at that time were still our allies and for another Sempill was a national hero, having established a world record flight from London to Stockholm in his De Havilland 'Moth' in 1930. In 1932 he was elected chairman of the Royal

Aeronautical Society, the guardians of the precious Schneider Trophy, and in reply to Lucy's request he came up with the same name as Blumenfeld – James Wentworth Day.

Wentworth Day was 33 years old at the time and had taken a degree at Cambridge University. He had been born and brought up in East Anglia, which gave him a life-long interest in the world of nature and country sports. He was extremely well connected, a member of the staunchly Tory Pratt's Club and an excellent shot, making him a welcome guest at weekend shooting parties. He had worked as a journalist on the *Daily Express* until 1930 when he took a two-year contract to edit and reorganise *The Field* magazine on behalf of Sir Leicester Harmsworth, the brother of both Lord Northcliffe and Lord Rothermere. Early in 1932 he rejoined the Beaverbrook newspaper empire on the *Sunday Express.* This was a somewhat roving commission that suited him well because above all he relished his spare time. He also had some private means, which meant that he only took on jobs that he really enjoyed. He shared a two-floor bachelor flat in a fine Charles II house on King Street, Pall Mall, with Arthur Portman, the proprietor of *Horse & Hound,* and Eric Bowater, the newsprint millionaire, who was then between marriages. Wentworth Day was also separated from his wife, Helen Gardon, whom he had married in 1925 after a number of unsuccessful engagements that echoed the experience of Theodore Brinckman.[7] The three single men shared a 'gentleman's gentleman' by the name of Stimpson.

Wentworth Day first learnt that he had been 'volunteered' for a new career when Colonel Sempill telephoned him on a bright summer morning in August 1932 and invited him to be his passenger on a flight to the Channel Islands. They landed on the island of Sark and lunched with the formidable Mrs Sybil Hathaway, known as the Dame of Sark, who ruled her domain as if it was a private fiefdom. After lunch, the Dame asked Wentworth Day where they were off to next, to which he had to reply that he did not have the slightest notion. Sempill answered for him, saying that they were going to meet another great lady.

Landing on the golf course on Jersey, the little plane was met by a long, sleek black car with drawn curtains, which drove them to Lucy's modest villa, Beaufield, a property that Wentworth Day described as 'a small, unpretentious house of the sort in which a prosperous doctor might live, not a mansion.' [see PLATE C7] Lucy's first words of greeting were, 'What do you think of Baldwin and MacDonald?' She laughed at her young guest's reply that he thought they made an unholy bedfellowship. 'Exactly right! That mahogany-faced old humbug Baldwin going to bed with that prinking hypochondriac MacDonald.' Lucy held no truck with the new so-called National Government. Wentworth Day later recalled how Lucy then invited him to sit down in the garden while she launched into a tirade, 'flinging the words like bullets among the roses'.[8]

'Do you realise that we're drifting towards another World War? Germany and Russia both hate us. The Russians murdered their Tsar and they would murder our King if they could. They want India. They want the Dardenelles, the Persian Gulf and the Middle Eastern oil, plus every warm-water port they can get their hands on. They want to dominate the world. Our air power is only sixth in the world – the army is miserably under strength and our navy is under manned and under gunned. I have a plan – a big plan. It will wake up Britain to the dangers that lie ahead. If we don't wake up in time we shall go down in the biggest war the world has ever known. I *must* tell the people the truth!'

After tea, she ushered her guests back to the car. 'Later, perhaps, I'll tell you more. Goodbye for the present. I like you.' Wentworth Day was stunned by the encounter – he had never been more impressed by any one at a first meeting. 'She looked like a handsome forty-five-year-old – she was sheer dynamite.'[9] Over the next few months she invited him up to shoot at her hunting lodge in the Highlands and for meetings at Byron Cottage. For Christmas she posted him a surprise cheque for £100. But no offer of any sort of job, probably because Lucy herself was gravely ill over Christmas. A communiqué from her doctors stated that she was suffering from vertigo, 'which so far has refused to respond to treatment. She must be kept absolutely quiet and no visitors are allowed.'[10] (Her illness was probably an attack of Ménière's disease, an infection of the inner ear that affects balance.)

Wentworth Day was still in bed early on Friday, 6 January 1933, looking forward to a weekend's shooting on Lord Mandeville's estate at Kimbolton when the telephone rang. It was a fully recovered but furious Lucy. 'Have you seen what they are doing to that poor man in East Fife? Will you go and fight for him?' The background to this inconvenient request was a by-election caused by the death of the incumbent MP, a National Liberal called Sir James Millar. His party's candidate was being opposed by a local farmer, Mr A. Anderson, standing as an Independent on behalf of local agricultural interests, though certain papers attacked him bitterly for being a closet Conservative.

Wentworth Day said that he could perhaps start doing something on Monday but Lucy snapped back 'that's not soon enough!' So, after an apologetic call to his host, he turned up at Byron Cottage to find that Lucy had already written a long pamphlet that she wanted printed and then taken up to Scotland for distribution. She had not got her own newspaper yet, but she knew there would be a lot of reporters covering this by-election and that she would be guaranteed publicity. He read through the document carefully, alarmed to find that it was utterly libellous. After considerable arguments he persuaded her to take out the most offensive items, but even then, as he recalled later, it was 'the hottest bit of political propaganda he had ever seen in print'. He then dashed off to a printer he knew who ran off thousands of the pamphlets and several hundred placards proclaiming 'Lady Houston's Advice to East Fife'. Armed with these, he took the first train to St Andrews, recruited twenty unemployed men and a Highland pipe-band and the next morning they plastered the town with the placards and put a copy of the pamphlet through every letter box. It was the first American-style, razzamatazz election campaign in the country and the residents of St Andrews could not believe what had hit them. The pamphlet was headed:

LADY HOUSTON'S MESSAGE TO THE WOMEN
(You may let your husband see this if he is good)

Underneath this headline was written (at Wentworth Day's insistence because he did not want the campaign to be accused of breaching any rules about candidate's expenses) the following:

> *Note: Lady Houston wishes it known that this is not an election message, but it is a message from her to all the women all over Great Britain and is being circulated everywhere.*

The document ran to well over 1,000 words, damning Socialism – 'the cause of the present ruin and bankruptcy in farming', the Liberals – 'barefaced swindlers and cast-off leavings of the nation', Free Trade, Internationalism and Russia in particular. She pleaded for a return to Conservative values of patriotism, strong defences and putting British interests first. The country had given the Conservative party a resounding mandate in 1931, so how had Stanley Baldwin been conned into this idea of a 'National' Government which was no more than 'a sham, a fraud, a humbug and a make-belief', with MacDonald still as Prime Minister?

A local paper reported that 'a comic element has been introduced by the appearance (in leaflet form) of the redoubtable Lady Houston who, having contributed £1,000 to the central funds of the Conservative party is now claiming the right to nominate the candidates.'[11] On the same day, the *Dundee Evening Telegraph* claimed that her intervention was 'an impertinence that Fifers will certainly resent. Ever since she deservedly won kudos by financing the Schneider Trophy contest, Lady Houston seems to have thought herself competent to run the whole British Empire.' The paper lambasted one of the other contesting candidates as well, a Mr Linklater who was standing as a Scottish Nationalist (SNP). 'It is about time that folk outside Scotland know how little that foolish movement appeals to Scotsmen.'[12]

Lord Beaverbrook himself turned up and made a speech on 10 January in support of Anderson, demanding that the Government's new-found stance on protectionism should not only apply to manufactured goods but to agriculture as well, otherwise British farming would be ruined. Anderson added that this applied to the fishing industry also. That evening Beaverbrook invited Wentworth Day, his ex-employee, to join him for dinner. 'My God, that old woman of yours is in it with both feet! If you handle her rightly she could sweep the country. She has the money, the power and the right ideas, but for heaven's sake curb her words.' Wentworth Day replied that he thought this was as impossible as putting a brake on the Ride of the Valkyries.[13]

The final result gave the National Liberals a comprehensive win (52%) with Anderson in third place – behind the Labour candidate – on 15%. Linklater for the SNP was bottom of the poll with only 3.6%. How things would change eighty years later.

Lucy had insisted that Wentworth Day kept her personally up to date with the campaign, which meant that he had made five overnight journeys back to London on the 'Flying Scotsman'. He had toured the whole of the constituency in deep snow and icy winds, organised six meetings a day and spoken himself hoarse. On the final day, 2 February, he held sixteen open-air meetings followed by a night spent duck shooting on the mud flats of the River Eden. Perhaps not surprisingly he then went down with double pneumonia. The following day he received an unpunctuated telegram from Lucy.

> So sorry hear you are ill dear boy all because you overwork I told you not to don't be a fool remember castor oil the panacea for all ills take teaspoon in half an orange then you won't taste it bottle follows by post get your own orange love Lucy Houston.[14]

The bottle duly arrived, together with a telephone call to the hotel manager to see that Wentworth Day took his medicine as prescribed. On top of his pneumonia he also had a black eye and a badly bruised shoulder because he had somehow found time to intervene in the Liverpool Exchange by-election of 19 January where he got involved in a fracas. The National Conservative candidate was Colonel Shute, well known in the constituency as the founder and patron of the Liverpool Repertory Theatre and for his work with deprived children. Wentworth Day felt it would be unkind to spoil his campaign and so concentrated his attack on his socialist opponent.

One wet and windy night he turned up at a Labour party meeting convened by the formidable virago Bessie Braddock, then at the start of her political career as a city councillor. The chief speaker was a socialist politician of Polish origin who had been a conscientious objector during the war. 'Speaking as a British working man on behalf of our gallant soldiers ...' he began, when Wentworth Day jumped up and bellowed out: 'Is it not a fact that you are a Polish Jew and not a Briton; that you have never done a day's work except as an agitator; that you have never fought anywhere except on a street corner and that your last hard day's work was in gaol?' The meeting erupted and a furious crowd chased Wentworth Day out into the street, where he slipped on the cobbles and received a glancing blow from a passing tram. When he rang Lucy the following morning with his daily report, she laughed. 'Splendid! That will show them that we mean business! Trams are such vulgar conveyances – you should avoid them. Catch a train and come and tell me all about it.'[15] The London evening newspapers carried a splash headline: 'LADY HOUSTON'S MAN WRECKS LIVERPOOL MEETING – THROWN UNDER TRAM BY RED MOB.'

Back in London that same evening, Wentworth Day was having supper at Pratt's club when one of its most frequent diners, Winston Churchill, came in with Admiral of the Fleet Sir Roger Keyes. Churchill introduced him with the words 'this is my young friend, Wentworth Day – Lady Houston's kept man.' Pointing to his black eye, he added, 'you observe the love token.' Lucy relished the account of this incident. 'Tell Winston that I am flattered – and so should you be! But also tell him that, alas, it is twenty years too late.'

Wentworth Day was not given long to recuperate from his pneumonia and his other injuries. Over a period of ten months he intervened with similar vigour in no less than eight by-elections, the first of which was at Rotherham in the industrial heart of south Yorkshire, the polling day being set for 27 February. At the general election in 1931 the National Conservative candidate had achieved a surprising win, though only by the smallest of margins, and now the socialists were hell-bent on regaining the seat. The country was still in the grip of winter with violent snowstorms affecting many outdoor meetings as Wentworth Day returned to the hustings, together with Lucy's novel innovation. Wentworth Day hired a small plane and had it repainted with the Union Jack on the wings and on the sides of the fuselage. 'The agents of Lady Houston are taking a prominent part in the election, denouncing the Prime Minister on the one hand and attacking Socialism on the other. Thousands of Lady Houston's leaflets are being distributed and her political organiser informs me that tomorrow morning the Houston "Air Special" will fly low over the whole of the constituency dropping pamphlets.'[16]

Another incident that added spice to the campaign was the arrival of Malcolm MacDonald MP, the son of the Prime Minister, who tried to speak in favour of the National Conservative candidate, Mr Drummond Wolff. He was booed off the stage by Labour supporters with cries of 'Judas!', 'Traitor!' and 'Get off home to your father!' Wentworth Day disrupted another Labour party meeting at Rawmarsh and was set upon by a horde of 'large and sinewy women' who threw him out into the snow and nearly succeeded in taking his trousers off. Lucy chuckled when told of the incident. 'Serves you right! Never let a woman catch you for money or anything else.' He had given her the excuse to roll out her favourite quotation from Rudyard Kipling. 'How many times do I have to tell you that the female of the species is more deadly than the male?' The final result of the election was a modest increase in the Labour vote but a collapse of support for the National Government which lost by a margin of nearly 16,000 votes.

Wentworth Day hardly had time to report to Lucy on this campaign before she packed him off again, this time to the normally peaceful and sedate country town of Ashford in Kent. Here the Conservative MP Michael Knatchbull had been elevated to the peerage as the 5th Baron Brabourne and a Mr Spens was defending the seat as a National Conservative at the by-election called for 17 March. 'Warm them up! Pitch into them!' Lucy declared. 'Find which side of the fence this Mr Spens is on – he may be a very nice man but he is in bad company! Now send me my needle and thread and plenty of ribbons and a white banner thirty-six feet long so that I can stitch your battle flag.' Wentworth Day described this encounter as being 'like Richard the Lionheart being exhorted by Berengaria as he set forth on the Crusades.' He enlisted the help of his young friend Captain Cecil Blacker,[17] a cavalry officer who relished the idea of a bit of sport and a possible punch-up. Together they canvassed the pubs and spread the word that Lady Houston was going to take a hand in Ashford politics. This aroused great interest, sufficient for Wentworth Day to hire the County theatre for a night. That morning Lucy's banner arrived, emblazoned in enormous red letters 3ft 6ins high with the words:

HEAR THE TRUTH ABOUT THE PRIME MINISTER.
COME TO LADY HOUSTON'S MEETING AT THE COUNTY THEATRE.

Wentworth Day hired twelve men, each with a long pole, to carry it around the town, and that evening 1,200 people packed the theatre. He harangued the crowd with Lucy's usual message about the threat of communism, how Ramsay MacDonald had been a traitor in the pocket of the Bolsheviks during the war, the desperate state of the country's defences, and the pitfalls of following the League of Nations along the line of disarmament. The meeting erupted with cries of 'Three cheers for Lady Houston!' and 'Down with Ramsay Macdonald!' while others shouted 'She's mad and bad!', 'Warmonger!', 'Enemy of the workers!', 'Up the reds!' and other comments not fit for printing. Wentworth Day's account of the meeting was no exaggeration when he claimed that 'policies were aired with a frankness unknown since the eighteenth century.' Lucy wanted him to be more explicit, adding that she had received a letter from a man denouncing her as 'the whore of Camden'. 'What impertinence!' she chuckled, 'and what ignorance! As far as I know I have never even set foot in Camden.'

A few days later David Lloyd George, the political hero of the Great War but now struggling to revive the fortunes of the Independent Liberals, was going to speak at another meeting. By the time Lucy was told of this she had obviously already done her homework. She had found out that a once famous Scottish footballer called Alec Jackson was due to play for Margate on the Ashford town football ground at the same time, so she ordered Wentworth Day to rush out sandwich-board placards declaring: 'THE BIGGEST BATTLE OF ALL! LLOYD GEORGE OR ALEC JACKSON? THE COUNTRY ONLY NEEDS ONE OF THEM. WHICH ARE YOU GOING TO SEE?'[18] When a somewhat deflated Lloyd George rose to speak he told his audience, with a wink at Wentworth Day, that he 'gathered his thunder had been stolen by a lady who knows her mind, so now I suppose we had all better go and watch the football.' Lucy was delighted by the outcome. 'The artful old dodger! He doesn't really like me but I think he respects me. Anyway, he's scared of me! What he needs is a haircut.'[19] Mr Spens won the election by a large majority.

The next two by-elections were going to be at Hitchin on 8 June and Altringham, near Manchester, a week later. They presented Lucy with a dilemma because in both cases the National Conservative candidates were known to be staunch Imperialists, as keen to preserve the scope and prestige of the British Empire as Lucy herself. At Hitchin the candidate was Sir Arnold Wilson who had been appointed as the colonial administrator in Mesopotamia after 1918. He initially gained local popularity by recommending the name change to the Arabic 'Iraq' but his general heavy-handedness led to riots that had to be suppressed with considerable loss of life. These events, with echoes of General Dyer's ill-judged massacre of unarmed protesters at Amritsar in 1919, embarrassed the Government and he was recalled in 1920 – and given a knighthood. He was known as a dull and pedantic speaker and the *New Statesman* dubbed him as a propagandist for Mussolini – which Lucy would have applauded – so she told Wentworth Day to keep out of the way.

Likewise at Altringham, where the National Conservative candidate was Sir Edward Grigg. Having served with the Grenadier Guards during the war, he had been military secretary to the Prince of Wales during his tours to Canada and Australasia before being appointed as the Governor of Kenya. He had achieved notable success during his time of office between 1925 and 1931. At the general election that year he had been elected as MP for Oldham as a National Liberal, but like Winston Churchill a few years earlier he was now changing horses. Wentworth Day was a personal friend and did not wish to cause him any embarrassment by intervening in his campaign.

If Wentworth Day is correct about the number of by-election campaigns he fought on Lucy's behalf, there must have been a few others in 1933, though he does not mention them in his book. What he does mention is the day he was summoned for a meeting with the Chairman of the Conservative Party, Lord Stonehaven. 'I have great admiration for Lady Houston,' were his opening remarks. 'Winston Churchill says she is the grandest, political gentleman-adventurer we have.' He continued: 'I realise that her attacks on the Government are activated by purely patriotic motives and most of the Ministers admire her courage and her patriotism. But she must not call the Prime Minister a traitor and neither must you, or the Home Office may prosecute and then both of you could end up in gaol.' Then he changed tack. He told Wentworth Day that he was obviously a man of strong convictions and a natural orator so would he not consider standing as a Conservative member of parliament? This was followed by a suggestion that Stonehaven could almost guarantee him a safe seat. Wentworth Day replied that he was flattered but could not possibly serve under Stanley Baldwin. (With Baldwin out of the way, he did stand as the Conservative candidate for Hornchurch in both 1950 and 1951, but did not get elected.) When he reported on this meeting to Lucy she chuckled. 'Well that would be great fun wouldn't it?

We would go to prison together and I wonder what the public would make of the sight of an old woman on a stretcher handcuffed to a handsome young man.'

Wentworth Day continued to speak vehemently against Ramsay MacDonald at by-election meetings and Lucy wrote a damning article about her *bête-noire*, followed up by a personal letter to number 10 Downing Street inviting the premier to sue her. Nothing happened. Then she was handed an opportunity to wade into an organisation that was one of the major paymasters of the Labour party. In April 1933 the Conservative Chancellor of the Exchequer was scratching around for ways to increase revenues to the Treasury and, as governments have done before and since, they looked at new regulations on businesses and possible changes to the tax laws. One target was the enormous reserves built up by the Co-operative Party. The 'Co-op' was exempt from taxation under mutuality rules, but perhaps the threat of changing the law might achieve what became known as the 'Lucy Houston trick', applying moral blackmail to persuade the Co-operative Party that it was their patriotic duty to volunteer a contribution – or else. Lucy penned an open letter to Mr Joe Compton, chairman of the Labour Party executive and at the time chairing the Co-operative Party conference in Nottingham, reminding him what this meant – how she had 'presented the nation with £1,515,000, not one penny of which could be claimed from her, as an act of grace on her part' – and commending a similar response. She did not get one. Instead the Co-op mitigated a potential tax bill of £1.2 million by sharply increasing the dividends they paid out to their members.

That summer of 1933 Wentworth Day paid his first visit to *Liberty* which was moored in Poole harbour. Lucy had set up her battle headquarters in her stateroom and, with a glass of Guinness in front of her on a Union Jack tablecloth, was plotting the next stage of her crusade. She told Wentworth Day that she had a straightforward little job for him, merely to go back to London and buy her control of a newspaper. He could edit it but she would run it. 'It must carry my message into every home in Britain. We must warn people of the dangers this Government is leading us into.'[20] She had already drawn up a list of 'wise people' that she would invite to write for it, people like the journalist and historian Ian Colvin. Also Meriel Buchanan, the daughter of the British Ambassador to Russia throughout the war, who had served as a nurse in St Petersburg under the most dreadful conditions. Wentworth Day was somewhat flabbergasted by his employer's new mission, and as he returned back to London he pondered on his employer's sheer audacity, a woman of 76 setting out to try and achieve nothing less than the undermining of the Government's authority and the downfall of the Prime Minister.

In the interests of continuity, I have taken the story of how Lucy recruited James Wentworth Day and his first year of buccaneering political activity well into 1933 and we will shortly return to recount how he found the solution to her journalistic ambitions. But during the spring of that year Lucy had hit the headlines again through another bold, pioneering aviation adventure, so now we need to go back a year and recall the heroic story of the Houston–Mount Everest expedition.

Chapter 14

Wings Over the Himalayas – the Houston-Mount Everest Expedition

Winning the Schneider Trophy in 1931 prompted a number of air-minded individuals and organisations to consider a new aviation challenge, namely flying at very high altitude. To have a height advantage over one's opponent in aerial combat had been well demonstrated in dogfights during the Great War, with the ability to swoop down on the enemy while at the same time gaining speed. Bombing from high altitude reduced the chances of being hit by anti-aircraft fire from the ground and defending fighters took longer to climb into range, a fact that stimulated the invention of devices, like RADAR, to give early warning of the approach of enemy intruders. On the other hand, it had to be admitted that as far as bombing was concerned these altitude advantages were offset by reduced accuracy in hitting specific targets. A major use of aircraft in the Great War had been reconnaissance over enemy lines, and all the major combatants had experimented with aerial photography, so that the results from such flights could be examined and analysed at headquarters. When viewed through a stereoscope, overlapping photographs could produce a 3D effect that allowed greater information to be extracted. In parallel with all these advantages of high altitude flying, there were also a host of technical problems to be overcome. Thinner air at high altitudes made engines less efficient, wings developed less lift, and less available oxygen had serious physiological and medical implications for pilots and observers, on top of which was the added problem of acute cold, with temperatures as low as minus 60 degrees centigrade.

The idea of tackling the ultimate altitude challenge, to fly an aircraft over the 29,029 foot summit of Mount Everest, was first put forward in March 1932 by Lieutenant Colonel L.V. Stewart Blacker, an officer with the Indian Army.[1] Blacker had once upon a time worked for the Bristol Aero-engine Company and had been a pilot in the Royal Flying Corps, being shot down and wounded on three separate occasions between 1915 and 1917. It was learning about the potential capabilities of the new supercharged, radial Bristol 'Pegasus' engine that triggered his appreciation that here was the key component that might make his vision a realistic proposition. He first submitted his outline plan to the Council of the Royal Geographical Society, an august organisation that was already interested in the concept of using aerial photography for surveying areas of the world inaccessible to traditional survey techniques on foot.

As a result of Blacker's approach the nucleus of an organisational committee was established at the College of Aeronautical Engineering in Chelsea. It included Lord Peel, a former Secretary of State for India and Blacker's father-in-law, and the author and adventurer Colonel John Buchan. From the very beginning, it was scientific advancement that was the prime motivation for taking on this daunting challenge. Mount Everest, the highest mountain in the world, was situated on the border of Nepal and Tibet and was as yet unclimbed, and if the expedition was successful it would greatly enhance the status of British science and aviation before a worldwide audience. It was also appreciated in certain political quarters that this would apply particularly in India itself, where British influence was being increasingly decried and undermined.

In April, the Air Ministry agreed to offer test facilities at three establishments, the Royal Aircraft Establishment at Farnborough, the RAF School of Photography and the RAF Experimental Establishment at Martlesham Heath, Suffolk. An official request was sent in May to the King of Nepal for permission to overfly his country and arrangements made for the expedition to have its base at the Army airfield at Purnea in north India, close to the Nepalese border. The Bristol Aero-engine Company was approached about the supply of the 'Pegasus S' engine and several aircraft companies were sounded out for the most suitable airframe on which to mount it. The committee's first choice was the Vickers 'Vespa', a large-winged biplane which had originally been designed as an army-cooperation aircraft. Fitted with the new Bristol Pegasus S engine, a Vespa VII had already captured the world altitude record of 43,976 feet on 16 September 1932. This was a remarkable achievement by the pilot, Captain C. Unwins, but it was a 'sprint' compared to what was planned over the Himalayas, in an aeroplane with only one crew member on board and no equipment except for his personal oxygen supply. The altitude record flight had taken off from an English airfield in the Vale of Evesham, on a day chosen to coincide with the best meteorological conditions, for which data was plentiful, a luxury that would be denied to the Everest Expedition. Crucially, however, this event had proved the capability of the new Bristol engine.

In a remarkably generous gesture, the Defence Department of the Irish Free State offered to donate, gratis, a pair of their Vespas, though these were fitted with the lower powered 'Jaguar' engines. Westlands of Yeovil had built a similar aircraft, provisionally called the P.V.3, based on their 'Wapiti' torpedo bomber, and after comparative tests this aircraft was chosen because it had a deeper fuselage, one that was more suitable for carrying the observer and all the extra equipment needed.

Through the summer of 1932 additional members were appointed to the management committee, including the former RAF pilot Lord Clydesdale MP, together with Lord Lytton (a former Governor of Bombay), Wing Commander Orlebar, who had been in command of the RAF High Speed Flight for the Schneider Trophy in 1931, and Lucy's friend Colonel Sempill, now Lord Sempill. The suppliers of heated clothes, oxygen cylinders and valves, additional instruments and the all-important cameras had been selected. Several organisations had offered practical help or concessions, such as Burma-Shell Ltd agreeing to supply special lubricating oils and P&O Steam Navigation Co offering cargo space to ship the aircraft out to India. The India Office agreed to grant customs exemption and the Gaumont-British Picture Corporation promised to buy the rights to any cine film that might be taken using their cameras.

In spite of all these generous offers of facilities, concessions and technical support, no one had yet come up with the most important ingredient of all – cash to pay for everything. And the timing of the project could not have been worse, because the economy was plunging from recession into depression. So in September Lucy received a visitor. 'I originally approached Lady Houston,' Lord Clydesdale wrote later, 'as an acquaintance of my mother and she had very kindly invited me to tea. She listened to my brief statement, but then turned away from it, to resume her discussion of political matters that were clearly her main interest. I was immensely impressed with the intensity of her patriotism and the fervour of her feeling for Great Britain and the Empire.'[2]

Lucy did not give an instant reply, but she invited Lord Clydesdale to join her at her hunting lodge in Scotland the following month. He also brought with him a letter from Lord Sempill, one that gave the project his own personal backing. 'It was then that she gave me her definite promise of support,' he recalled, 'and it was the prospect of raising British prestige in India through the expedition that appealed to her enormously.' From that moment she started to take an almost motherly interest in the health, safety and wellbeing of everyone involved. Lord Clydesdale, soon to celebrate his 30th birthday, spent a bitterly cold day stag shooting and returned to Lucy's lodge chilled to the bone. She told him that if he was going to be the chief pilot, he should start going into serious physical training to ensure he was absolutely fit. She was not going to be responsible for anyone getting themselves killed through amateurish over-enthusiasm, and virtually demanded that the committee appoint a chief executive officer to be in charge of seeing that every detail was tested and checked to the highest professional standards. The man chosen was Air Commodore Fellowes, recently retired from the RAF, and 'the expedition became a band of brothers, bound together by a mutual confidence in their leader.'[3] Lucy also required that her friend from the press, R.D. Blumenfeld, be invited onto the committee as 'her eyes and ears'. The headquarters of the expedition, now officially called the 'Houston-Mount Everest Flight', were transferred to Grosvenor House and Lucy had a banner made proclaiming the title in large red letters on a white background, to fly from the flagpole on the roof. She wanted to make certain that the people of London were aware that she was once again backing British aviation.

With an initial £10,000 from Lucy, and a guarantee that she would cover all future costs, two aircraft were ordered from Westland, the original P.V.3 prototype that was renamed the 'Houston-Westland' and a specially modified 'Wallace', the name given to the production version that was about to go into service with the RAF. After testing at Yeovil, both were crated up for shipment to Karachi on the P&O Liner SS *Dalgoma*. At the same time three de Havilland Moth aircraft were acquired – including one comfortable and refined 'Puss Moth' version donated by Fry's Chocolate – to provide local communication and transport supplies in India. These were flown from England, via North Africa and Persia, by Clydesdale and the reserve pilots, accompanied by Air Commodore Fellowes and Lt Col Blacker, while Lady Clydesdale enjoyed the journey by sea in company with the two Westlands in the hold of the P&O liner. Before the pilots set off, Gaumont-British sent a camera team to Byron Cottage to film a conversation between Lucy and Lord Clydesdale in which she explained why she was financing the expedition. It took several takes before Lucy was happy that it was exactly as she wished, and in it she stated that 'the people of India will then know, from this success, that we are not the decadent people their leaders try to make us out to be.'[4]

The liner docked at Karachi early in March 1933, the aircraft were uncrated and assembled, and then they set off for New Delhi. Lucy had sent a telegram to the Viceroy, Lord Willingdon, asking him to welcome the Expedition and 'give it every assistance required', to which he had replied that he would 'gladly receive members of the Expedition so generously financed by you and wish them God-speed on their great adventure.' So the planes arrived in Delhi to be met with a viceregal reception, inspection and appropriate hospitality.

One other key member of the expedition had flown out to Karachi by the faster and undeniably more comfortable means of an Imperial Airways airliner. This was Colonel P.T. Etherton, a colleague of Blacker in the Indian Army and, most importantly, a personal friend of the King of Nepal. Etherton headed straight off to Kathmandu to confirm the initial offer of allowing the planes to overfly his country on their 160-mile flight path from Purnea to Everest – not just once, but possibly a second time if things did not go according to plan at the first attempt. (This was a very wise back-up plan but it never formed a part of Lucy's understanding of her commitment.)

The remote and very primitive airstrip at Purnea, base camp for the expedition, was forty miles from the nearest railhead and any supplies that could not be flown in on the de Havilland Moths were transported in lorries that took ten hours to traverse the rough road. By the end of March, however, everything was assembled and all the equipment had been tested again under local conditions. The scientific details of the heated clothing, the vital oxygen supplies and the sundry cameras and their related equipment are fascinating but largely irrelevant to the theme of this story.[5] Equally fascinating is the ingenuity that had to be employed to fit them all into a cramped, confined space while keeping weight down to an absolute minimum. All equipment had been tested in the RAE low-temperature chamber at Farnborough, but would the observers, wearing masks, goggles and bulky gloves be able to operate the cameras in the slipstream of an aircraft possibly thrown around by turbulent air at a height of over 30,000 feet? Little was known of the meteorological conditions around the Himalayas, though flying around the Alps had demonstrated that mountains could produce startling down-draughts which could cause a plane to plunge thousands of feet in a few seconds.

With everything in place, it was now a case of waiting for suitable weather conditions. The broad, synoptic situation over north India could be received by telegram from Calcutta but there were no local forecasts available. Crucial to the success of the venture was a knowledge of the likely wind speeds near the summit and these could be roughly checked by sending up weather balloons and tracking them from the ground with theodolites. Clear skies were essential for good photography but these were usually associated with the highest wind speeds, far above the calculated safety limit of 60 mph; when these wind speeds dropped, the clouds rolled in. The first day that provided acceptable flying conditions was Monday, 3 April, and at dawn that morning the die was cast.

Because of the all-pervading dust, the survey cameras in the floor of the aircraft could only be mounted at the last minute and then linked to the manual shutter-release mechanisms in the cockpit. Donning the cumbersome heated clothes and oxygen masks had been rehearsed again and again but it was not until 8 am that the two planes and their crews were ready for take-off. (The main purpose of the 'Wallace', piloted by Flight Lieutenant McIntyre, was to provide a photographic record of whatever the lead aircraft achieved.) Blacker, the observer in the 'Houston-Westland' piloted by Clydesdale, noted in some dismay that it took them a long time to climb above the dust haze in the valleys before they broke out into the icy, crystal-clear sky around the mountains. After each photograph was taken, the back of the camera had to be released and a fresh plate inserted, not easy in thick gloves. It was while he was standing and leaning down to perform this task on one of the floor-mounted survey cameras that they hit a down-draught and plunged 2,000 feet. For a few seconds he experienced weightlessness, and when Clydesdale regained control and resumed the climb Blacker admitted later that it was a miracle that he had not broken anything or severed any of the oxygen pipes or electric cable connectors. Between taking the regular vertical shots, he had to thrust his upper body out into the icy slipstream and take oblique shots with the handheld camera, again reloading a fresh plate each time. They made three circuits over and around the summit before an uneventful return to base. The most sensational objective, the one that would hit the press headlines around the world, had been achieved and it seemed that the only piece of equipment that had failed was the telephone link between pilot and observer.

A potentially more serious accident had happened in the second aircraft, the Westland 'Wallace', whose main role was to provide the cine film. The pilot was McIntyre and the acting observer was S.R. Bonnett of the Gaumont-British Corporation. At the peak of the climb, while filming the 'Houston-Westland' flying over the peak of Everest, Bonnett accidently stood on the tube to his oxygen supply, severing it from its supply valve. As he struggled not to lose consciousness while he battled to make a temporary join by tying the two pipes together with his handkerchief, he missed the chance to take a vertical sequence looking down on the summit itself.[6]

The following day the opportunity was taken to fly over Kangchenjunga, the mountain on the borders of Sikkim and Assam that until 1852 had been believed to be the highest of all, at 28,169 feet. Telegrams of congratulations flooded in, from King George V, the Prime Minister, the Royal Geographical Society and the organising committee in London. Lucy's own telegram read as follows: 'Delighted to hear the glad news of our great victory over Everest. Send you my warmest congratulations and appreciation of your great achievement and of the pluck and courage you have shown. God bless you.' In return, she received one from the committee, expressing their warmest thanks for 'having once again been responsible for putting Britain in the forefront of world aviation.' When asked by a reporter why she had financed the expedition in the first place she told him, 'I want it to be thoroughly understood by everyone that our chief aim in this adventure was to show India that we are not the degenerate race that their leaders present Britain to be. India will now be forced to realise that the British lion is still full of pluck and courage and this conquest of Everest is a splendid achievement by we Britons, and the people of India can be justly proud of it.'

After the photographs from the hand-held cameras on both flights were processed, the results were shown to be excellent, but those from the survey cameras were useless, obscured by the low clouds and dust haze that had extended right up to 19,000 feet. Scientifically, and from the point of view of the Royal Geographical Society, this was the main objective of the whole expedition, so it became an absolute necessity to repeat the exercise. When this was reported in *The Times*, together with the fact that the King of Nepal had confirmed his permission for a second flight, Lucy penned another telegram: 'The good spirit of the mountain has been kind to you and brought you success. Be content. Do not tempt the evil spirits of the mountain to bring disaster. Intuition tells me to warn you that there is danger.' This was followed by a further telegram: 'Planes uninsured. Nor will be.' At the same time she contacted every member of the committee in London, imploring them to forbid another flight. The British Aviation Insurance company had agreed to underwrite one flight only; Lucy was aware that if any disaster were to occur on another, she would be responsible not only for any material costs but also possibly the lives of crew members. This preyed heavily on her conscience. The result was a yet another telegram sent from the committee to Air Commodore Fellowes prohibiting a further flight.

Then, just after he had informed his team at Purnea of the gist of his latest instructions, Fellowes was struck down with fever. The team were on the point of mutiny anyway. They knew the importance of the survey photographs and furthermore the cine camera team were desperate for more panoramic footage of the wild mountain scenery to entrance cinema audiences back in England. It was the PR value of this aspect of the mission that they took to Fellowes and, still semi-delirious, he gave his permission for one last flight, stipulating that the aircraft must not go beyond a range from which they could not glide back to base in the event of an engine failure. So on 19 April, when the visibility over the lower levels in the valleys leading up towards Everest was clear, in spite of clouds massing around the highest peaks, the final flight was undertaken and completed successfully. This time the survey photographs were excellent, covering a corridor one hundred miles long and six miles wide. [see PLATES B16–18]

Jubilation, however, would be short lived. 'Bidding hasty farewells to the many Indians, from rajah to ryot, who had welcomed, cheered and entertained us most nobly, we came galloping to Calcutta – to meet a legal call from London, where an avalanche, or maybe a whirlwind, of writs was ready to fall … and we discovered our funds in London frozen and bills to pay.'[7]

The story is now taken up by Blacker who flew back to London in advance of the rest of the team.

As good luck would have it I found Lady Houston's solicitor, one Willie Graham, to be a most fair-minded and reasonable man. I called upon him with the Field Service Regulations of the Army in my pocket. To begin with, like most civilians, he was obsessed with the belief that our wooden-headed Army is cast-iron in its methods. Much to his surprise, I showed him those paragraphs, inspired originally by the Duke of Wellington, which lay down that a formal precise order must not be departed from when the giver is present. On the other hand, in the absence of the giver, and change of circumstances so require it, the recipient is *not only permitted to depart from the letter of the order but is enjoined to do so.* When Willie Graham had got over this shock to his civilian instincts, he grasped the point and told Lady Houston to forgive us, which forgiveness took the form of large boxes of cigars.[8]

On his return to England, Lord Clydesdale immediately went to visit Lucy to tell her all about the great adventure, even before he reported more formally to the Royal Geographical Society.[9] All the members of the expedition were treated like conquering heroes, luncheons and dinners were organised for them, commemorative medals and stamps were issued and learned papers were read to learned societies. The Pope sent Lucy a personal message with his congratulations and in grateful acknowledgement she published a picture of him in the *Saturday Review*. Underneath it she impishly added, 'His Holiness the Pope has sent his blessing to Lady Houston for her patriotism. She still awaits the Archbishop of Canterbury's message.'[10]

She did not like Cosmo Lang, partly because he had spoken sympathetically about the German Kaiser at the start of the Great War but more particularly because he was openly disapproving of another of her heroes, Edward Prince of Wales. One of the more sensational discoveries from the aerial survey of the mountainous ridges around Everest was a lake that appeared to contain warm water, and Lucy was especially delighted when the Nepalese government chose to name it Parvati Lal, 'the Lady of the Mountain' in her honour. Blacker went on the wireless to give two talks about the flights and how they had proved that pin-sharp photographs could be taken from 30,000 feet, ending with a warm tribute to Lucy's generosity.

The Times gave a complimentary lunch in their offices for all the expedition members on 1 June. Lucy had received an invitation but had been forced by ill health to send a letter of regret that she would be unable to attend. Attached was a request that a message from her should be read out to the guests, a message that reiterated the reasons why she had financed the venture. There was no mention of potential scientific rewards, only her controversial political angle on promoting British prestige. She had been inspired to donate her money, she wrote, because she had heard that a relation of a friend of hers, a British police officer in India, had been murdered and that this was becoming a more common occurrence since 'agitators have been permitted to preach treason … and make the people of India think that we Britons have lost our courage.' She believed that 'some great deed of heroism might rouse India and make them remember that though they are of a different race, they are subjects under the King of England, who is Emperor of India.' She went on say that 'they should remember all the advantages and privileges that they have enjoyed under English Rule … and our forefathers, who fed them when there was famine, nursed them when there was plague and administered absolute justice to them in every way.' John Astor, the proprietor of *The Times* and host of the luncheon, wrote her a letter that evening.

It gives me the greatest pleasure to send you *The Times* commemorative medal of the Houston-Everest Flight Expedition. I feel sure that you will be pleased to hear that my references to your generosity and your message, as well as the tributes paid you by Air Commodore Fellowes and Lord Clydesdale, were very warmly received.

In fact though, and for quite understandable reasons perhaps, Astor had not read out Lucy's message at all and when this was reported back to her she became extremely angry and wrote a further letter to Astor telling him that she felt deeply hurt by the omission. At the same time she sent the text of her 'message' to three other rival newspapers, the *Morning Post*, the *Daily Mail* and the *Daily Sketch*, who sniffed a populist story with which to prick the pomposity of *The Times* and printed it in full. There followed an increasingly testy correspondence between Lucy and Astor that did neither party much credit. *The Times* had negotiated the sole publicity rights for the Expedition – 'I regret to say without my knowledge or consent' – and had enjoyed a great boost to its circulation as a result, so why, Lucy asked, had he insulted the person who had made it all possible? 'I am sometimes very simple, for I foolishly imagined that you would be a gentleman and a man of honour.'

There was a partial rapprochement when *The Times* organised an exhibition of photographs taken by the Expedition at Sunderland House on Curzon Street in November. Opened by the Secretary of State for Air, Lord Londonderry, *The Times* had agreed that all the profits from the exhibition would be donated to the National Association of Boy's Clubs, a charity warmly approved of by the Prince of Wales.[11] Lord Londonderry's speech congratulated everyone involved in the 'intrepid adventure', concentrating on the technical achievements that would enhance British prestige around the world. In the afternoon Colonel Etherton gave an informal lecture on the 'human side' of the expedition, explaining that 'hundreds of natives came and camped around the aerodrome at Purnea. They could not conceive that anybody could fly over the mountain and return in safety. Apart from the scientific and geographical results obtained, he thought they had established some moral ascendancy over the people in that part of the world by flying twice over Everest and also over Kanchenjunga, and in the present state of affairs in India that was all to the good.' It was a script that Lucy might well have written herself.

Figure 3. The Houston–Mount Everest medal presented to Lucy by the French Societé de Geographie. *(Saturday Review)* (The gold medal presented to her by *The Times* is locked in the vault of the RAF Museum, Hendon).

There was, however, one other sour note left by the Everest Expedition and that concerned the cine film that had been taken at great expense on behalf of the Gaumont-British Film Corporation. Somewhat surprisingly, the film of *Wings over Everest* was not exhibited for over a year. Before being launched in the cinemas, it was shown at a private première to members of the expedition and afterwards Lord Sempill reported to Lucy that the introduction, over which she had taken so much trouble, had been completely omitted; it had 'ended up on the cutting-room floor'. Lucy was incandescent and promptly sent her 'managing director' Warner Allen down to the studios to confront the director. In his pocket he carried a letter from her stating that unless her introduction was restored she would brief her friend Sir Patrick Hastings KC to sue the company for defamation of character. Allen was passed from one minor executive to another, none of whom seemed able to provide an answer as to why the introduction had been cut out. The footage had been lost; the sound recording had not proved satisfactory; it had been someone else's decision etc. Eventually, by waving Lucy's letter, he was ushered into the office of the managing director. Now there were profuse apologies and assurances that the matter would be looked into immediately. A little later, Lucy received an invitation to visit the studios where she was promised a private screening of the restored version of the film. She took Allen with her in the Rolls-Royce on the appointed day, was ushered into the director's viewing room and offered a seat, one that she found very uncomfortable. There was a long delay and then the director assigned to look after her began to get on her nerves. Lucy became increasingly fractious. Finally the film started to roll, but now the soundtrack on her introduction was not synchronised to the film itself. After a few minutes Lucy stood up, grabbed her walking stick and stomped out, exclaiming: 'This is disgraceful – you will be hearing from my solicitors.'

There was as usual a large crowd by the studio gates, autograph hunters and film-fans hoping for a glimpse of their screen idols. On this occasion they were treated to a scene of rich drama as Lucy, draped in furs, stood by her Rolls-Royce and tore a monumental strip off the unfortunate director, lambasting him and his company as if he had been Ramsay MacDonald. The crowd loved it and 'cheered her on to fresh flights of indignation'.[12] After several minutes Lucy allowed herself to be helped up into the back seat of her Rolls, at the same time commanding Foster to drive her away from the horrid place as fast as he possibly could. She gave Warner Allen a beaming smile and reflected on her acting skills and how she had held her audience transfixed. 'Did you hear how they cheered me?' she crowed, 'the people are always on my side because I am one of them myself.' Allen wrote later that the incident reminded him of Nell Gwynne's rapport with the London mob when she was Charles II's mistress, declaring delightedly that they must not confuse her with his other Roman Catholic mistresses and that she was proud to be 'the Protestant whore'.[13]

The whole episode did, however, have a happy ending. The film, including Lucy's introduction, was going to have its public premiere in the Curzon cinema on 3 June 1934,[14] and beforehand a lunch was given in Lucy's honour. It was one of the rare occasions when she felt robust enough to appear in public. At the end of the lunch, in reply to her health being toasted, 'to the patriot whose generosity made the great adventure possible', she made the one and only prepared speech of her life. It was very well delivered, short, modest and gracious to everyone involved in the expedition and the making of the film. Perhaps surprisingly, it contained not a single word of politics. It was a triumph. (A copy on the film has been posted on YouTube by Blacker's grandson under the title *Wings over Everest 1934*. Unlike the copy held by the British Film Institute, it does not include Lucy's contentious introduction.)

The technical and medical achievements of the Houston–Mount Everest expedition were very considerable and should never be underestimated. Aircraft instrumentation, oxygen apparatus, clothing and cameras had been tested in a practical manner that could never be done under simulated laboratory conditions alone; likewise the endurance of aircrew under the most extreme conditions. The science of aerial photography had been advanced dramatically, with potential benefits both for the RAF and surveying in general, while the prestige of British science had been boosted in the eyes of the whole world. Lucy could revel in the results of her contribution to another great patriotic adventure.

Chapter 15

The Saturday Review

In early 1933 Lucy's fury was aroused by another incident that had hit the headlines, namely the arrest of six British engineers working for Metropolitan-Vickers in Russia. The men had been helping the Russians to build an electricity generating plant and they were arrested on trumped-up charges of spying and inciting sabotage. A 'show trial', of the sort that became common in later years, was arranged and so-called confessions extracted. The Foreign Office demanded their immediate release and, failing to receive satisfaction, placed a total embargo on trade with the USSR. Two months later the engineers had still not been freed and Lucy leapt into action, printing one of her pungent leaflets, 'which were distributed by well-dressed men and women throughout the principal hotels and theatres of the West End'.[1] It was headlined, 'Why is the Prime Minister not in Russia?' and declared, 'I accuse the Prime Minister of being personally responsible for the agony and merciless persecution six unhappy Englishmen are now going through. They are the victims of his insistent propaganda to treat a gang of murderers and thieves as a civilised and dependable people.' If she expected that this would provoke an injunction for libel she would be disappointed, but to everyone's relief no death sentences were handed out; there was one three-year prison sentence, one two-year, three expulsions from the country (a dream punishment in the eyes of most Russians) and one acquittal.

Writing letters to the press and printing pamphlets still did not satisfy her craving to reach a wider audience and she yearned to have her own daily newspaper. Her admiration for the industry led her to donate £500 to the Company of Newspaper Makers – better known as the Stationers' Company – for long service awards, including one to a Mr Cox who had worked on the *Western Gazette* for an incredible 52 years.[2] It has already been mentioned in an earlier chapter that she had set Wentworth Day off on this trail in spite of the discouragement from her friend R.D. Blumenfeld who had gently pointed out the total impracticality of this wild concept even for someone of her wealth. But she modified her ambition slightly and turned her attention onto possibly starting her own weekly journal. She already had in her mind a punchy title. But this was a field of journalism with which she was totally unfamiliar, so who could she turn to for expert guidance?

Lucy first approached Comyns Beaumont, the editor of an illustrated weekly called *The Graphic*, which had published an editorial strongly critical of Stanley Baldwin. This gave him instant credibility in her eyes. Would he, she asked, with her financial backing start a new weekly journal that she wanted to call the *Pepper Pot*? The selling price would have to be no more than two pence and she asked him if such a journal, with an eye-catching, patriotic cover, could achieve sales of a quarter of a million per week. She even offered to underwrite an initial £100,000 if he could find investors prepared to put up another £50,000. Comyns Beaumont was one of England's great eccentrics, believing that the British Isles constituted the fabled land of Atlantis, that Jerusalem had originally been located in Edinburgh and that Jesus Christ had been born at Glastonbury. He also suggested that the ancient Egyptians were originally Celts from South Wales and that there was a Zionist plot to undermine the British Empire. But he held shrewder and more conventional views on newspaper finance, and told Lucy that the concept would be a certain money-loser and a most unattractive investment opportunity.

Lucy admired women journalists, particularly Lady Milner who had recently taken over the editorship of the Conservative weekly *National Review* from Leo Maxse and she donated £14,000 towards its running costs. She also helped finance a long-forgotten journal called *The Patriot*.[3] And she received an offer from Oswald Stoll who wanted to sell her his obscure weekly called *The Referee*; but, as she told Oscar Pulvermacher, she had turned it down in spite of the fact that Winston Churchill had offered to take a share and be the editor for £100 per week, because she felt its reputation had been 'all mucked up and ruined for years'.[4] Pulvermacher tried to advise her against the whole idea of buying a weekly journal, 'which might be a pretty – and costly – plaything, but you would soon become impatient at its infrequent appearances.'[5] Then there was speculation that she might get involved with Oswald Mosley's journal for the British Union

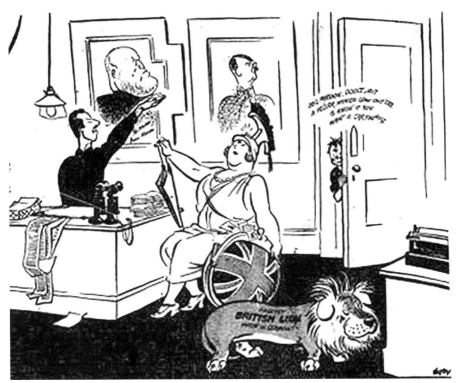

Figure 4. Cartoon by David Low when it was rumoured that Lucy might consider financing Oswald Mosley's BUF journal, *Blackshirt*. Low himself creeps into the meeting, asking if there would be a job for a cartoonist. *(Evening Standard, 11 September 1933)*

of Fascists, *Blackshirt*, a rumour that prompted David Low to publish one of his wickedly satirical cartoons. [See FIG 4] Lucy's answer was to write that 'Mosley wears a black shirt while mine is red, white and blue. His lion is made in Germany – my lioness is British through and through.'[6]

As she looked elsewhere, Wentworth Day came up with the idea of the *Saturday Review*, another weekly that had already printed contributions from her. It had been founded in 1855 and was, in its day, a respected literary organ that attracted contributions from the likes of Anthony Trollope, H.G. Wells, Oscar Wilde, George Bernard Shaw and Dante Gabriel Rossetti. The controversial roué Frank Harris had been the editor during the 1890s when it adopted a very strong anti-German attitude, with the Latin slogan 'Germania est delenda' ('Germany needs to be destroyed'), being almost alone in predicting a future war between the nations 'because of their conflicts of interest'. The editor from 1924 had been Gerald Barry (1898–1968), who then resigned in 1930 when the management board ordered him to support the new United Empire Party founded by Lords Beaverbrook and Rothermere. (Barry subsequently set up the *Week-End Review* which soon merged with the *New Statesman*.)

By 1933 the *Saturday Review* was owned by two cousins, Guy and John Pollock. Guy Pollock, 'a man of high principles and inflexible courage', had been editor of the *Sunday Express* when Wentworth Day had been a journalist on the paper, while John Pollock was already well known to Lucy from the time they had worked together on the Galicia Charity during the war. The third shareholder – and the one most relevant to our story – was Warner Allen. A writer and journalist, he became Paris correspondent of the *Morning Post* in 1908 and then in 1914 an official war correspondent covering the fighting in France and later on the Italian front. When the Americans arrived on the Western front he was attached to their headquarters and stayed with them until 1919. In 1920 he was awarded the CBE and made a Chevalier of the Legion d'Honneur. After the war he was appointed foreign editor of the *Morning Post*, then London editor of the *Yorkshire Post*, before retiring in 1930 to concentrate on writing about his favourite interest and hobby – wine. He had already published *The Wines of France* in 1924, drawing on his experiences of living in Paris during the last great days of the Edwardian epoch. He followed this with *The Romance of Wine* in 1931.

Together with the Pollock cousins he had tried to revive the fading fortunes and the fallen prestige of the once famous *Saturday Review*, and 'had been highly successful – in losing our money.'[7] Lucy now appeared on the scene and on 6 May 1933 bought out John Pollock's controlling interest in the company for £3,000, a deal negotiated on her behalf by Wentworth Day. Initially Guy Pollock stayed on as editor, trying to act as a buffer between Warner Allen and, to use the latter's own words, their 'eccentric proprietor'. Soon the incompatibility between Guy Pollock's ideals for the journal and 'her unorthodox and inflexible intentions' became all too obvious and he resigned in October. So Lucy appointed James Wentworth Day into the editorial chair, and during his first few months in this role he landed a tremendous scoop.

A friend of his from Fleet Street, who ran a small foreign news agency, came to him with the proof of an article written for a Nazi newspaper by Hitler's Minister for Propaganda, Doctor Goebbels.[8] It was even signed in ink with Goebbels' own signature. Wentworth Day's friend doubted whether any British Newspaper would touch it, but how about the *Saturday Review*? The article outlined in detail the Nazi plan to 'provide more lands for the expansion of our race' and their right to rearm. 'The revision of the Peace Treaties has become our principal political programme … to obtain a revision of our eastern frontier. The Danzig Corridor must once again belong to Germany; and that part of Silesia which was given to Poland must be restored to us.' It ended with a clear warning. 'After that, the rest will be *purely a matter of power*.' Wentworth Day grabbed the opportunity and had it printed in the *Saturday Review* that night.[9] On the opposite page was a response from André Tardieu, the former Prime Minister of France, under the heading 'The Menace of Germany; a Policy that Aims for War'. In it he argued that other nations must convince Germany that they will not allow her to follow the policy Dr Goebbels outlined, and expressed his fear that a socialist government in France would leave her defenceless. 'Hitlerism, which began with violence at home, will, unless something is done, sooner or later end in violence abroad.'

The article caused a sensation. The Polish Embassy ordered several hundred copies, while Goebbels published a furious denunciation in the German press, naming Wentworth Day as a 'journalistic well-poisoner', who would be barred from ever entering Germany. The only person who did not seem thrilled was Lucy herself, not because of the exposé itself, which she applauded, but because to her mind Wentworth Day had overstepped his authority by not giving her the chance to edit the article in her own way. She gave him an icy reprimand.[10] Lucy expected him to be at her beck and call day and night, becoming increasingly irritated when she found that she could not contact him to take her telephone calls in the small hours of the morning, the time when her chronic insomnia seemed to make her mind most active. So she summoned Warner Allen to a meeting on board *Liberty* which was then moored off Sandbanks in Poole Harbour. On arrival he was given a drink and invited by the captain to wait below decks until she was ready for him. He soon found out the reason for this delay.

She was engaged at the time in one of those daily mysteries of health and hygiene in which she was apt to indulge excessively for a woman of her age. She was promenading on the starboard deck, away from the shore, with no clothes on, and on a cold and chilly day absorbing all the sea air she could through lungs and pores. She carried out a similar ceremony wherever she might be, standing naked before an open window and breathing deeply in all weathers.[11]

When she did greet him it was all flattery. She knew his reputation as an epicure and gourmet and gave him a fine lunch of partridge, washed down by a bottle of 1911 Mumm Cordon Rouge champagne which Lucy claimed was the last one left in her late husband's cellar. Then she tried to cajole him into taking over the editorial chair, but although he fundamentally agreed with her politics he was not prepared to have his name, and reputation, attached to her wilder outbursts. He declined, suggesting that since she felt so strongly about how the journal should be edited, why did she not do it herself? He had fallen into the trap – this was exactly the move she was planning. They parted with the agreement that he should be her 'managing director' – whatever that might mean – and she would be the editor.

Back at the offices of the journal at 20 York Buildings in the Adelphi, with a raft of instructions, the 50-year-old Warner Allen later confessed 'that he could see rocks ahead'. Lucy insisted on editing virtually every contribution submitted to the journal, changing the meaning here, scratching out paragraphs there, the only exceptions being those submitted by her journalist friends Ian Colvin and Colin Brooks. She designed a new cover in vivid stripes of red, white and blue, [see PLATE C18] and if an issue contained one of her virulent attacks on either Ramsay MacDonald or Stanley Baldwin, the cover would include an unflattering photograph of the victim. Allen soon found himself working late into the night, accommodating Lucy's last minute alterations and then making sure that the journal was printed in time for delivery to the main distributors, newsagents like W.H. Smith and Lavells. He also had to deal with Lucy's other foibles. Although she had been an ardent campaigner for women's rights, she did not approve of any of them working in the journal's offices, so he had to keep the female typists screened off in an area safe from Lucy's observation when she arrived for unannounced inspections.

One day Warner Allen was approached by a group of people who claimed that they had uncovered a sinister plot to subvert the *Saturday Review*, asking whether they could discuss this with him in secret before they took their revelation to Lady Houston herself. Once inside his office, and having made sure that the door was locked, they started murmuring about black magic, Bolshevist plots and Jewish secret societies. 'Just look at that,' their spokesman said, pointing to the latest cover, one of Lucy's more flamboyant designs in the colours of the Union Jack. Warner Allen was completely baffled until a finger tapped on a small red, five-pointed star in the top right hand corner. 'See what we mean? It must be a secret code.' Warner Allen then had to explain that it was indeed a code-symbol printed on those copies to be posted to individual subscribers, rather than the bulk that were sent out to the newsagents. His guests departed somewhat deflated. But to avoid any future ambiguity, Warner Allen decided that the printer's mark should be changed to a simple asterisk.[12]

Exactly how much money Lucy spent on the *Saturday Review* over the next three years is uncertain but it was probably in the order of £60,000 a year, the major costs being overtime for the printers as she made endless last minute alterations to text and layout.[13] This, at a time of high unemployment, actually made her very popular with the workforce, particularly as she also gave them a generous annual party and shared out any of the winnings from her racehorses. Circulation had declined to only 3,000 copies per week before she bought the journal, but overnight 'this hitherto acid spinster of critical journalism was transformed into a flamboyant, hard-hitting, hoydenish termagant … bristling with hard home-truths.'[14] At its height, circulation reached over 60,000 copies per week.

The bulk of the articles had a very strong, right-wing political flavour, with an emphasis on international affairs and the weakness of the country's defences both at home and abroad. 'Get on with the Singapore base!' and 'Britain must build more aircraft!' were typical headlines, while four pages each week were devoted to 'News from the Empire'. To emphasise Lucy's conviction that money spent immediately on rearmament would pay long term dividends, she printed a special supplement devoted to her friend and hero Lord 'Bobs' Roberts of Kandahar VC on 11 November 1933. In it she reminded readers that in 1903 he had implored the Government to give him

£3 million to form an army sufficient to prevent Germany starting the war that then cost us £6 *million per day*. Feats of British aviation were given wide coverage, like winning the race to Australia and the intercontinental flights of Amy Johnson. Contributors included Nesta Webster, Benito Mussolini, and a Russian professor who had suffered imprisonment in the Gulag after the purges of 1930; articles about Russia were always highly critical. The most pungent articles were written under pen-names such as 'Kim', 'Historicus' and 'A.A.B', and those by Lucy, calling herself the 'truthsayer', were printed in capitals with a larger typeface. To retain its traditional readership, the journal did still maintain its interest in the arts, with incisive reviews of new plays, films and books, while a whole page, usually disapproving, was devoted to the output on the BBC wireless service.

Sometimes the distributors demanded that certain sentences be 'blacked out'[15] while on several occasions the newsagents, on the advice of their solicitors, refused to handle the distribution of the journal at all when Lucy had penned an article that bordered on the libellous. She then had to face up to the expensive alternative of selling the journal directly on the streets of London. Wentworth-Day was still on her pay-roll as a sub-editor, so on these occasions she ordered him to take up the challenge, which involved recruiting troops of unemployed men armed with sandwich-boards and placards, just like her political campaigns at by-elections. [See PLATE B19] One group headed for the City via the Strand and Fleet Street before returning along Cannon Street while the second group converged on the West End, covering Piccadilly, Marble Arch, Oxford Street and Leicester Square. Then it was back to a pub near the Adelphi where the foot soldiers were plied with generous amounts of beer and pies in lieu of payment.

The first occasion when these tactics were necessary was on 11 November 1933, after Lucy had written an editorial headed 'Lest we Forget'. In this article she recounted how, before the Great War, Lord Roberts had 'warned, implored, beseeched and entreated the Government to prepare for the war he knew was coming, but all in vain.' She went on:

You children, who have no fathers to love and guide you, should remember that you were orphaned because of this. And today, can we say that all this misery, all the loneliness in our hearts has been a lesson to us? No – it has taught us nothing. We have been forced into disarmament. Millions of our money has been squandered on peace conferences, while the demolition of our forces of defence has been very carefully thought out and very thoroughly accomplished.

Then she lashed out: 'Our Prime Minister today, Ramsay MacDonald, is the same man who, when our soldiers were being mown down … preached far and wide to munitions workers to strike. How can any of you … be sure that your dear one's life was not sacrificed through the treachery of this traitor?' She followed this up with a personal letter to Ramsay MacDonald inviting him – again – to sue her for libel, but nothing happened.[16] This issue sold like hot cakes and went through several reprints, finally achieving sales of 50,000 copies.

Lucy's journal reached its pinnacle of popularity during the general election of November 1935, when Lucy's simple, blunt style of journalism, her eye-catching slogans and her forthright warnings struck a popular chord of doubt and disenchantment; some examples will be quoted in later chapters. She never used long words, while her frequent use of capital letters, exclamation marks and underlining may have offended more conventional editors, but it hit home with the same impact that was recognised in the advertising industry. 'It was the smart thing to have the *Saturday Review* in a Mayfair flat, a ducal mansion or a stockbroker's home. Equally, you found her paper and pamphlets in the solid households of the suburbs and the cottages of working people.'[17] A cockney taxi driver dropping Wentworth Day off at Byron Cottage one day remarked, 'Cor! That old Jemima's got guts. I won't charge yer.'

But Lucy still yearned to reach a wider audience. When she was on Jersey she used to tune her wireless in to Radio Normandie and this gave her the idea of replicating it herself. So she ordered Wentworth Day to 'buy her one of the Channel Islands … and some aeroplanes', so she could have fast communication for news flashes from London and other European cities.[18] When he found that there were no islands for sale, he started negotiations to rent one. Somehow or other the Privy Council got to hear of this and the owner was advised in the strongest terms not to conclude a deal. Lucy then came up with the idea of turning *Liberty* into a floating wireless station that she could moor somewhere just outside the British three-mile territorial limit and bombard the populace with political propaganda from her own cabin. (She was anticipating the 'pirate' radio station Radio Caroline by thirty years.) Over dinner one evening, her concept was discussed with Winston Churchill who was somewhat alarmed. 'Much better to keep your paper going,' he growled. 'I read it. It's the English *Action Francaise*. Keep it alight!'[19] Meanwhile in Germany, Hitler had already taken over the *Reichs-Rundfunk-Gesellschaft* with its massive headquarters in Berlin. Under the control of Dr Goebbels it became the most potent weapon in his propaganda war.

Between bursts of feverish activity, Wentworth Day could relax over lunch with the journal's other sub-editor Lieutenant Commander Peter Kemp, 'a boyish, gallant fellow' who had lost a leg while serving on submarines.[20] Their favourite haunt was Rule's restaurant on Maiden Lane. Here they had a regular table underneath a marble statue of an ancient Greek philosopher in conversation with some muse or goddess. When Wentworth Day asked Lucy to remind him who the characters were supposed to be, she chuckled: 'Oh! that is George Bernard Shaw refusing Mrs Patrick Campbell's proposal of marriage.' This well-known fable was supposed to have been terminated by GBS's refusal to contemplate an affair on the grounds that he could not bear the thought of any child of such a union having his looks and her brain. In spite of his being a committed socialist, the incident prompted Lucy to write to GBS requesting him to submit an article for inclusion in the *Saturday Review*, a request he refused on the grounds that she surely did not want the outpourings of 'a decrepit ghost crawling across her pages'. In fact he was less than a year older than Lucy and would live to the age of 94. Wentworth Day even went in person to visit him to try to persuade him to change his mind, suggesting that a piece about the help to his writing that he must have received from his wife would be of great interest to readers. GBS said that this would be a very short article indeed because his wife had only once ever been of any use to him in this respect – when she had married him. 'And why did I marry her? For her money of course.' (He had married the fellow Fabian and wealthy Irish heiress Charlotte Paige-Townshend in 1898, a marriage that was never consummated.)

The *Saturday Review* and its increasingly dramatic interventions into British politics after 1933 became Lucy's overriding passion, so perhaps this is a suitable moment to stand back for a while and look at the more personal aspects of her character, before plunging back into the maelstrom of world events which would soon lead to the Armageddon of another European war, a calamity that she had been prophesying with such shrewd insight.

Chapter 16

Domestic Matters and More Racehorses

Lucy's year was divided between winter in Hampstead, spring in Jersey – to retain her domicile – summer cruising on her yacht and then a few weeks in the Highlands during the autumn. She was a demanding and sometimes irrational employer which meant that the turnover within her staff was high. She was, however, intensely loyal and generous to those who were loyal to her, like Miss Ritchie and her chauffeur Foster. For tax reasons, Byron Cottage was registered in the name of her sister Florence Wrey; Lucy used to tell visitors that she was merely 'the lodger'. The garages there contained a white, open Rolls-Royce and a large black Buick for rainy days. Lucy loved speed – I am certain that if her health had allowed it, she would have implored Colonel Sempill to take her flying – and on the road she was perpetually urging Foster to go faster. He once told Wentworth Day how he had been driving Lucy down London's Southampton Row at 60 mph when they were overtaken by a much smaller car. Lucy had slid back the communicating window and ordered him to pass it. 'Call yourself a chauffeur? Get a move on! You're crawling along like going to a funeral!'[1]

She assumed that Wentworth Day and Allen would always drive at maximum speed when they were on her missions, becoming very testy if they were ever late. If she was plotting a new article for the *Saturday Review* she would order Foster to take her for a drive out into the country in the Rolls-Royce, wrapped in one of her many fur coats and displaying a large emerald pendant on her turban-style hat. The route was immaterial; she claimed that the wind in her face and the fresh air rushing past stimulated her brain. Back in London, she told him to stop outside any pub that took her fancy, go inside and bring her out a pint of Guinness, which she then drank while the local children crowded around the car and stared at the strange sight.

Somehow she never managed to make satisfactory arrangements for local delivery of provisions when she was entertaining guests at her hunting lodge in Scotland. Instead she telegraphed orders to the Army & Navy store in London, arrangements that sometimes went badly wrong. Warner Allen once received a frantic telegram claiming that she had had no food for two days and asking what was he going to do about it. So, for the next fortnight he coordinated matters with the manager of the Army & Navy and personally saw that every hamper, every package, was clearly labelled and put on the night train from Kings Cross. Beef that had originated in Scotland had to make a two-way journey of nearly one thousand miles. Arrangements to stay at other locations around the country usually turned out to be a disaster. On one occasion, for reasons unknown but perhaps to do with a by-election campaign, she rented a house in Ramsgate. It proved to be too cold even for her and Wentworth Day found himself being soundly castigated.

Ever since her years with Frederick Gretton and Theodore Brinckman, when she became an able horsewoman, she had retained a love of racehorses and owned several over the years. Watching them race was probably her favourite recreation, but when in her later years her health kept her increasingly housebound, her inability to get to the racecourses became a major frustration. She sent her horses to be trained either by a Mr Darling or by Jim Russell at Mablethorpe in Lincolnshire, a small village right on the coast. Russell found himself under strict instructions. None of her horses were allowed to race as two-year-olds, a practice she considered cruel. They must do training gallops not only along the beach but actually through the breakers, her theory being that the salt water and iodine would help build up their muscles. Not convinced that her instructions were being carried out, she ordered Warner Allen to rent her a cottage in Mablethorpe one spring so that she could keep an eye on matters, but after a few days she found the location so remote, the telephone and telegraph system so inadequate that she promptly returned to London. Why hadn't Allen warned her? It was all his fault.[2]

In 1932 she bought a filly called Silver Belle for 3,100 guineas, 'one of the highest yearling prices of the year.'[3] Its maiden race was a triumph. Ridden by Gordon Richards in the Several Stakes at Newmarket in April 1934, it romped home at 100–1. But the horse later proved to be somewhat of a disappointment; she telegraphed Russell threatening to rename it 'Silver-plated Belle'. Among her string in 1934/6 were Winsome Boy, Min Lee, Mythical Ray, Rubicon, Red Park (her only steeplechaser) and Red, White and Blue, which won a 'thrilling finish in the Willow Plate at Haydock, coming home at 100–8'.

Another of her horses was Mistress of Arts, the winner of the King's Prize Handicap at Epsom in April 1935. She was furious that Russell had not told her in advance that it had been very well handicapped and stood a good chance of winning, and she had only backed it herself with a modest amount. Even so, her staff on the *Saturday Review* were delighted when she distributed her winnings amongst them. Colin Brooks, editor of the *Sunday Dispatch* and one of her closest confidants, was surprised to receive an envelope from her enclosing five £5 notes but with no explanation. He telephoned her. 'I tried to get hold of you to tell you to back my horse but couldn't get through,' she told him, 'so I placed a fiver on for you and that is your winnings.'

By far the best horse she owned was called R.B. Bennett (by Salmon Trout out of Irish Mint), named after the tough, no-nonsense Conservative Prime Minister of Canada from 1931 to 1935. Lucy admired him hugely. His robust response to the economic depression that affected his country as badly as its neighbour was to introduce selected import tariffs on goods coming from outside the British Empire. In 1932 he had convened, and dominated, the Ottawa Conference comprising all the independent dominions of the Empire, later collectively known as the Commonwealth of Nations. Noble though its objectives were, disagreement among the leaders led to its failure. 'Iron Heeled' Bennett was virulently anti-socialist and introduced an amendment to the Canadian constitution following the Winnipeg General Strike, an amendment that dispensed with the presumption of innocence in cases where threats to the security of the state were perceived. He particularly targeted the Communist Party of Canada, eight of whose leaders were jailed. Lucy thought this was just the sort of medicine with which to treat communists, though she might not have applauded his means of tackling unemployment, a system that had echoes of the Russian Gulags. This involved sending unemployed men off to forest labour camps, where they worked in the logging industry for 20 cents a day. Bennett also cut unemployment benefits, believing they stifled initiative.

Lucy's eponymous racehorse is probably best remembered, if at all, for completely failing to turn up at the start of a race in November 1936 where it was certain to be the clear favourite and it had been heavily backed. The weather at Windsor that day was atrocious, driving rain keeping most of the punters under cover, so the horse's absence in the collecting ring initially went unnoticed. The trainer and jockey waited expectantly; the horse was stabled just a few minutes away from the course so it was impossible that it had got lost in transit. But had it been kidnapped by unscrupulous bookies? They set off for the stables in panic only to discover that the stable lad had merely fallen asleep; but by then the race had started.[4]

Towards the end of her life, Lucy found it increasingly difficult to attend race meetings in person, but in June 1934 she wrote to Oscar Pulvermacher in girlish glee:

> Here is an adventure! I am horribly ill, but two days ago I decided to see Ascot once again and have rented a house and a box, no. 110. So if you go, do look me up. I have also got a Royal Enclosure ticket too, but no fancy dress. So if you see someone looking very nautically attired you will know it is me. I haven't seen anyone in London for eight years – so I shall be an unknown quantity. What fun![5]

While she enjoyed watching the horses run, she deplored the dress standards of some of the women there, particularly those wearing 'hideous, enormous hats that blew off onto the racetrack'. She went on to say, 'Everyone's sympathy went out to the poor men who had to accompany these frights, who, posing as women of fashion, only succeeded in being figures of fun.'[6]

Her racehorses were the only luxury indulgence of her later life and doubtless cost her a significant part of her fortune, particularly as she never kept any of her winnings, distributing them among her staff and the crew of *Liberty*. She was fond of other animals as well; she had a small, pet Belgian griffon that she called 'Benito' after her Italian hero. When her favourite stepson 'Naps' Brinckman's second son was born in 1933, he asked Lucy if she would be godmother, to which she replied: 'Delighted – provided you call him Mussolini.' In spite of the potentially lucrative prospects, the child's mother put her foot down and he was christened John Francis instead.[7]

In earlier years, Lucy had adored dressing in flamboyant clothes. One of her greatest friends in the 1920s was the beautiful, Australian-born Ranee of Pudukota, universally admired for her gorgeous silk saris. Lucy had visited her following the death of her husband the Rajah in 1928, 'Now, my dear,' she had said, 'you will no longer be needing any of your pretty coloured dresses, so you can give some to me.' Which she did, and Lucy had them remade into classical day-dresses. But by the 30's she had adopted the simple day fashions of the time – plain skirts and coats, 'Mary Jane' style bar shoes and the universal cloche hat or a form of a simple turban. Indoors, she wore on her head a knotted silk scarf, always adorned by a single jewelled pendant, but whatever her headgear she teased out a cheeky kiss-curl over her forehead. Her one concession to vanity concerned her hair, once her crowning glory. When it started to go grey she took to wearing wigs with the hair colour of her youth. Evidence that she could still look stunningly stylish when the occasion demanded is amply demonstrated in the photograph taken of her with the winning Schneider Trophy team in 1931. [see PLATE B13] During the winter months, in the privacy of Byron Cottage which never had central heating, practical comfort was her prime consideration. Wentworth Day recounts how she wore men's long woollen pants and padded around the house wrapped in a Turkish towelling bathrobe.

When she was feeling well she took a keen interest in food and cooking, Warner Allen claiming that her own recipe for steak pie was a sensation, though as a considerable connoisseur himself he deplored her lack of interest in wine and her preference for 'wallop' – draught beer. Her favourite foods, apart from her own pie, were traditional British fare: venison, grilled salmon, mutton cutlets, pheasant, plain lobster, herrings and oysters. She had no truck with salads but loved asparagus, broad beans and globe artichokes. Everything was washed down with pints of Guinness or Burton-brewed beer. Tea invariably consisted of sandwiches made with 'Gentleman's Relish' anchovy paste, while after a hard day's work she would make a pick-me-up of a raw egg whisked into a tumbler of brandy. She paid her chef of the moment and his assistant well over the odds, but never trusted them to make porridge, a task always assigned to Miss Ritchie. Often the entire kitchen staff at Byron Cottage would be sacked over some trifling misdemeanour, only to be rehired a few days later, with Lucy apologising profusely for her irritable nature and bad manners. And during these hiatuses she would live on a diet of oysters, ordered daily from Scott's restaurant. On Jersey, whatever the weather, she insisted on going down to the beach for a picnic, carried up and down the cliff by Foster, who also had to deal with her folding bed. Once in position she would discard her old 'modesty' coat and lie down to expose herself to the sun, or the wind and the rain, wearing nothing but a bra and the very briefest of shorts, an early precedent for the bikini.[8]

This was all part of her unique health regime. She could not bear to live with closed windows, visitors often commenting that the rugs in her various residencies would become airborne in particularly windy weather. Warner Allen wrote that 'few well-to-do women can have lived more uncomfortably than Lady Houston did during the years I knew her.'[9] She believed that colds must be tackled immediately the first symptoms appeared, preferably by going to bed with a shawl round the head and a succession of hot-water bottles packed around the body. At the same time, the patient was advised to gargle and take nasal douches of Listerine or table salt dissolved in boiling water; then two tablespoons of castor oil, immediately followed by the sucking of half an orange to disguise the taste. Most crucial of all was to drink large tumblers of very hot water every two hours, preferably with fresh lemon juice added and lots of sugar. Gee's Linctus was the treatment for coughs by day and a teaspoonful of Vaseline taken before going to bed at night. She claimed from her own long experience that these treatments were infallible, and printed them on the back page of the *Saturday Review* throughout the winter months. This was how she treated minor ailments, but for the underlying problems with her health – exceptionally low blood-pressure and insomnia – she resorted to treatment by the most expensive doctors, as we have seen on a number of occasions. Eva Thaddeus had noted that her health, even in her youth, was 'not robust' and, as mentioned earlier, she had been advised to go abroad for the winter during her marriage to Theodore Brinckman. At her wedding to George Byron she was reported as being in frail health, and her frequent bouts of illness became more serious as she grew older. She found it all very vexing. As she became increasingly housebound and unable or unwilling to take physical exercise, her once exquisitely slim figure became rotund and matronly, a fact that was cruelly satirised by David Low in a number of cartoons for the *Evening Standard* between 1933 and 1935. [see FIGS 4 & 6]

Her favourite cartoon, one that she had framed to sit on her desk, depicted her in typically pugilistic mode. [see FIG 5] It was published in 1935 at the time of debates within the Labour party to choose a leader to succeed Ramsay Macdonald. The leading contenders were Clement Atlee (pictured behind Lucy) and Herbert Morrison, and the caption read, 'For goodness sake keep the contest going, Herbert. Look who's coming now!' To the right of the ring stands Winston Churchill, waiting to act as 'second' to Lucy in the next bout.[10]

Lucy was, in her own private way, deeply religious. She had a simple faith in the goodness of God, who had answered her prayers when she was in the depths of depression at the time she had been certified as mad, following the death of Robert Houston. She had vowed then that she would cast aside vanity and the trappings of personal wealth and devote her future life to the good of others, a creed that informed her legion acts of charity and her love of her country. None of her political actions were for her own advancement; she would chide herself cruelly if anyone suggested that her motives had been in any way selfish. The same applied to her abiding patriotism, and when she learnt that the Oxford Union debate on 8 February 1933 had passed a motion (by 275 votes to 153) that 'this House will in no circumstances fight for King and Country', she summoned once again her chariot of fire and her arrows of indignation, penning an excoriating article about the foppish decadence of contemporary British undergraduates.[11]

Figure 5. Lucy's favourite depiction of herself in a political cartoon. *(Author)*

Chapter 17

Lord Lloyd and the India Bill

Apart from Winston Churchill, the man Lucy lionised as the potential saviour of British politics was the Conservative peer Lord Lloyd. He was, to her mind, the 'strong man' that the country desperately needed to lead it out of the morass into which it was being taken by the ineffectual politicians of all parties sitting at Westminster. She had started having correspondence and meetings with him in 1930, at the same time writing to Oscar Pulvermacher, the night-editor of the *Daily Mail*, imploring him to actively promote Lord Lloyd in his newspaper.[1] Pulvermacher had replied that he wondered whether Lloyd wanted to put himself forward as a political leader. Lucy replied, '*He is the man England wants*, I am sure. That he is ready to do this is one thing, but if the public do not have his name and his sayings pushed down their throats again and again they would not listen to him if he were the Archangel Gabriel. He must be advertised and rubbed into their thick intelligences. He cannot do this himself – *but you can*.' In a later letter she reported that 'Lord Lloyd has been to see me and has just gone. He thinks the outlook *very black*, but *no one* will believe it or realise the gravity of it.'[2] Again in May 1931 she reported that 'she had had a most despairing letter about the outlook from Lord Lloyd.' To this she added, 'I see nothing but a second Russia coming here by leaps and bounds, and that mischievous old creature Lloyd George is going to do his best to help.'[3]

From the opposite end of the political spectrum, Lord Lloyd believed passionately in the British Empire and all it stood for, how it could exercise firm government according to Christian ethics, its perpetration of justice without corruption and its commercial potential for the benefit of the rulers and the ruled alike. Disillusioned by his own experiences of democracy based on a broad franchise, he was an unashamed elitist, convinced that matters were best handled by a governing class, either of aristocratic birthright or proven skills in diplomatic, military or commercial administration. 'In his eyes, politics were not the "great game", but a means of saving and regenerating that great instrument of civilisation, the British Empire. Such a seriousness of approach would render him forever an oddity in British politics.'[4] It was precisely these unique, forceful characteristics and his conviction that Britain needed strong military defences that Lucy found so appealing. Lloyd has been effectively airbrushed from the roll call of great British patriots, only faintly remembered – if at all – as a dinosaur from a past era, and so to understand Lucy's fascination with this complex man it is perhaps worthwhile to recollect his strong personality, his past achievements and his not inconsiderable contribution to the pages of British history. I make no apologies for devoting a whole chapter to this diplomatic and political giant.

George Lloyd was a man of modest stature but impressive appearance, his black hair, dark complexion and piercing, dark brown eyes proclaiming his Welsh, Celtic origins though some people might easily mistake him for a Turk or an Armenian. Like many families of landed gentry in Wales, the Lloyds of Dolobran, Montgomeryshire, could trace their decent from one of the Welsh princes of the dark ages. George's ancestors in the sixteenth century had served as Justices of the Peace and local worthies, but later generations in the seventeenth century became Quakers, which led to their being denied public office and persecuted, even imprisoned, for their beliefs. They migrated to the Midlands in 1698, leaving behind them the ruins of Dolobran Hall, their ancestral home, and becoming high-church Anglo-Catholics. One branch of the family started the bank that still bears their name while another branch became ironmasters in the Birmingham area, founding the business that developed into the steel tube makers Stewarts and Lloyds. The two branches of the family had been reunited when Sampson Samuel Lloyd II married his cousin Emilia Lloyd, a great-granddaughter of Charles Lloyd the banker in 1868. George Ambrose Lloyd was their sixth child and third son born in 1879. He was educated at Eton and Trinity College Cambridge where he achieved sporting success when he coxed the university eight to victory over Oxford in the 1899 and 1900 boat races. But he went down without bothering to take his final exams and getting his degree, traumatised by the loss of both his parents within weeks of each other the previous year. With his happy family upbringing shattered and finding the prospect of working for his elder brother in the family business most unappealing, he set out on his travels to try and satisfy an inherent wanderlust that would remain with him for the rest of his life.

Through the influence of his university friend Samuel Cockerell in the commercial department at the Foreign Office he went to Istanbul, where he became an unpaid and unofficial research agent for the embassy, drifting around Palestine and taking a special interest in the Hejaz railway that the Germans were building as part of their ambitious rail route from Berlin to Cairo. The reports he wrote about the details of the route of the railway, and the motives behind it, together with his investigations into the Turkish economy, received favourable comment when they were forwarded back to London and would prove invaluable during the British campaign against Turkey in the First World War. In the years leading up to this conflict, the concerns of the Foreign Office were focused on the intentions of Russia in the region and their lust for a warm-water port on the Mediterranean, an extension of the FO's obsession with Afghanistan that had led to the disastrous military campaigns of the previous century. Lloyd's perceptive analysis pointed out the errors of this policy, insisting that Germany was the real potential threat. In 1907 he was appointed as a special commissioner to investigate trading possibilities for Britain in the whole of the region around the Persian Gulf.

Lloyd was elected as the Unionist MP for West Staffordshire in 1910 and the following year he married Blanche Lascelles, a niece of the Earl of Harewood. Nine months later their son – and only child – was born and christened David Alexander, the latter name in honour of his godmother Queen Alexandra. The birth presented no problems, but shortly afterwards Blanche developed a serious kidney infection and for several weeks was close to death. In January Lloyd, already disillusioned with what he saw as the impotence of his role as a mere backbencher and increasingly finding himself at odds with his party's leadership over tariff reform and Irish independence, took his wife on a voyage of recuperation to East Africa. In Kenya he was staggered by the potential for the country and how rich the English settlers were becoming, even deciding to buy a couple of plots of land himself. On his return he pressed the Government to do more to support the colonists and build more railways; he wrote articles for the newspapers about the country's prospects and seriously considered giving up his seat in Parliament and embarking on a new life for himself and his family. 'I hate the House of Commons so badly that I despise myself for not having the initiative to abandon it.'[5] But his political allies urged him to stay and as matters in the Balkans deteriorated, reaching a climax with the assassination of Archduke Ferdinand of Austria at Sarajevo in June 1914, he was alarmed to hear from the French Ambassador that Britain seemed mindful not to honour their obligation under the 'Triple Entente' with France and Russia in the event of Austria declaring war on Serbia. When General Wilson confirmed to him that this did indeed seem to be the attitude of the Liberal Foreign Secretary, Sir Edward Grey, who feared it would push Germany into invoking its alliance with Austria, Lloyd swung into action, lobbying his friends on the right of the Conservative party to make their political leaders stand up for Britain's honour and reputation for keeping her word. Lloyd therefore became a crucial catalyst in arranging the 'Lansdowne House' meeting that persuaded the Liberal Prime Minister, Herbert Asquith, that the Conservative opposition would support him if he did decide to go to war.

Soon after the outbreak of hostilities, Lloyd was commissioned into the Warwickshire Yeomanry and was assigned to the staff of Sir Ian Hamilton during the Gallipoli campaign, later joining up with T.E. Lawrence in his support of the Arab Revolt and working with him in the desert on the disruption of Turkish supply lines along the Hejaz railway.[6] [see PLATE B21] His personal bravery in action was rewarded with a DSO in 1917. When hostilities ceased, he wrote an influential book entitled *The Great Opportunity* in collaboration with Edward Wood (later to become Lord Halifax) which set out a Tory manifesto against the continuation of the wartime coalition under Lloyd George. He made speeches in the House of Commons in support of the Montagu-Chelmsford proposals for devolving more power in India from the centre to the Provincial Governments and was delighted when, in October 1918 just after his 39th birthday, he was appointed as the next Governor of the Bombay Province and made a Knight Commander of the Indian Empire as Sir George Lloyd.

Lloyd's period in Bombay was stressful but extraordinarily productive. His relationship with the Foreign Office and the permanent staff they assigned to him was strained, because they considered him an 'amateur' and not 'one of them'; they resented the fact that he reported directly back to the cabinet. Nor were his dealings with the Viceroy any easier, since Lord Chelmsford changed his attitude once he attained that role and now wanted to centralise more power to Simla and away from the regions, while Lloyd was equally committed to exerting his independence and local authority to get things done. He inherited tentative plans for two great infrastructure schemes: land reclamation, the Back Bay project, to provide land for more housing; and a dam across the river Indus, the Sukkur Barrage, to supply both electric power and water for irrigating many thousands of acres in the hinterland. Neither had progressed off the drawing board through lack of finance on the one hand and motivational inertia on the other. Lloyd solved the first by raising loan capital from the local money markets and the second by his own dynamic drive and commitment. He also had to deal with local strikes and civil unrest stirred up by Ghandi's rhetoric and the campaign to press for Indian independence. Lloyd's initial attempts at mediation suffered a serious setback in April 1919 when General Dyer ordered his troops to open fire on an unruly but unarmed demonstration in Amritsar, causing the death of 370 people, including women and children, and injuries to hundreds more. Ghandi became increasingly intransigent and Lloyd finally ordered his arrest and trial on charges of sedition, leading to a prison sentence of six years. This firm action had precisely the effect that Lloyd wanted, in spite of dire predictions from his advisers, and for the remainder of his tenure civil unrest was markedly diminished.

He had inherited a very run-down residence from his predecessor, and with his wife Blanche's assistance had restored it to its former magnificence and outward display of Imperial splendour. He took every opportunity to dress himself in his robes of state, writing to friends back in England that he was convinced his 'subjects' were not impressed by a Governor in a grey suit. The Prince of Wales, later to be Edward VIII, remarked that 'he had never known what regal pomp was until he visited Lloyd in Bombay.'[7] And he enjoyed a certain degree of reconciliation with the Viceroy when Blanche's brother Tom, who was serving as a temporary ADC to her husband, announced his engagement to Lord Chelmsford's daughter Joan Thesiger. Throughout his four-year tenure Lloyd had pushed himself to the limit and suffered frequent bouts of ill health, mainly brought on from overwork. On their return journey to England in late 1922, the Lloyds stopped off in his beloved Cairo and he could enjoy a brief skiing holiday in Switzerland, while he could also reflect on a job well done under very difficult circumstances.

Arriving back in England, he rather assumed that his political masters would make good the tentative promise, made to him by his friend Stanley Baldwin, of an elevation to the peerage and appointment as High Commissioner for Egypt, but he was disappointed on both counts. Andrew Bonar Law had won the general election of April that year with a majority of 74 for the Conservatives, but he was already a sick man and was forced to retire in May 1923, handing over the leadership of the Conservative party to Stanley Baldwin and precipitating another general election in June. The country was in the grip of industrial unrest with strikes in the coal industry. Ireland was in turmoil following the so-called settlement. The Conservative party itself was disunited over questions of tariff reform, the white paper in advance of the Independence for India Bill, defence spending and the repayment of loans the country had been forced to take on from the USA during the war. Baldwin struggled to head a minority Conservative government for a few months until forced to hand over the reins to Labour's Ramsay Macdonald. Lloyd meanwhile was left kicking his heels and forced to try and recover his own finances – he was not a wealthy man and his time as Governor of Bombay had left him with considerable debts – so he accepted a directorship at Lloyds Bank and another at Shell Oil, while his letters requesting a new diplomatic role were submerged by more pressing matters at Whitehall. At least his past services were recognised in January 1924 when he was appointed a member of the Privy Council, and three months later by being made a Knight Grand Commander of the Order of the Star of India.

Ramsay MacDonald in turn had to go to the country in October 1924 to seek a new mandate from another general election. Lloyd, increasingly disillusioned with the democratic process as it was playing out in the British parliament, had not put his name forward as a candidate, but the death of the Conservative candidate for the safe Tory seat of Eastbourne two weeks before polling date threw up an unexpected opportunity to get back into political notice, an opening that he was persuaded by friends to grab with both hands. Lloyd was formally adopted as the Unionist candidate and he immediately set off on the campaign trail, which his wife Blanche found 'very interesting', though he found it 'badly distasteful'.[8] He intensely disliked speaking in public, but his brief appearances on the hustings were enough to ensure his election by a massively increased majority due to his charisma and the strength of his personality alone.

Lloyd did receive the offer to be Governor of Kenya from the Colonial Secretary, Leo Amery, in March 1925, implying that 'it was all he was likely to get', since the Foreign Office favoured another candidate for Egypt in the form of Lawrence Dundas, Earl of Ronaldshay, who had been Governor of Bengal at the same time that Lloyd had presided over Bombay. And Lord Birkenhead, the Secretary of State for India, had earmarked himself as the next Viceroy. As Blanche Lloyd recorded, 'It is no less an issue than whether the brilliant crooks in the cabinet are to continue to dupe the Prime Minister into disregarding the claims of loyal service in order to arrange appointments to suit their own convenience.'[9] Lloyd now appealed in writing directly to both Austen Chamberlain, now the Foreign Secretary, and Stanley Baldwin, reminding them of his unique qualifications, his deep understanding of the problems across the whole Middle East and past promises. Chamberlain's reply was a schoolmasterly ticking off, but Baldwin telephoned him to say that 'it would be all right' and the following day Lloyd received notification that he would be the next High Commissioner for Egypt – with the title of Baron Lloyd of Donobran.

British interests in Egypt centred around the Suez Canal which had been finally completed by the French engineer de Lesseps in 1869 after ten years in construction. It provided a vital short cut for trade with India and the Far East. The building of the canal had been financed largely by French business syndicates, with the Egyptian Royal family owning 44%, a stake that was acquired on behalf of the British Government by the Prime Minister Benjamin Disraeli in 1875 for £4 million – without seeking prior approval from Parliament. By an agreement in 1882, Egypt became a Khedivate 'within the sphere of British influence', though the precise nature of Britain's role in Egypt was never clearly defined. In 1888 the Convention of Constantinople reconfirmed the right-of-passage by ships of all nations through the canal under International Law. A threat of invasion by Turkey in 1915 forced the British Government to step up its military presence in the country and declare the country a British Protectorate with the appointment of the first High Commissioner, Sir Reginald Wingate. Wingate refused to allow an Egyptian delegation headed by Saad Zaghloul Pasha to attend the Versailles peace conference to argue the case for Egypt to be recognised as a separate state, and from then on Zaghloul and his nationalist movement, the Wafd, became the focus for increasingly vociferous and violent opposition within the country. Serious rioting in 1919 led to Wingate's replacement as High Commissioner by Viscount Allenby, the victor of Britain's campaigns in the Middle East during the First World War, who held the post until 1925.

Egypt was a despotic monarchy and King Fuad, a descendant of Mohammed Ali, who had established Egypt's independence from the Ottoman Empire in the early nineteenth century, appointed all the ministers to his government. Any opposition to his rule, usually in the form of street riots, had to be suppressed by force, resulting in major increases in the number of police and the size of the army. This latter development caused the British government considerable anxiety, both in terms of cost and the diversion of troops from other regions, and they had sent the Colonial Secretary Lord Milner to try to establish a dialogue with Zaghloul in 1920. The resulting 'Milner Declaration', never cleared by the cabinet, stated that Britain's aim was to 'reconcile the aspirations of the Egyptian people with the special interests which Britain has in Egypt'. These interests were enumerated as control of the Suez Canal, the defence of Egypt's borders, the protection of foreign interests and the continuance of the status of Sudan as a British Protectorate. Another part of the declaration stated that the British intended to remove all their officials in 1927. King Fuad had been persuaded to appoint Zaghloul as Prime Minister, but when the commander-in-chief of the army, Sir Lee Stack, had been assassinated in 1924, Allenby had blamed the Wafd movement – and by implication Zaghloul himself – and ordered Fuad to dismiss him, whereupon Fuad suspended the constitution and chose to rule with the sole assistance of his cronies Ziwar Pasha and Nashaat Pasha, the latter not even being an elected deputy. The minister for Egyptian affairs at the Foreign Office, Nevile Henderson, took the view that Allenby had, by his heavy-handed actions, only made matters worse and forced his resignation.

So the role of his successor would be a very delicate one indeed and Lloyd's appointment was seen by many of his friends as a poisoned chalice.

Blanche, who entertained ambitions for her husband even as far as a seat in the Cabinet, wrote in her diary, somewhat prophetically, that his acceptance meant 'a definite goodbye to home politics as far as one can foresee'.[10] But at least he could now rely on the wholehearted support of the Prime Minister, Stanley Baldwin, and the new Chancellor of the Exchequer, Winston Churchill. The Lloyds' arrival in Cairo in October 1925 was a very public statement of intent. He had been warned that he should never travel except in an armoured car but two days later, wearing the shimmering white ceremonial dress uniform of his office, with the blue sash and star of his knighthood across his chest, he insisted that he and Blanche be driven through the streets of Cairo in an open horse-drawn carriage with a mounted escort of cavalry. He was delighted that this display of pomp was greeted with more cheers than jeers. Lloyd was appalled by the poor state of the Residency that 'gave no impression of permanence to the British presence in Egypt'.

His arrival coincided with a united show of strength by all the Egyptian opposition parties, who met in the Continental Hotel and declared themselves to be a new parliament. Lloyd now showed considerable diplomatic skills. He managed to get King Fuad to set a date for new elections in the spring – though he believed that Western-style democracy was totally inappropriate for a country like Egypt – and held private talks with Zaghloul to persuade him to do nothing until then, while at the same time requesting the Admiralty to send a battleship from Malta to Alexandria. As expected, the elections provided massive support for the independence movement though, as luck would have it, Zaghloul declined the premiership on the grounds of ill health. Lloyd returned to England to receive new instructions, which in essence were that he must reopen negotiations with the new Prime Minister, Sarwat Pasha, for an unequivocal acceptance of all the points in the 'Milner Declaration', which had been the sticking point on all previous attempts at a new treaty. In a memo to Winston Churchill, Lloyd summarised the impossibility of what he was asked to do:

> First to protect British and foreign interests at all costs and secondly not to interfere in the internal affairs of Egypt!! Each one contradicts the other.[11]

Sarwat, who had unofficially indicated that he might be prepared to accede to the British demands, then prevaricated, while the Foreign Office in London became increasingly concerned that Lloyd might decide to take some unilateral action to break the deadlock by an impulsive show of force. Without informing Lloyd, they invited Sarwat to London for secret negotiations, in which they made a number of concessions that diluted the British demands as long as the British army retained control of the 'canal zone' and that some British officials remained after 1927. When Lloyd heard that this was the new official policy, one that would be presented to Parliament for a vote, he was utterly disgusted, and wrote to friends that he could foresee the collapse of the British Empire and that he felt it was like the 'legions being recalled to Rome'. The rift between Lloyd and his political masters widened and he considered tendering his resignation, but the general election in 1929 that handed power to the Labour party took the decision out of his hands; the new Colonial Secretary was Arthur Henderson and one of his first actions was to force Lloyd to hand in his resignation or be given the sack.

For the next few years, Lloyd was consigned to the political wilderness along with his friend Winston Churchill, both of whom were seen as representing the unfashionable 'diehard' wing of the Conservative party, urging rearmament, rather than appeasement and the disarmament policy of the League of Nations. Both men were shunned for voicing their vehement opposition – Lloyd in the Lords, Churchill in the Commons – to the Independence for India Bill that was now being revived in committee and promoted by Ramsay Macdonald's Foreign Secretary, Sir John Simon. Lloyd was particularly critical of the Government's invitation to Ghandi, the man he had once consigned to prison, for round-table talks in London. He saw it as another nail in the coffin of the British Empire that he had devoted the best years of his life to serving.

His restless energy would not allow him to be idle however. He learnt to fly, and he became the dynamic chairman of the Empire Economic Union that he had founded to provide links between Business and the Conservative party and to campaign for Imperial Preference in trade. With Churchill, Leopold Amery and Sir Henry Page-Croft he became a leading light in the Indian Defence League (IDL), men who believed that independence would inevitably lead to murder and mayhem, the march of corruption and opening the door to Communism. These views coincided precisely with those of an elderly firebrand of a lady in Hampstead.

In October 1933 Lucy sent Lloyd a long telegram urging him to form a new political party 'based on good old-fashioned Conservative principles', one that would attract those on the right of the Conservative party and be a popular, sensible alternative to counteract the rise of Oswald Moseley and his British Union of Fascists. While Lucy admired Moseley for his robust denunciation of Communism, she distrusted his thuggish methods and deplored his overt anti-Semitism. 'You are the right man to be Prime Minister',[12] she told Lloyd, at the same time offering to provide initial funding of £100,000 for the IDL, with the promise of more to come. After making a telephone call and writing out a cheque for £10,000, she summoned the long-suffering Wentworth Day and ordered him to drive round to Lloyd's house in Portman Square and deliver it to her hero in person. But first of all she gave him a ticking off. Wentworth Day himself moved in an eclectic social circle that included politicians of all parties, and two nights before had attended a private dinner party at the famous old eating-house, the Cheshire Cheese. Among the guests enjoying a gastronomic feast of oyster and game pie, fine burgundy and vintage port had been his friend Lady Lymington, the wife of Lord Lymington, a founder member of the right-wing, agrarian group called the 'Mystery' – and Sir John and Lady Simon. Lucy had vented her fury that he should have dined with the 'monster who is handing over India to Communism', adding that she 'hoped the pudding had choked him'.[13]

Wentworth Day's encounter with Lloyd made a vivid impression on him. 'He strode across the room like a panther ... I had never met, and never shall meet again, a man who made such an instant impact of purpose, courage and magnetic personality.' Lloyd invited him to sit down and said, 'I know Lady Houston well – a great woman, a great patriot. I admire her immensely.' He then went on to say that he could never accept any money that came with strings attached, particularly the idea of a new political party with the aim of overthrowing the Government. But he added that he would accept the cheque as a contribution to the IDL campaign, to fund the expenses of his planned lecture tour around the country to warn people of the dangers of the Government's policies towards India and home defence. He then added the caveat that his acceptance was conditional on no interference from Lucy in what he said or did. The two men then chatted for an hour and established a lasting friendship. Lloyd told him that he was going to make an important speech on 21 November at the *English Review* dinner, an event at the Savoy hosted by its editor Douglas Jerrold and presided over by 'that idol of true-blue Conservatism, Lord Carson'. As a result of Wentworth Day's report back to his employer about his meeting, she may have leaked the news about Lloyd's upcoming speech to friends in the press. The *Sunday Despatch* commented that 'Lloyd was going to launch a back-to-Conservatism campaign', while the *Daily Herald* announced that he intended to 'make a bold bid for the leadership of the growing number of Tories who are sick and tired of the alliance with the Simonites and the MacDonaldites.'[14] In fact his speech turned out to be something of damp squib; not the rallying call that his supporters had hoped for at all, but a reasoned argument for adopting a policy more akin to President Roosevelt's 'New Deal' for the USA. He started off by agreeing that the formation of the National Government in 1931 to tackle the problems of a weak economy and soaring unemployment had been a sensible one, a decision endorsed by the electorate as a whole. Now though the political leaders had to unite in a programme of positive action: youth training, the revival of basic industries, agricultural protection by tariff reform and investment in rearmament.

> I have seen it suggested that it is my intention to form a new party or a new section of an old party … but I have no such intention. It is not new parties that we need, but principles and the pluck to pursue them.[15]

Lloyd was no tub-thumping orator and when he sat down he was 'very depressed', knowing that his supporters would be disappointed by his performance. But over the next few months he used Lucy's money to set up a propaganda office for the IDL and, together with Winston Churchill, Lord Hailsham and others, toured the country giving twenty-one speeches to packed audiences on India and his concepts for National Policy. Someone else who joined the campaign was Winston's 24-year-old son Randolph Churchill who, without informing his father or Lloyd, decided to stand as an IDC candidate in the Liverpool Wavertree by-election of 6 February

Plate C1. Byron Cottage, the Georgian house that Lucy bought in Hampstead around 1909. Her bankrupt husband, the 9th Lord Byron, lived in rooms at the back. (*Author 2012, by kind permission of the present owners*)

Plate C2. No.11 Targa Road, Hampstead, the house that Lucy turned into 'The Bluebird's Nest' convalescent home for nurses in 1915. (*Author 2012*)

Plate C3. The garden with the doorway opening onto Hampstead Heath. (*Author 2012, by kind permission of the present owners*)

Plate C4. Thrumpton Hall, Nottingham, the family home of the Byrons, now a popular wedding venue. Lucy and George were rare visitors. (*Les Garland photography*)

Plate C5. Preparatory montage for a portrait of Lucy as Lady Byron by the Irish artist Henry Jones Thaddeus in 1904. For some reason it was never completed.

Plate C6. Lucy's CBE medal. She thought the official ribbon, in a shade of salmon pink, was vulgar and devised her own in the form of a purple bow. (*Author, RAF Museum, Hendon*)

Plate C7. Beaufield House, Lucy's home on Jersey. The extensions at left are modern. (*Author*)

Plate C8. Memorial cross erected by Lucy over the grave of her 3rd husband, Sir Robert Houston. (*Author*)

Plate C9. The contentious inscription on the plinth, stating that he had 'died most mysteriously'. (*Author*)

Plate C10. Supermarine S.6B S1595 with Flight Lieutenant Boothman taking off for his winning circuit in the 1931 Schneider Trophy race. (*Courtesy of Solent Sky Museum, Southampton*)

Plate C11. Silver replica of the Schneider Trophy. A winged zephyr embraces another riding a wave, the symbolic triumph of speed over the elements. (*Courtesy of Solent Sky Museum, Southampton*)

Plate C12. The Schneider Trophy. The British victory in 1931 meant that the trophy would remain in this country in perpetuity. (*Science Museum, London*)

Plate C13. Landing the pilot from the winning Supermarine S.6B, with Lucy's steam yacht *Liberty* in the background. Artistic licence has brought *Liberty* over from Cowes to Calshot. (*Painting by David Wilson in the author's collection*)

Plate C14. Cover of official souvenir programme for the Schneider Trophy race, 1931. (*Courtesy of Solent Sky Museum*)

Plate C15.
The winning
Supermarine
S.6B serial
S1595. (*Author,*
Science Museum,
London)

Plate C16.
The reserve,
serial S1596.
Trophy replica
in foreground.
(*Author, Solent*
Sky Museum,
Southampton)

Plate C17. The Rolls-Royce 'R' engine, which was later used to power land-speed record-breaking cars for Donald Campbell and Captain Eyston. Lessons learnt during its development were incorporated into the iconic 'Merlin' engine. (*Author, RAF Museum, Hendon*)

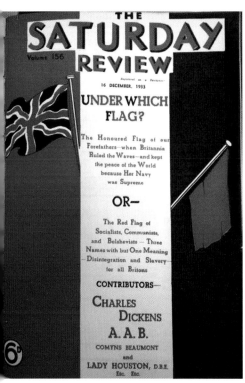

Plate C18. Front cover of the *Saturday Review* designed by Lucy and used, with textual variations, July 1933 to 1935.

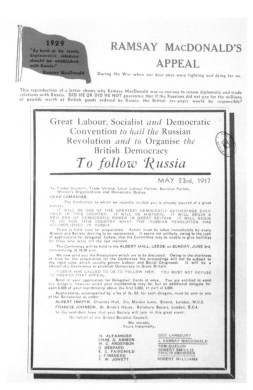

Plate C19. Rear cover of the *Saturday Review* April 20, 1935, reminding readers of Ramsay MacDonald's activities in 1917 during World War I.

Plate C20. Cover of the *Saturday Review* July 6, 1935, during the Abyssinian Crisis.

Plate C21. Lucy's tombstone in East Finchley cemetery. (*Author*)

IN
VERY LOVING MEMORY
OF
DAME FANNY LUCY HOUSTON, D.B.E.
WHO PASSED TO HER REST ON DECEMBER 29th. 1936;
WIDOW OF THE LATE
ROBERT PATTERSON HOUSTON, BART.
SHE WAS ONE OF ENGLAND'S GREATEST PATRIOTS
AND HER GENEROSITY WAS UNBOUNDED.
ALSO TO ARTHUR HENRY WREY,
BROTHER-IN-LAW OF THE ABOVE
WHO DIED DECEMBER 26th 1940.
AND ALSO TO FLORENCE.
WIDOW OF ARTHUR WREY.
WHO DIED APRIL 29th 1959.
SHE FIRST GAVE HER OWN SELF TO THE LORD
AND UNTO US BY THE WILL OF GOD.

Plate C22. The 'Cowdray' pearls, sold by Christie's in London in June 2012 and again for a record price by Sotheby's, Hong Kong, October 2015. (*Sotheby's catalogue*)

1935 caused by the death of the sitting Conservative MP. Lucy admired Randolph as 'a chip off the old block' and funded his campaign. She had been particularly impressed by his response to the notorious 'King and Country' debate at the Oxford Union. Three weeks later, Randolph Churchill proposed a resolution that the report of the debate should be deleted from the records of the Union, and when he lost this in a rowdy debate – by an even larger majority – he took matters into his own hands and tore the relevant pages out the ledger. He had to be escorted back to his hotel by the police. Soon after the original debate, the President of the Union received a box of 275 white feathers, the traditional symbol of cowardice, from an anonymous donor. Mindful of her proposal to send the parrots to the House of Commons in 1912, one guesses that Lucy had been behind this gesture.

Randolph Churchill's intervention in the Liverpool Wavertree by-election, 'which exhibited in equal degree the courage which warmed the hearts of his friends and the lack of judgement which made his enemies rejoice,'[16] merely had the effect of splitting the Tory vote in half, thereby handing victory to the Labour candidate on only 35% of the votes cast. On 11 February, Sir Samuel Hoare, Secretary of State for India, introduced the second reading of the India Bill which was approved in the House of Commons by 404 votes to 133, and it then went into its committee stage which lasted until May. Winston Churchill led the opposition but the vehemence of his oratory began to frighten even his most ardent supporters; Lord Salisbury declined to chair his public meeting in the Albert Hall.

Lloyd's speech in Exeter on 25 May was reported in *The Times* under the headline 'Black Shirt on White Paper':

Whenever Parliamentary government has been tried in the East, it has led to chaos or tyranny, generally both, and in India local government invariably spells corruption. I agree that we are honestly pledged to make the experiment in self-government in India, but not at any particular moment or in any particular way. India is a country with a hundred Irelands inside it. It has been ruled not so much by the sword as by British impartiality. No Indian Minister could or would be trusted, because he would have to belong to one of the warring factions. What right has Mr MacDonald or Mr Baldwin, the transient figures of a fleeting moment, to hand over our great heritage without consulting the people of this country? Surrender in China, in Ceylon, and in Egypt is closing avenues of employment for our own people. If the Conservative Party will not look after the interests of this country, as well as those of India, they should not be surprised that more and more people in this country would prefer a black shirt to a White Paper.[17]

His well reasoned address to a meeting at Liverpool in June 1935, acknowledging the quandary the Government faced, was applauded to the rafters and widely reported in the press, but it did not impress Lucy. She felt that the IDL campaign was altogether too slow and 'too sedate' and she vented her frustrations on Wentworth Day. 'Lloyd shouldn't give the Government *any* credit whatsoever – or show them any mercy. He should have blown them sky high. I am going to send him a telegram.'[18] When Wentworth Day saw what she had written he was appalled and implored her not to send it, knowing that it was tactless at best and deeply offensive at worst, implying that Lloyd was a traitor to his own principles. Lucy was not to be persuaded: 'I am paying for this campaign so I have every right to say what I feel!'

Lloyd phoned Wentworth Day with an invitation to breakfast the next morning – he was seething with indignation. 'I won't put up with this sort of thing! She must understand that I won't be dictated to. I don't mind what she says in a letter, but I will not be browbeaten by a telegram that could be read by anyone in the Post Office.' He then went over to his desk and wrote out a cheque to refund the whole £10,000 Lucy had given him. When Wentworth Day returned to Byron Cottage and related what had happened, Lucy burst into tears. 'Oh what have I done!' she sobbed, suddenly transformed from Boadicea into a pathetic child who knows she has been naughty. She tore up the cheque and told Wentworth Day to go back to Lloyd and beg for his forgiveness for her impetuous stupidity, with the promise that he could have whatever money he needed to rouse public opinion against the India Bill. Lloyd was still too hurt to even consider such an offer, though he did write her a letter of conciliation.[19]

I do not deny that I was disappointed with the immediate result and I realise that if a better speaker than I had been available [at the Liverpool meeting] swifter progress might have been achieved. None the less, I do feel that a great deal was actually achieved at rather a critical moment in influencing opinion. The present anxiety of the Government shows that this is the case, and I believe that when the crucial struggle over India comes on in the autumn, we shall find that we have gained more ground than we knew.

But without any alternative source of major funding,[20] the IDL campaign lost momentum and effectively ran out steam, and the third reading of the India Bill was carried by 386 votes to 122, including 84 Conservative rebels who followed Winston Churchill into the opposition lobby. This action sealed his political exile, taking Lloyd with him. T.E. Lawrence, his buccaneering companion from the First World War desert campaign and now living out his own exile as Aircraftsman Shaw, wrote to him with his own analysis: 'To be sacked by the Labour party was glorious; to have been at odds with the Tory chiefs is less assuring.'[21]

Several historians have speculated that if the IDL had been more successful in the 1930s, Parliament might have been forced to take more care with the details in the preparation of the final precipitous Act of 1947, thereby saving the lives of some of the millions who died in the massacres following Indian partition. Lloyd and Lucy were reconciled and remained friends for the rest of her life. Nor would Lloyd forget his meetings with her loyal emissary James Wentworth Day as we will see shortly. But for now Lucy had another campaign to fight, another crusade on which to attach her banner and Wentworth Day would once again be thrown into the thick of it. This time her target was the League of Nations and particularly the new Foreign Secretary, Sir Samuel Hoare.

Chapter 18

'Our Champion Hoare', the Abyssinian Crisis and the General Election of 1935

We want no more of Samuel Hoare,
He isn't the man for Chelsea.
We've had our fill of the India Bill
And the Red Geneva Rag.

Chelsea voters don't be fooled
We're weak on land and sea,
And up in the air where Sam Hoare ruled
We're weak as weak can be.

Lucy Houston, November 1935

Before diving into the meaty issues of this chapter and the events that would define the year 1935 as a watershed in world politics, Lucy packed Wentworth Day off to Norwood in south London to intervene in the by-election taking place in March. The main contenders were Edwin Duncan-Sandys for the National Conservatives, and Mrs Gould on behalf of the Labour Party. At the last minute a Mr Findlay entered the contest as an Independent Conservative, sponsored and encouraged by Winston Churchill's journalist son Randolph. On 8 March, Lucy wrote a letter to Winston urging him to 'enter the fray himself', to which she received his reply stating that he thought 'the ground at Norwood was ill-chosen'.[1] Randolph's intervention was made even more controversial when it became known that Findlay was a member of the BUF. Not only that, his only campaigning leaflet was one written by Lucy under the title 'Thrown to the Wolves',[2] supported by placards and posters outside his headquarters. The leaflet was one of Lucy's fiercest attacks on the leaders of the National Government and 'officials' soon stepped in to confiscate the lot on the basis that it contravened Electoral

Law. Wentworth Day's soapbox oratory failed to save Findlay from losing his deposit, while Duncan-Sandys won with more than half the votes cast. He would shortly marry Winston Churchill's daughter Diana.

In March 1935, Lucy penned a particularly excoriating piece about the National Conservative MP Anthony Eden.[3] He had been Parliamentary Private Secretary to the former Foreign Secretary, Sir Austen Chamberlain, from 1926 until his promotion to Under Secretary for Foreign Affairs in 1931. What damned him in Lucy's eyes was his recent acceptance of the post of Minister for the League of Nations. The members comprising the League had changed since its formation in 1920. Germany had been admitted in 1926, but had left in 1933 along with Japan, while to Lucy's absolute horror the Union of Socialist Republics (USSR) had been allowed to join in their place. By 1935 Italy had resigned as well, leaving Russia as the only superpower in a collection of mainly small nations who could not agree unanimously about anything. The exiled Haile Selassie was still the official representative for Abyssinia, which Lucy later took as the cue for questioning whether, in that case, the correct man to represent Russia should surely be Grand Duke Cyril, the heir to the Romanoff dynasty?[4]

Lucy included some highly personal and potentially libellous suggestions that Eden's extraordinary good looks – 'this nancified nonentity' – threw doubts on his sexuality. His first move had been to visit Moscow for talks with his opposite number Maxim Litvinoff and the soviet dictator Joseph Stalin. Lucy suggested that the welcoming band should have played the tune 'Cheer up, smile and be gay'. 'Stalin himself was greatly taken with Eden's straightforwardness and "simplicity" of character,' she wrote. 'In this case, character has had its just reward.' This was all too much for the distributors of the *Saturday Review* who once again refused to handle the journal, while ministers got very hot under the collar.

The cover of the following issue of the *Saturday Review* was edged in black and showed a photograph of Lucy 'mourning the truth'.[5] [see PLATE B20] The banner headline declared, 'We have been warned that if THEY have much more of our nonsense (meaning our habit of revealing the truth about politicians) they will close us down.' The next week's issue had the same cover but now with a muzzle superimposed.

On 20 April 1935, Lucy stepped up her campaign to denigrate Ramsay MacDonald by printing on the back cover of the *Saturday Review* a pamphlet of 23 May 1917, signed by him and other leading socialists, inviting Trades Unionists and Women's Organisations etc to attend a Convention in Leeds on 3 June. (see PLATE C19) Its objective was to 'hail the Russian Revolution and to Organise the British Democracy ... Russia has called us to follow her. You must not refuse to answer that appeal.' Inside the journal, Lucy reproduced the accompanying letters with the 'resolutions that will be discussed', including one that urged workers, soldiers and sailors to set up their own Councils or 'Soviets'. Ramsay Macdonald was furious and had meetings with the Attorney General (Sir Thomas Inskip) about what legal action to take.[6] A few weeks before, an American journalist by the name of Walker had been sentenced to six months in prison for forgery and had confessed that these 'letters' had in fact been his work. There now followed a terse correspondence between the Attorney General and Lucy (who was in cahoots with the Duke of Atholl) about handing the 'letters' over. Sir Thomas pointed out to the Prime Minister that they did not want to stir up too much publicity, because one of the resolutions 'passed unanimously' at the Convention had indeed been the suggestion that servicemen should set up 'Soviets' to question the authority of their officers. His final advice to the PM was that he might consider 'taking proceedings against Lady Houston for trafficking with a purveyor of forged documents.' The matter fizzled out.

Sir Samuel Hoare, in his role as Secretary of State for India, had been the Government Minister driving the India Bill through Parliament, which cast him as an unpatriotic villain in Lucy's eyes in spite of the fact that his aunt was her greatest friend and the wise advisor on her charitable work. Lucy wrote an article that included the following paragraph:[7]

This man is treating England and India as if they were his own private property and their inhabitants his galley slaves, to be given away with a pound of tea according to his wishes. Why this persistent, insistent pigheadedness over India by him and his gang? Can it be that they are in the power of Russia? Is it possible that in order to placate their master they have promised India to Russia as a little 'bonne bouche'? There is something dark and dirty in all this which ought to be unearthed. Who is going to do this? Must it be left to a woman?

The India Act received the Royal Assent in September 1935, and while it broadened the electoral mandate and brought more Indians into regional government, it never gained the cooperation of the Princely States, an essential requirement for moving India towards Dominion status. Further action stalled. Hoare's reward from Stanley Baldwin was to be promoted to Foreign Secretary on 7 June 1935 and this appointment riled Lucy even more. What other parts of the Empire – like Egypt – would he now give away? What other actions might he take to weaken our defences and put the borders of the Empire at risk? Would his policies be determined by the toothless, ineffectual League of Nations that Baldwin referred to as his 'sheet-anchor' and Lucy called the 'Red Geneva Rag'?

Lucy had a further gripe against Samuel Hoare. He had been Minister for Air during much of the 1920s and she felt that he had not done enough to promote the interests of the aviation industry and defend the Royal Air Force against the cutbacks in its budget. In fact he had done much good with the limited resources available to him, maintaining the RAF's separate identity from the army, founding the University Air Squadrons and re-establishing the air cadet training college at Cranwell. If he could not deliver squadrons of new aircraft, he could help ensure that there would be new generations of fledgling pilots, a far-sighted move for which the country would be extremely grateful within a few years. Lucy's narrow, blinkered outlook could not recognise his many fine qualities, particularly his reasoned, pragmatic approach to solving problems in a world of rapidly changing national aspirations.

On 3 October 1935, and without any formal declaration of war, Italian troops had invaded the ancient kingdom of Abyssinia (Ethiopia) in the Horn of Africa, a fellow member of the League of Nations. This precipitated an international crisis of unprecedented proportions; not only did it involve a major European nation but it might, if Italy ever became our enemy rather than ally, threaten Britain's control of the trade routes to the east down the Suez Canal and the Red Sea. The League had shown its complete impotence in 1931 when Japan had invaded the Chinese province of Manchuria; what was it going to do now? Samuel Hoare and his fellow counterparts assembled in Geneva and talked. They wrung their hands and generally agreed that it was a terrible thing and that something had to be done. Largely through the initiative of Anthony Eden the League notionally agreed with the concept of trying to impose economic sanctions against Italy as a way of wagging its finger at Mussolini and telling him he had been a very naughty boy. [see PLATE C20] Most nations only paid lip service to this idea, but Britain 'played the game with a straight bat'; it would mean the loss of £4 million a year in exports of coal and the jobs of 16,000 miners.[8] To reinforce the Government's commitment, a Royal Navy fleet was dispatched to exercise in the Mediterranean off the coast of Italy.

Lucy initially took a very different view of the 'Abyssinian Crisis'. Italy had been our staunch ally in the Great War and was now strenuously fighting the spread of communism. Why shouldn't Mussolini try and recreate some of the past glories of the Roman Empire, the regime that had provided stable prosperity to the Mediterranean region for hundreds of years, while defending itself from 'uncivilised' tribes that threatened its borders? Moreover, Abyssinia was seen by many as a cruel, primitive nation that still embraced slavery. And wouldn't the sanctions policy merely make Mussolini question who his allies should be in the future? When Hoare seemed to be spending more and more time in Paris, she assumed – wrongly as it turned out – that he was sealing the sanctions agreement in collusion with the French.

So when the date of 14 November was announced for the 1935 general election, Lucy swung into action. Hoare had been the Conservative MP for the Chelsea constituency since 1910, retaining his seat in the 1931 general election with a massive majority of 18,289 votes over the Labour candidate. There was no way that Lucy could do much to dent this and indeed she had no intention of encouraging his Labour party opponent. Her main objective was to cause him maximum discomfort by a campaign of pamphleteering and personal ridicule much more akin to electioneering of 100 years earlier, while at the same time urging Stanley Baldwin to ditch his National Coalition with the Labour Party and lead the country back to 'true Conservative values'. She pointed out quite reasonably that on the basis of the number of seats in the House of Commons the ratio of cabinet ministers should be 19 Conservative, 2 Liberal and only 1 Labour party. Why, therefore were there so many socialist ministers in the cabinet? She was not alone in seeking a tougher new Tory leader, an undercurrent picked up by the cartoonist David Low. [see FIG 6]

Her most potent pamphlet, of which she had half a million printed and distributed, was entitled 'If I'd been Mr Baldwin'.[9] In it she lambasted him for toadying up to Ramsay MacDonald, for adopting a policy of friendship to Russia and not using his massive majority in 1931 to build up the defence forces and make the Royal Navy once more the peace keeper of the world, rather than relying on the toothless League of Nations. 'How can you be surprised that all this anti–British unreality has brought such apathy as never was before known at any election?' she asked, ending the pamphlet with the prophetic plea, 'Turn over a new leaf, Mr Baldwin, and make the people

Figure 6. David Low's suggestions for a new Tory leader. Lucy's policy (3) is suggested as 'Rule Britannia and damn the details!' while that of the bellicose Lord Lloyd (4) is 'Putting a stop to all this Peace!' *(Evening Standard, reproduced in the Saturday Review, 3 August 1935)*

forget all this Socialistic and League of Nations "sheet-anchor" nonsense – that has brought us only bitter enmity and *will surely bring war*.' Lucy's pamphlet made a considerable impression on the public. It was written in simple, hard-hitting language understandable by everyone and quite unlike the wordy platitudes in most politicians' election speeches and campaign leaflets.

She wrote a satirical song – two verses of which are quoted in the chapter heading – and personally trained a negro minstrel band to sing it outside Samuel Hoare's house and through the streets of Chelsea. She published a scurrilous pamphlet entitled 'Our Champion Hoare'[10] and ordered Wentworth Day to recruit new teams of men with sandwich-boards to parade placards proclaiming 'Why send our Champion Hoare to Paris?' which 'swept the West End of London on a wave of ribald laughter.'[11] This was the entertaining, mass-media aspect of her campaign; in the *Saturday Review*, however, she published a very serious article indeed that went straight to the very heart of the problem. But before quoting from this at some length, it is relevant to delve into the background of Europe's tortuous relationship with Abyssinia over the previous century.

The country lay to the south of Egypt across the Nubian desert, bordering Sudan to the west and Somaliland to the south-east, with a coastal strip to the north-east along the Red Sea. Topographically it consisted of three distinct regions: the flat-lands bordering Somaliland, the region of Eritrea along the coast and the mountainous plateau in the centre. The history of the region was complicated, going back to biblical times and the legend that the Queen of Sheba, believed by many to have been the ruler of Abyssinia, visited King Solomon in Judea and returned to her country bearing his child. (This legend inspired the Rastafarian movement in the 1930s to believe that Ethiopians were the 'lost tribe of Israel', and that the Emperor known as Haile Selassie, one of whose titles was the 'Lion of Judah', personified the second coming of the Messiah as foretold in the Old Testament.) Adding to the mythology was confusion with another legend concerning the mystical Christian monarch Prester John and his fabulous goldmines, which formed the basis for the popular novels of the author Rider Haggard.

In 1862, Emperor Tewodros of Abyssinia was confronted by numerous internal uprisings against his despotic rule, but his pleas for support and military assistance from the major European powers fell on deaf ears. Most of the world viewed it as a barbaric, primitive nation of slave-owners. To add leverage to his demands to the British Government, Tewodros took a British missionary hostage and then imprisoned a number of consular officials who went to his rescue. When word got back to London that these men had been led through the capital in chains and then beaten and whipped before being thrown into a dungeon, the Government sent various delegations to parlay for their release. Negotiations of a sort lingered on over many months until Queen Victoria authorised a military rescue expedition in August 1867. She may have envisaged a quick dash by a small task force, but the high command in London demanded a mission of revenge, with the objective of showing other nations that the British Lion was not to be provoked without harsh reprisals. (A similar attitude had driven Britain to go to war with China in 1839 and 1857 in what became known as the Opium Wars.)[12]

> The British expedition of 1868 … proceeded from first to last with the decorum and heavy inevitability of a Victorian state banquet, complete with ponderous speeches at the end. And yet it was a fearsome undertaking; for hundreds of years the country had never been invaded, and the savage nature of the terrain alone was enough to promote failure.[13]

General Sir Robert Napier, a battle-hardened campaigner from the Sikh wars and the Second Opium war in China, methodically assembled a force of 13,000 British and Indian soldiers – mainly the latter – together with a supply train of 26,000 camp followers and over 40,000 animals, including elephants. He had learnt important lessons from the logistical failings of the British army during the Crimean War and he was not prepared to launch his invasion until everything was in place. He faced a 400-mile trek to his objective through hostile territory. His force would have to fight off ambushes along the way, but his major obstacle was the terrain as he headed inland and eventually prepared for the final assault on Tewodros's mountain fortress at Magdala. At the last minute Tewodros tried to negotiate terms in exchange for the release of the hostages, but General Napier demanded nothing less than unconditional surrender. Spurred on by the prospect of rich booty, his troops scaled the citadel in a bloody assault, and when Tewodros committed suicide rather than face defeat and capture, his defending army ran away. The subsequent sacking and looting of Magdala was not a proud moment in the annals of British military history but Napier returned to London as a great hero, showered with honours and commemorated by a magnificent statue that stands in Kensington Square off Kensington High Street.

And what had been achieved? Parliament had authorised £2,000,000 for the operation but it had cost a staggering £8,600,000.[14] The Prime Minister Benjamin Disraeli declared that the financial cost was immaterial since the venture had been morally correct, the rescue of the hostages had been the successful outcome and the cost in terms of human life had been minimal. Only 35 Europeans had been killed and 333 badly wounded (though the – unrecorded – number of casualties suffered by the Indian troops was undoubtedly much higher). Unlike the outcome of the First Opium War, by which Britain won the concession of Hong Kong as an important trading post and military base, Britain had neither sought nor gained any territorial advantage. 'Regime change' had admittedly been achieved by eliminating a tyrant, but the legacy had been to leave the country destabilised and at the mercy of rival claimants to fill the vacuum. (Politicians in the twenty-first century who ordered the invasion of Iraq and supported the overthrow of Colonel Ghaddafi of Libya had not learnt their history lessons – or chose to ignore them.)

During the 'Great Dash for Africa' in the 1880s, when the major European countries carved up the Dark Continent for their own colonial purposes, much of Somaliland was divided between the administrations of Britain, France and Italy. Italy had already colonised Libya on the Mediterranean coast and now decided to expand its empire by threatening to invade Abyssinia from Italian Somaliland. Emperor Menelik II promptly signed the Treaty of Wuchale with Italy which appeared to grant Italy control of the province of Eritrea along the Red Sea in exchange for their recognition of Menelik's title to the rest of the country. But each interpreted the terms of the treaty in different ways, and in 1895 Italy launched a full-scale invasion to start the First Italo-Abyssinian War. In the succeeding campaign,

Menelik managed to recruit support in the way of money and armaments from France, who wanted to curb Italy's expansion in Africa, and Russia, who just wanted to stir up enmity between the two European rivals. Without the careful planning that had preceded Napier's operation, the Italian army underestimated Abyssinian resistance and suffered a catastrophic defeat at the battle of Adwa in March 1896. Italian losses amounted to 7,000 killed, 1,500 wounded and 3,000 taken prisoner, and this humiliation led to rioting in many Italian cities and the collapse of the Government in Rome. The Treaty of Addis Ababa in October did at least define the borders of Eritrea and confirm Italy's right to rule over this new colony but it also restricted that country's ambitions for further adventures in Africa. At least for the time being.

In 1926 a joint Italian-British commercial initiative had been presented to Empress Zewditu's heir apparent and plenipotentiary, Ras Tafari Makonnen, by which the Italians sought to build a railway into the heart of the country and the British hoped to construct a mighty dam. The Abyssinian heights provided the headwaters for the Blue Nile and this scheme would have provided much-needed irrigation into the British Protectorate of Sudan. Having agreed initially, Ras Tafari soon had second thoughts and went to the League of Nations for arbitration. His eloquence on this occasion so impressed the people of Britain that the Government was forced to drop the waterworks scheme altogether, leaving the Italians on their own. But in August 1928 Zewditu signed the 'Treaty of Friendship and Arbitration' with Italy, which gave landlocked Abyssinia concession to a port on the Red Sea at Assab in Eritrea, called for cooperation in constructing a road from there into the interior, and clearly defined the precise borders between Abyssinia and Italian Somaliland. Two months after the treaty was signed, Zewditu died and Ras Tafari was declared as the new Emperor with the title of Haile Selassie I. And he believed that the road would merely provide an invasion route for the Italians and determined that it would not be built.

Tensions between the two countries rose and the Second Italo–Abyssinian War was provoked by a deliberate Italian military incursion across the border from Italian Somaliland at Wal Wal in December 1934. What became known as the 'Abyssinian Crisis' was taken to the League of Nations but got bogged down by lack of condemnation from Britain and France, both of whom were anxious to show friendship to Italy and secure it as an ally in any future disputes with Germany now that Adolf Hitler was rising to power. In January 1935, France signed an agreement effectively giving Italy a free hand in Africa in exchange for a promise of such cooperation. In April, Italy strengthened her hand still further by joining the 'Stresa Front' with France and Britain, a new pact to curb German violation of the terms of the Versailles treaty as originally laid out in the Locarno Pact of 1925. Ramsay MacDonald, Mussolini and the French Prime Minister Pierre Laval met at a hotel in the Italian town of Stresa on Lake Maggiore and concluded the pact on 14 April. [see FIG 7] So when the League finally gave its ruling in September that neither side could be held responsible for the 'Wal Wal' incident and washed its hands of the tiresome matter, Mussolini felt emboldened to launch a full-scale invasion of Abyssinia. Without any declaration of war, General Emilio De Bono ordered his forces to cross the river Mareb from Eritrea at dawn on 3 October 1935. Which brings us back full-circle to Samuel Hoare, the British general election of November 1935 and the resolution passed by the League of Nations to impose sanctions against Italy.

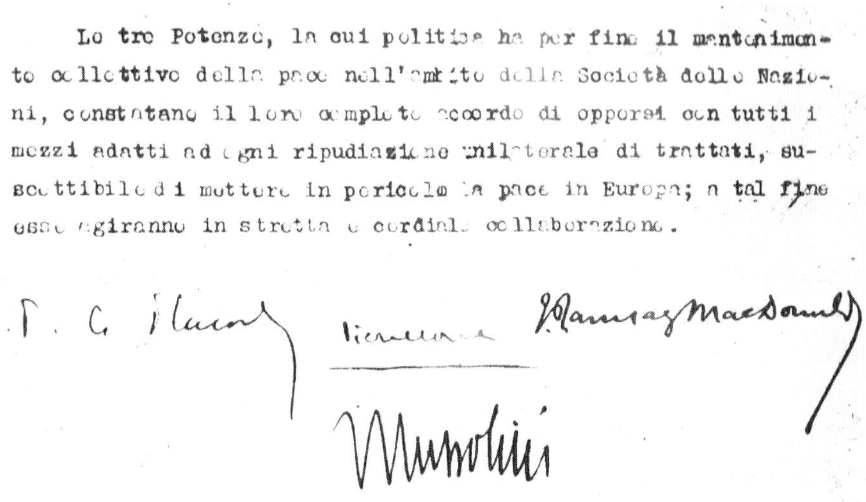
Le tre Potenze, la cui politica ha per fine il mantenimento collettivo della pace nell'ambito della Società delle Nazioni, constatano il loro completo accordo di opporsi con tutti i mezzi adatti ad ogni ripudiazione unilaterale di trattati, suscettibile di mettere in pericolo la pace in Europa; a tal fine esse agiranno in stretta e cordiale collaborazione.

Figure 7. Unlikely bedfellows. The signature of Ramsay MacDonald alongside that of Mussolini on the Stresa Agreement, 14 April 1935, together with that of the French Prime Minister, Pierre Laval. *(Author)*

In the *Saturday Review* of 9 November 1935 Lucy published her 'scoop', an article written by the distinguished Italian, Commendatore Luigi Villari, a writer, historian and diplomat who had served many years in the Italian Foreign Office. He had made a lifelong study of relationships between Italy and the English-speaking nations of the world.

> What Italians cannot swallow is that it should be Great Britain who has taken the lead in promoting this preposterous policy of sanctions, and that it should be the British delegate who, inspired by venomous spite, should with unremitting persistence have forced it on the unwilling representatives of other countries. The Italian people had, for generations, been accustomed to regard Great Britain as a traditional friend, whose Government, even when pursuing its own national interest, did so in a gentlemanly way and in a spirit of fair-play … For them the British Empire represented one of the bulwarks of our common civilisation.

He then went on to write that Italians had also taken deep offence from the menace threatened by the fleet of British warships. He concluded:

> Those of us who know the British well still believe that, if the politicians have misbehaved and there is a good deal of hypocrisy in sections of the British public, there is also sincerity and honesty in other groups. But it will, in future, be immensely difficult to convince any Italian of this fact.

In retrospect, it is easy now to recognise that Britain's handling of the Abyssinian Crisis would prove to be a major factor in Italy deciding to opt out of the 'Stresa Front' agreement, resign from the League of Nations in 1937 and ally itself with Germany in the upcoming conflict that Lucy was predicting. While she was right about this, she was on the other hand utterly wrong about the motives for Samuel Hoare's meetings in Paris. Behind closed doors and without consulting his colleagues, Hoare was hatching a plot with the French Prime Minister Pierre Laval to bypass the League of Nations completely in an attempt to resolve the crisis. The Hoare-Laval Pact as it became known would have seen the two nations agree that Italy might annexe the southern half of Abyssinia provided that he left Haile Selassie to rule the other half. It was a highly pragmatic solution, but when news of it leaked out in early December, there was uproar in the British Cabinet and Hoare was forced to resign from his post as Foreign Secretary, to be replaced by Anthony Eden. (It has often been quoted that King George V, during his first interview with Anthony Eden, had said, 'So, no more coals to Newcastle – no more Hoares to Paris.') Lucy had campaigned against Hoare to cause him discomfort; he himself had now completed the job for her. But if Lucy had known about the secret pact, she might have seen him in a far more sympathetic light. (History now condemns Laval as a Nazi collaborator during the Second World War, being executed for crimes against humanity in October 1945. Somewhat unfairly, the legacy of Samuel Hoare has been tainted by his association with this man.)

The Italian invasion from Somaliland made slow progress, so they opened a second front from Eritrea. A critical moment as far as world opinion was concerned occurred at the end of December 1935 when the Italian air force bombed a Swedish Red Cross hospital and then dropped mustard gas bombs, and later phosgene gas, on civilian targets. Both actions were in direct contravention of the Geneva Convention, though the Italians tried to claim they were merely retaliating against the enemy's use of 'dum-dum', squash-head bullets and the murder of one of their pilots, Tito Minniti, who had been shot down, captured, tortured, and executed (an incident cruelly echoed in the fate of a Jordanian pilot at the hands of ISIL in 2015). The Abyssinian forces were worn down in a number of battles through February, March and April largely due to superior Italian weaponry on the ground and control of the air. On 2 May, Haile Selassie boarded his royal train, taking with him the country's gold reserves, and slipped out of the country via French Somaliland (now Djibouti) and Jerusalem to set up a 'government in exile' in England. Three days later General Badoglio marched his troops into Addis Ababa and the war was effectively over, though the formal surrender was only signed on 18 December 1936.

In May 1936, Haile Selassie was invited to address the League of Nations in Geneva and newsreel cameras from around the world would record his dignified speech. In this he denounced Italy's illegal invasion and the war crimes they had committed, while at the same time criticising the international community for impotently standing by:

> It is collective security: it is the very existence of the League of Nations. It is the confidence that each State is to place in International treaties … In a word, it is international morality that is at stake. Have the signatures appended to a Treaty value only in so far as the signatory Powers have a personal, direct and immediate interest involved? … It is us today. It will be you tomorrow.

Readers may wonder why I have devoted so much space to the Abyssinian Crisis; but it was a crucial trigger point in world politics in the 1930s. Mussolini was at the peak of his Imperial ambitions with almost the entire Horn of Africa now incorporated into Italian East Africa. Previous alliances were crumbling, such as the Anglo-French-Italian 'Stresa Front', and new allegiances were to be forged between the fascist dictators in Europe. France was angry with Britain for signing the Anglo-German Naval Agreement in June 1935, while Japan, once a supporter of Abyssinia at the League of Nations, declared in favour of Italy if it would recognise the legality of Japan's invasion of China following the 'Mukden Incident'. It too would soon align itself with the Axis powers.

Most importantly for our story was that Lucy had to face up to the fact that her hero Benito Mussolini was behaving very badly and acting like a demonic tyrant, one that posed a threat to her beloved country and its Empire. She would have to look for her 'strong man' much closer to home.

Chapter 19

Patriotism, Charity and the Prince of Wales

Lucy had renewed her offer of donating £200,000 to buy squadrons of new fighter aircraft for the air defence of London in April 1935, but it had been rejected yet again. Neville Chamberlain, still the Chancellor of the Exchequer, explained that he would be delighted to accept the money 'as a contribution towards general Exchequer revenues' but that he could not allow restrictions to be imposed on how it was to be spent.[1] The Conservative MP for Henley-on-Thames, a Mr Hales, raised the matter in the House of Commons, asking whether in future 'donors might be allowed to allocate their offer to a specific purpose.' Duff Cooper, the Financial Secretary to the Treasury replied, 'No Sir! It is the duty of His Majesty's Government to submit to parliament estimates for the annual expenditure on defence. Any increase in such expenditure by private donations would constitute an interference with the authority of parliament and could not be permitted.'[2] Lucy was furious, seeing it as yet another example of weak, petty-minded, bureaucratic inflexibility, an aspect of what is now known as 'political correctness'.

She sent a telegram to the Prime Minister, by now Stanley Baldwin, that included the following stinging indictment:

> You have treated my patriotic gesture with contempt such as no other Government in the world would or could have been guilty of towards a Patriot … the safety of London is of the gravest National importance to every Englishman and every Englishwoman the wide-world over and as such the Prime Minister should consider it.

And she made sure that her readers knew what she had done, publishing the full text in an article under the heading 'England Arise and Know what to do!'[3] Other newspapers applauded her offer: 'Let us pay tribute to the outstanding imagination and patriotism behind this gift.'[4] Then she followed up her campaign with an open letter to the Prime Minister, circulated to newspaper editors around the country:

> Poor Mr Chamberlain! The safety of London – how it bores you. With a gesture of utter contempt, without even deigning to ascertain the wishes of the people of London – you have flung the safety I offered them on the dung-heap of the House of Commons.[5]

There was, perhaps, another rather flippant reason why the Government refused her offer. It came to her notice that some members of the Privy Council thought that if they accepted it, the country would expect that Lucy should be given some sort of high honour. She already held the title of 'Lady' and she had been created a Dame of the British Empire in 1917, but the thought of giving her a peerage in her own right was just a step too far. Members of the House of Lords quaked at the thought of having such an outspoken harpy in their chamber. Like a naughty child who sticks her tongue out at her elders and betters, Lucy wrote: 'The deaths of the Dukes of Wellington and Marlborough have created an unexpected problem for filling the two vacancies in the Order of the Garter. As one would be no use to me, I modestly suggest that I might be given both!'[6] Her irreverent sense of fun never left her.

Lucy withdrew her offer to the Government in a huff and redirected her benevolence to more grateful recipients.[7] She had previously donated £5,000 to the National Council for Maternity and Child Welfare, £5,000 to the London Lock Hospital which specialised in the treatment of venereal diseases,[8] and £3,000 for the restoration and reopening of Kew Gardens after they had fallen into dilapidation. Now she donated £1,000 to the London Society for Teaching and Training the Blind, £50,000 to St Thomas's hospital for its rebuilding programme and £1,000 each to the 'Not Forgotten' Association and the Xmas Fund for Soldiers still in Hospital. Lord Lloyd was President of the Navy League which set up a fighting fund to 'urge the need for an adequate Navy', and at their dinner in the Grosvenor House Hotel in October he announced that she had pledged £10,000. An item in a newspaper that ignited her fury reported that the Town Councillors in Nelson, near Burnley in Lancashire, had refused to contribute a single penny towards the Jubilee celebrations in the town and so she sent off a cheque for £50. The fund-raising committee reported that this generous donation had enabled them to meet their target of £450 'for the children and old folk of the town', adding rather caustically 'in spite of the action of the Socialist Town Council'.[9] The Ferrybridge Farm Schools appeal received £2,000 to build two new cottages on one of their farms,[10] while her sporting instincts spurred her to provide prize money for the Ulster TT motor races when other sponsors backed out.[11]

She posted £5,000 to the Papworth Hospital for Tuberculosis and sent the Prince of Wales another £3,000 for his Toc H building fund, making £9,000 over three years.[12] When she read that a 17-year-old Miss Doris Lever, who was battling to support her widowed mother and crippled brother, had been up before the magistrates and fined £5 for non-payment of rates, Lucy sent her a cheque for £25.[13]

Then she decided to take up the cause of the British herring-fishing industry which was going through a very bad time, partly because of a poor harvest in the autumn of 1934 but mainly because a massive order from Russia, the main export market, had been effectively cancelled by the Government who refused to guarantee payment. The excuse was that Russia was in debt to the UK to the extent of £1.3 billion, in spite of the fact that we were buying 13 million cwt of wheat and barley from them every year, plus 0.5 million cwt of butter. As Lucy acidly pointed out, these were goods that 'could have been produced by British farmers' and warned that 'Socialism is the cause of the present ruin and bankruptcy of farming.' The fishermen, being self-employed, were ineligible for unemployment benefit, so she donated £1,000 to the English Herring Catchers Association at Lowestoft and a similar amount to the Scottish equivalent in Inverness. 'I want everyone to eat fresh herrings one day a week,' she wrote in the *Saturday Review*, 'to keep our fishermen from the dole and despair.' She even came up with a wild scheme to sell herrings around the country in the winter using the insulated cycle barrows that sold ice-cream in the summer, but the logistics of arranging the rail transport defeated it. But at least her campaign of letters to the press did give the humble fish some snob value, persuading a few top-class restaurants to put them on the menu.[14]

Politics, however, remained her prime concern. That summer there had been a by-election in Robert Houston's old constituency of Liverpool West Toxteth and Lucy sent the Conservative candidate Mr Cremlyn, not money, but a telegram of encouragement.

> Bravo Cremlyn! You are the man for West Toxteth – a fit and proper successor to my late husband Sir Robert Houston. Good luck and may God be with you. Fight for Conservatism and you will fight for right. Yours, in deep admiration, Lucy Houston.

But in spite of Lucy's endorsement, the seat went to the Labour candidate Mr Cribbins who then retained it at the general election in November.

Lucy even flirted with the idea of diverting the £200,000 spurned by the Government towards the political movement that fitted most closely to her own concepts and which, in spite of its crude methods, was gaining considerable public momentum: Oswald Mosley's British Union of Fascists. Might Mosley be her 'strong man' after all? In May 1934, Lucy had met him in person when she attended a fund-raising dinner at the right-wing January Club, a discussion group founded by Mosley to attract Establishment support for the BUF. The speaker on that occasion was Commandant Mary Allen, co-founder of the women's police force, who had just returned from a visit to Germany studying policing methods under Adolf Hitler. Fellow guests had included Lord and Lady Russell of Liverpool, Wing Commander Louis Greig, several generals and Major 'Fruity' Metcalf, close friend and confidant of the Prince of Wales. Lucy's female companions included the madly eccentric Jeanne Camoys Stonor – another mistress of the German diplomat Joachim von Ribbentrop – Lady Ravensdale and the Russian emigrée Anna Wolkoff, who was later tried as a Nazi spy.[15] (Anna was a talented seamstress whose dress designs were featured in *Vogue* and who numbered many aristocratic wives among her clients, including the American divorcée Wallis Simpson, who will figure later in Lucy's story.) This was not the first time Mosley had hoped to tap Lucy's financial support. Harold Nicholson wrote in his diary after Mosley addressed a lunch-hour meeting at the Cannon Street Hotel in June 1931 that 'the Prince of Wales was sympathetic [to the New Party] and that his name might be used to get money out of Lady Houston, the snobbish, eccentric, right-wing millionairess.'[16]

She published a portrait of Mosley in an issue of the *Saturday Review*, with a few quite flattering paragraphs of text. Wentworth Day took a copy round to the luxurious house where Oswald was living with his mistress Diana Guinness, formerly the most beautiful of the remarkable Mitford sisters, and was invited to stay for dinner, during which Mosley expressed his wish for a meeting with Lucy.[17] However this idea was very quickly stifled by a singularly vicious, very personal attack on her by one of his lieutenants in their house journal, *Blackshirt*. The writer sneered at her journalistic style, her punctuation, her grammar and her jingoistic patriotism. At her 'advanced age', he wrote, she should know how to behave better. Lucy reacted with typical vigour, writing a personal letter to Mosley with a pen dipped in vitriol, demanding an apology and ordering Warner Allen to deliver it to the headquarters of the BUF in person and not return until he had a reply. After an interview that lasted half an hour, Mosley gave Warner Allen a letter in which he chided Lucy for having lost her sense of humour. Why, when she spoke plainly and outspokenly on political issues, should she object to other people doing the same? Lucy was furious; this was no apology but a lecture. How dare he, she snorted, teach his grandmother how to suck eggs, declaring that never, ever was he to receive a penny from her.[18]

Lucy was by no means finished with supporting British aviation. In the summer of 1935 she decided that she would like to have her own aeroplane. Back in July 1933, designers at the Bristol Aeroplane Co had sketched the outlines of two possible twin-engined passenger aircraft, planes that might compete with those being developed in the USA by both the Douglas and Boeing Corporations. The second design, powered by two 'Mercury' engines, was designated as the Type 142 and was estimated to have a cruising speed of 240 mph at 6,500 feet, a phenomenal figure at that time. So when Lord Rothermere, proprietor of the *Daily Mail*, was told the details that had leaked out to the local press, he informed the company that he would like to sponsor the prototype for his private use, 'to encourage prominent firms and businessmen to make proper use of civil aviation and, not least, to point out to the Air Ministry how their existing fighters might be no match for a high-speed transport used as a light bomber.'[19] He was quoted a price of £18,500 and the prototype, which he insisted was called *Britain First*, made its maiden flight in April 1935. Transferred to the RAF test-flight airfield at Martlesham Heath, it created a furore, being 50 mph faster, even with a full load, than the latest fighter prototype, the biplane Gloster Gladiator. Two months later, a modified and improved version specifically designed as a light bomber was on the drawing board, and this aircraft became the famous Bristol Blenheim of the Second World War. Air-minded Lucy felt a pang of jealousy when she read about Rothermere's inspired generosity and made it known that she would like to do a similar sponsorship as a private venture, but it seems that no company took the offer seriously.[20] Boards of directors were doubtless concerned, with some justification, that she would wish to interfere personally in every detail of the design.

Returning to Lucy's charitable work, her largest single donation of the year was a birthday gift of £40,000 to Edward Prince of Wales in June. This he forwarded to the Jubilee Trust, which had been set up to 'support existing youth organisations and encourage the setting up of new ones'. In gratitude for this and to show his deep appreciation, Edward visited Lucy at Byron Cottage in person. Some years earlier she had been presented to him at court and had been invited to visit him privately both at Clarence House and St James's Palace.[21] It appears that they each regarded the other with great respect. Lucy's grand political scheme envisaged a key role for the mercurial Prince once he became King, but, through the rose-tinted lenses of her admiration for this charismatic but unreliable man, Lucy only saw a Prince Charming and conveniently overlooked his shortcomings. She saw his tours of the Commonwealth as proof of his patriotism and love of the British Empire, rather than the reality of his father's wishes to keep him out of the country to avoid the embarrassments of his unconventional love life with various married women. And Edward himself seems to have viewed the tours as very tedious duties, enlivened only by the chance of some shooting and polo-playing, together with a few brief affairs along the way. (The true extent of his boredom only became public knowledge when his copious letters back to Freda Dudley-Ward were published.[22])

Animosity between monarchs and their eldest sons was a tradition that stretched back in English history to the reign of Henry II, while that between Henry IV and the wayward Prince Hal would become notorious two centuries later. It was particularly disruptive during the Hanoverian period. George II wished that his radical son Prince Frederick had never been born, while George III's madness was made even worse by the louche antics of the Prince Regent, later to be George IV. As Prince of Wales, he had entered a form of marriage with a widowed lady, Maria Fitzherbert, though she had only agreed to the match after he had threatened to commit suicide if she had refused. What made this union even more scandalous was the fact that Maria Fitzherbert had been a Roman Catholic; a century later, the idea of the Prince of Wales marrying an American divorcée would be equally contentious. Nor should it be forgotten that Queen Victoria had a distant and disapproving relationship with her eldest son Prince Edward, eventually to be Edward VII, blaming his youthful sexual adventures for contributing to the death of her beloved husband Prince Albert of Saxe-Coburg and Gotha.

One enlightening example of how Lucy became indirectly involved in the family feud between King George V and his eldest son occurred during the King's Jubilee celebrations in the summer of 1935. Lucy, a staunch monarchist, found her loyalties sorely tested, since she felt that the King was being unreasonably stubborn in not recognising and supporting Edward's extrovert efforts to modernise the institution of monarchy. For the naval review at Spithead, *Liberty* had been given the singular honour of having the number one buoy at the head of the line. When the order came to 'dress ship' the day before, Lucy refused to get the flags out and instead instructed her captain to weigh anchor and sail for France.[23] Once out in the channel, she ordered a cask of rum to be brought up so that she, along with all her crew, could sing 'God bless the Prince of Wales' to the tune of the National Anthem, and drink his health.

Highly conscious of his own ancestry, Edward made no secret of his feelings that there remained a natural affinity between the establishment figures – the 'old families' – of Germany and England. He once told an equerry that 'every drop of blood in my body is German'. Queen Victoria's grandson Kaiser Wilhelm had obviously been a most unfortunate aberration, allowing his acute inferiority complex and his jealousy of his cousin George V's empire and navy to lead his country into the disaster of the 1914–18 war. Now was surely the time to rebuild relationships. It was as a result of a speech by Edward in 1935 that the Anglo-German Fellowship (AGF) was formed in London, attracting leading figures from industry, the press and both Houses of Parliament. Included in their number were the Governor of the Bank of England, Geoffrey Dawson (the editor of *The Times*), the Marquis of Clydesdale, Duncan Sandys, Lords Nuffield, Redesdale and Londonderry and the Duke of Wellington. 'Corporate' members came from the directors of Unilever, Price Waterhouse, the Midland Bank and Lazard Bros amongst many others. The German equivalent was the Deutsche-Englischer-Gesellschaft, which emphasised the fact that both were primarily concerned with business links rather than politics. But the possibility of any sort of closer alliance between Britain and Germany rang alarm bells in Moscow, so the KGB made certain that their two leading operatives in London, Guy Burgess and Kim Philby, became members of the AGF.[24]

Away from the official diplomatic routes between the two countries' embassies, Adolf Hitler was using a number of aristocratic 'go-betweens' to sound out the true extent of Britain's commitment to either pacifism or belligerence, and the leading character here was another grandson of Queen Victoria, Charles Edward (1884–1954) the son of the haemophiliac Leopold, Duke of Albany, Victoria's eighth child. Brought up in England, he had inherited the title of Duke of Saxe-Coburg and Gotha on the sudden death of his first cousin Albert in 1899, whereupon he moved to live in Germany and adopt the name of Carl Eduard. He later became a covert member of the Nazi party but remained on friendly terms with the British Royal family, being welcomed to tea at Windsor Castle and a popular guest at AGF dinners. He is quoted as saying that his cousin Edward, Prince of Wales, 'saw a German-British alliance as an urgent necessity, [one that should be] a guiding principle of British foreign policy; not an alliance against France, but preferably one that included her.'[25]

Anglo-French relations with Germany had suffered a serious blow in March 1935 when Hitler had ordered his troops, in defiance of the League of Nations, to reoccupy the Rhineland, the demilitarised zone of fifty miles on either side of the River Rhine that had been established under the Treaty of Versailles. Hitler knew that this was a massive gamble and worried that France would take a military stand against this incursion, confessing later that if the French had offered any form of resistance, 'we would have had to withdraw with our tails between our legs.'[26] Instead, the lack of any French reaction, as well as speeches in the League of Nations, convinced him that he would not need to worry about his western borders if he launched an attack to the east. France's only response was to extend the time that army reservists 'served with the colours', an action that Hitler took as his excuse to increase the size of the German army to 500,000 men and threaten to increase its fleet of warplanes from 4,500 to 8,000; by contrast, Britain at that time had fewer than 600, most of which were obsolete, while Russia had 4,000 and Italy 1,900.

Edward Prince of Wales was particularly impressed by the way Germany was tackling its unemployment problem, in stark contrast to what he saw from his visits to deprived areas of Britain. Joachim von Ribbentrop, soon to be appointed as German ambassador to Britain, told Prince Kyril of Bulgaria that he believed Edward was at heart a National Socialist,[27] while Adolf Hitler himself 'looked upon Edward as a man after his own heart, and one who understood the *Führerprinzip* and was ready to introduce it into his own country.'[28] This was precisely what Lucy hoped he would do when he became king. King George V was known to be in poor health and it would not be long before he passed away, but before that 'end-of-an-era' event Lucy had to face a relationship crisis of her own.

To use his own words, towards the end of 1935 James Wentworth Day 'gave Lady Houston the sack.'[29] He went on to write that 'two years in the mud and blood of the First World War were an admirable baptism for five formative years on the hot-plate of Fleet Street ... but working for Beaverbrook in the days of his youthful fire was nirvana compared with Lady Houston in her late seventies.' Overworked, exasperated and driven to distraction by her tantrums, the camel's back had finally been broken. Not by overwork on political causes nor by her endless demands on his time, but because of Lucy's disapproval of some of the company he kept. Wentworth Day had taken a rare weekend off to accept an invitation from Alexander Montagu, Viscount Mandeville and heir to the Duke of Manchester, to join his pre-Christmas shoot at Brampton Park near Kimbolton in Huntingdonshire. He had already had to refuse five previous invitations on account of Lucy's demands, but now he could enjoy 'high pheasants by day, mallard flighting in the dusk of evening skies and dinner under the gaze of Van Dycks and Lelys, in the company of old friends, old claret and vintage port.' He was blissfully unaware that Lucy had spent the weekend frantically telephoning around the country to track him down. When he turned up at Byron Cottage on the Monday morning, 'Medusa herself confronted me.'

Lucy demanded to know where he had been and, on being told, launched into a tirade about the old Duke. 'That disgraceful old man! He kept a little music-hall girl, Bessie Bellwood, when I was young. She had the effrontery to drive around in her own Hansom cab with a bee painted on the side and the motto "Poor but Busy". He's been broke twice; gone through a million. You've no right to mix with such people.' Wentworth Day's protestations that his son 'was worth ten of his father and had successfully managed to pull the estate round' fell on deaf ears. 'Liar!' she spat. This proved to be the last straw. He headed for the door with the parting shot that he was finished with her and that she could get someone else to fight her battles for her. Then he added that she also owed him £600 back pay. 'You won't get a penny!' Lucy snapped, 'How dare you leave a poor, defenceless old woman like me in the lurch. And you'll come back when I want you. They always do. Miss Ritchie walks out on me every now and then – she always comes back. Poor dear, I know I overwork her.'

Wentworth Day went to see Lucy's lawyer Willie Graham, 'a man of infinite but peppery charm, great personality and immense humanity.' One of the leading lawyers in London, he was also chairman of the Illustrated Newspapers Group and Wentworth Day had often dined with him. He chuckled when told what had happened. 'Serve her right!' he commented. 'Thought of doing it myself several times! But I can't afford to lose her business. Perfect old terror – gives me hell. I always say that I will not put up with her nonsense any longer, but I do. Can't help admiring her.' Wentworth Day agreed, but said that she was now behaving like a furious old woman with more money than sense. All he wanted now was a quiet, steady job that would not make demands on his spare time. So Graham invited him to take over editing and reviving one of his journals entitled *Sporting and Dramatic News*, an organ that was losing money. It was agreed that Graham would pay him the same salary that Lucy had, plus regular expenses.

Both Graham and Wentworth Day received letters from Lucy three days later. To the former she wrote: 'I hear you have given my young man a job.

Look after him well. He's a good sort and a hard worker – but a bit peppery. I may need him soon, so you'll have to give him time-off when I want him.' Wentworth Day's letter contained a cheque for £600 and a brief note. 'I know I am a tiresome old woman, but I am fighting this fight single-handed and don't spare myself so why should you grumble?' There was an ominous PS: 'I shall have a little job for you soon.'

Over the following months Wentworth Day did indeed manage to turn around the fortunes of the *Sporting and Dramatic News*, which 'had almost ceased to be sporting and was scarcely dramatic' by means of a subtle journalistic trick. Wentworth Day introduced new contributors and good photographers, but his real success, one that 'brought a blush to the old lady's faded cheeks', was to fill a page with sensational gossip and several rather risqué, bawdy jokes. In this respect, it took over the mantle of *The Sporting Times*, popularly known as the *'Pink 'Un'* and foreshadowed journals such as *Private Eye* many years later. Two major public schools banned it – a parson preached a sermon against it – but the circulation soared. However, Wentworth Day found himself hauled before the managing board for a ticking off. 'These so called jokes are preposterous!' fumed one director. 'They're blue! I won't let my wife and daughter have the paper in the house!' 'Quite right!' agreed Willie Graham, 'neither will I, but my wife and daughter smuggle it in when I am not looking. You ought to be ashamed of yourself Day, though my client Lady Houston says it's making her feel quite young again.' Censure fizzled out.

This was all sometime in the future; it was only a few weeks after Wentworth Day had taken up his appointment that he was summoned to Graham's office for quite another reason. 'Lady Houston tells me that I have to send you on leave, so there's nothing we can do about it. She wants to see you on Monday.' On arrival at Byron Cottage, 'she was charm, sweetness and blandishment personified.' She informed Wentworth Day that there was going to be a by-election in the remote constituency of Ross & Cromarty in Scotland and that Randolph Churchill was intending to stand as an Independent Unionist against the National Labour candidate, Ramsay MacDonald's son, Malcolm MacDonald. 'I have great faith in Randolph,' Lucy declared, 'if only he wasn't so headstrong, and I am going to finance him. Here's the money and give it to him once a fortnight, just as long as he preaches my doctrine. He makes a magnificent speech – he'd make a dead bishop sit up and pray.'

So once again Wentworth Day found himself taking the sleeper from King's Cross to Scotland, this time to Dingwall, arriving in a flurry of snow on 7 January wearing a suit of tweeds and carrying a pair of shotguns. He told journalists that he had 'come for a holiday to shoot wild geese', and though he assured journalists that this should not be taken as a metaphor for political character assassination, he stated his opinion that 'Malcolm MacDonald is a political nonentity electioneering on his father's coat-tails.'[30] Another paper noted his arrival under the headline, 'He's gunning not for ducks, but for the MacDonalds, with Lucy Houston's dynamite!' Although Malcolm MacDonald was still a member of the Cabinet as Colonial Secretary, he had lost his parliamentary seat as MP for Bassetlaw in the last general election.

Four weeks of hard campaigning in bitter weather followed, with Wentworth Day driving Randolph Churchill over icy roads through blinding snowstorms as they traversed Scotland from the North Sea to the sea-lochs on the Atlantic coast. A total electorate of 30,000 voters was spread over an area of several hundred square miles. On the opening night of the campaign at Dingwall, Wentworth Day wrote that 'Randolph swept a typical hard-headed, cautious, disbelieving and essentially "Liberal" Scottish audience of tradesmen, farmers, fishermen and labourers to a crescendo of spontaneous applause.' Some newspapers, however, saw it differently. 'The Unionists are permitting themselves to be led by such exotic influences as the redoubtable Lady Houston, as a cat's paw in the bitter feud of the Churchill family against the maker of the National Government.'[31] The declaration on 10 February returned Malcolm McDonald for National Labour by a large margin over his Labour Party opponent, and the Liberal candidate lost his deposit. Randolph Churchill only managed to retain his by a narrow margin.[32]

Ross & Cromarty was not the only by-election in Scotland at the time, so Wentworth Day also had to find time to take Lucy's message to the dons and graduates of the universities in Edinburgh and Glasgow. The Combined Scottish Universities seat became vacant on the death of the Unionist MP Noel Skelton, presenting the Tories in the National Government with a dilemma. There were strong pressures put on Stanley Baldwin, the new Prime Minister, to allow his predecessor, the elderly, ailing Ramsay MacDonald (who had lost his seat in 1935) to be the National Government candidate, and there was a 'gentleman's agreement' that National nominees would not contest one another. So the Conservative Unionists put up no opposition, a decision that Lucy found appalling. The press reported that 'Lady Houston has sent copies of her pamphlet "What the late Prime Minister has done for England" to every graduate of the Scottish Universities,'[33] and it was Wentworth Day who had to see that this was achieved. The pamphlet was largely a reprint of one she had issued at the last general election and he must have wished that it had been re-edited to change the word 'England' to 'Great Britain'. At its core Lucy had written, 'For the last three years, while Mr Ramsay MacDonald was Prime Minister, the National Government preached disarmament, and during that time they dragged the Navy, the Army and the Air Force down, down, down to the depths of despair.' Then, harking back to the controversy over his involvement with the Socialist Convention of 1917 she had added:

I accuse him of being on the committee, the primary objective of which was to bring the Great War to an end through the outbreak of a Revolution that would paralyse our military operations. In 1918 he was encouraging strikes in munitions factories, while in 1928 he wrote that the General Strike was one of the most glorious things this country has produced.

Once again Ramsay MacDonald asked the Attorney General if there was a case for a libel against Lucy, or the London publishers of the leaflet, this time under the Representation of the People's Act of 1918. He would have been disappointed by the AG's reply: 'I confess that I have some doubts as to whether an offence has been committed, or whether it is expedient in the public interest that proceedings should be initiated.'[34] (The Lord Advocate for Scotland had written to him with a very radical suggestion, namely that 'the only possible alternative would be the heroic expedient of arresting Lady Houston in the Channel Islands.') Lucy had made her point but Ramsay MacDonald won the election easily, his nearest rival being a Glasgow University professor standing for the Scottish National Party. Two years later he would be dead.

This excursion into Scotland was the last occasion on which Wentworth Day worked for Lucy to carry out her bidding, but they remained friends and kept in touch regularly over the next twelve months, and it is thanks to him that we know an intriguing detail about her personal relationship with the man who was by then King Edward VIII. This will be revealed in the following chapter, but 1936 would be a year of such turmoil, when so many of Lucy's Cassandra-like warnings would begin to come true, that we must see her last, increasingly lonely months in the context of world events.

Chapter 20

King Edward VIII, the Engagement Ring and a Broken Heart

George V died during the night of 20 January 1936 and the accession of Edward to the throne was widely seen as the dawn of an optimistic new era. The economy was recovering from the depression following the Wall Street Crash of 1929, and there were widespread expectations that Edward would purge the stuffiness of his father's court, encourage employment schemes and inspire the younger generation to grasp the opportunities offered by science and new technologies. Lucy greeted the new King early in his reign by printing a 'Humble Petition to His Majesty from his Loyal and Devoted Subjects, who Honour Him as their ONLY LEADER.'[1]

> You are a great and mighty Monarch, but you are much more to us than that, a dearly beloved King who reigns by love in the hearts of his people; and I am writing the thoughts of millions who look to you, their King, in this terrible time of stress to deliver them. We want to hail you as our Man of Destiny who will free us from our perplexity – to reinstate us – and heal our wounded pride which has been dragged down so low.

She then warned that 'your throne and perhaps your life are in jeopardy – remember Russia.' She later urged him to become a 'benevolent despot', pointing out that Benito Mussolini and Adolf Hitler had risen to become the 'men of destiny' in their own countries.

> We who love you, our beloved King, look to you to be our leader we can trust to save us, and we implore you to do for your Empire what these two men have done for their countries. The British constitution does not exist except as a snare and delusion to entrap you, Sire, but its true

spirit would pervade, unite, invigorate and vivify every part of your realm if you were our leader instead of those knaves who are dragging us down. Use, Sire, your Royal Prerogative to get rid of the political hacks who would destroy you and your Kingdom. Queen Victoria commanded her ministers and they had to obey – you have the absolute right to do the same.

Lucy's exhortation could not be plainer, but any optimism for a new national dynamic was very quickly squashed, as the months leading up to Edward's planned coronation were dogged by a constitutional crisis that set him in conflict with his Prime Minister, by now Stanley Baldwin, and the head of the Church of England, Archbishop Cosmo Lang. Furthermore, Edward became casual about his appointments, he was late in returning his Red Boxes of official papers and he infuriated his staff by ignoring established protocols. His known interest in modernisation and social reform assumed a very low priority compared with his determination to marry an American divorcée named Wallis Simpson – and make her his Queen Consort.

The British public knew virtually nothing about Wallis Simpson owing to a conspiracy of silence mutually agreed by the press, but those people with access to foreign newspapers could learn that she was in fact currently still married to her second husband, Ernest Simpson, and that she had a somewhat shady past, involving exotic sexual experiences in China when she was 29 years old. Her then husband, Win Spencer, was an officer in the US Navy. After a promising start as a dashing pilot, he was promoted to commander of a new flight-training station, but his problems with alcohol began to make him a liability to his superiors. In 1924 he was in command of a modest supply ship, ferrying troops and provisions from the Philippines to the various treaty ports on the Chinese coast such as Canton and Shanghai. Mainland China at that time was a dangerous place in the chaos of civil war, with the foreign enclaves and legation areas having to be heavily guarded. Officers' wives were virtually forbidden from joining their husbands, so there is a mystery as to why young Wallis was allowed to follow him virtually everywhere. The answer was that she had been recruited by the US Intelligence Agency and was being employed by them to deliver secret documents to US Naval Command posts, because wireless codes had been broken and the telegraph system was being tapped.

It was while she was visiting the British colony of Hong Kong that she is reputed to have been introduced to 'perverse practices' in one of the high-class brothels known as 'purple mansions'.[2] Apart from being encouraged to watch lesbian displays, Wallis was taught the ancient courtesan art of *Fang Chung*, a technique that combined stimulating a partner while massaging certain muscles around the genitals to delay premature ejaculation.

In Peking Wallis had a brief affair with the 'suavely handsome' Italian Naval attaché, Alberto da Zara[3] and a much more serious one in Shanghai with the 'moody, proud' 21-year-old Count Galeazzo Ciano, by whom she became pregnant.[4] An illicit, but very necessary, abortion landed her in hospital in Hong Kong and meant that she would never be able to have children in the future. Ciano's father had been a leading fascist at the time of Mussolini's 'march on Rome' and the son would later be appointed by Mussolini as his Foreign Minister. Also in Peking Wallis had met up with a woman who had befriended her six years earlier in California, a young widow then called Kathleen Bigelow but now married to a US Intelligence officer by the name of Herman Rogers. Wallis and Win had by now drifted apart – eighteen months later she would start divorce proceedings against him on the grounds of desertion, the divorce being finally granted in 1927 – and she entered into a bizarre *ménage à trois* with the Rogers which nearly broke up their marriage.[5] However, matters were soon patched up and the couple remained Wallis's best friends right through her courtship by Edward.

By 1934 Wallis had superseded all the other women in Edward's life, such as Freda Dudley-Ward and Lady Thelma Furness. Freda Dudley-Ward, the wife of an MP, was precisely the same age as Edward, level-headed, sensible and a steadying influence on the Prince, first as his mistress from 1918 till 1923 and then as his close confidante until Wallis forbade him to speak to her ever again. Very different had been the American beauty and minor film star Thelma Morgan, whose second marriage in 1926 had been to the elderly Viscount Furness, founder of the eponymous shipping line. She and Edward met in 1930, and for the next four years she was his regular weekend guest at his house in Fort Belvedere in Windsor Great Park, while also entertaining him at her own houses in London and Melton Mowbray. Ten years younger than him, she opened his eyes to the dynamism of youthful America and its burgeoning technologies, and at the same time introduced him to the American concept of democracy, one that admittedly discriminated against its own citizens who had a different coloured skin. It was through Thelma Furness that Edward had met Wallis Simpson and it was she who, before departing for a visit back to America, famously asked Wallis 'to look after the little man for me while I am away'. It was a request she would deeply regret, because by the time she returned Wallis had completely supplanted her in Edwards's affection.

Lucy must have been aware of the rumours circulating in London about Wallis Simpson and of her unsuitability to be Edward's consort, but for her the romance of the situation was of prime importance. If her Prince Charming was truly in love, then he should be allowed to marry the object of his affection. An interesting light was thrown on the relationship by an entry in Duff Cooper's private diary.[6] Duff Cooper (married to the society beauty and actress Diana Cooper), a cabinet minister who would rise from Financial Secretary to the Treasury to become Secretary of State for War in November 1935, was considered to be one of the shrewdest politicians of his generation and an acute judge of character.

> We dined with Freddie Lonsdale at the Garrick Club. He had quite a large party and I sat next to Wallis. She talked very sensibly – said she had not allowed Edward to come to her flat since his father's death … and even suggested that it would be better if she were to go away altogether. I think she is a nice woman and a sensible one – but she is as hard as nails and she doesn't love him.

On Edward's part, it seems that Wallis somehow satisfied a deep-seated psychological need, various biographers attributing it either to a version of sadomasochism or some other form of control that released him from an undefined sexual dysfunction.[7] Edward's earliest sexual experiences had taken place while he was on leave in Paris in 1917 when he was introduced by some French friends to an ambitious courtesan called Marie Marguerite Meller.[8] She was four years older than Edward and an experienced practitioner in recognising the sexual peccadilloes of her clients, photographs of the time often showing her with a whip or a riding crop. [see PLATE B12] Whatever the technique she used, it triggered an immense, life-changing emotion in the immature young man. Edward fell desperately in love. Over the following months he wrote 'Maggie' a number of passionate, indiscreet letters, letters that she kept. In July 1923 she was charged with murdering her latest husband, a rich sadistic Egyptian 'Prince', by shooting him dead in London's Savoy Hotel. Before her trial in September, her barrister, Sir Edward Marshall-Hall, let it be known to Buckingham Palace that he might have to disclose the content of these highly indiscrete letters as part of her defence, and so Edward was hastily packed off to spend a few weeks on a ranch in Canada to avoid the embarrassment of his being called as a witness, and it is believed that a deal was struck to purchase the letters. On 17 September, the trial judge in effect instructed the jury that they should consider whether this had been what the French called a *crime passionnel*. It took the jury less than an hour to bring in a verdict of 'Not Guilty'.

Various biographers have highlighted Edward's immaturity – the 'Peter Pan' syndrome – including the fact that he seldom if ever needed to shave. 'In the face of parental admonition, or hostility of any kind, his first thought was flight.'[9] This was his default position, one that he would employ to catastrophic effect within twelve months of becoming king.

Gossip about Wallis was rife; it was said that she was conducting a simultaneous affair with the pompous German diplomat, Joachim von Ribbentrop, passing on to him extracts from government papers that Edward left lying about at Fort Belvedere, while he sent her daily bunches of roses or carnations.[10] The fact that they were always made up with seventeen stems was taken to imply the number of times they had slept together. Nor was he her only suspected lover, with the name of a 'suave adventurer' called Guy Trundle hinted at by some commentators.[11] As the constitutional crisis escalated, opinion in the country became polarised, with support for Edward's cause being aired by the *Daily Mail* and *Daily Express* while the other newspapers, particularly *The Times*, printed leading articles of robust opposition. Winston Churchill led the group of Edward's friends in parliament, informally known as the 'King's Party', that included Duff Cooper and Lloyd George, while outside Westminster support came from the unholy political alliance of Oswald Mosley and the British Communist

Party. Other advisors suggested that if Wallis could be persuaded to go back to America for a year, the coronation could take place and perhaps the solemnity of his oath, combined with separation, might cool his ardour. This would never have worked, because Wallis, to her credit, had tried to break off their relationship in June by going abroad for a week. She had only agreed to return when Edward had written letters threatening to commit suicide if she did not come back to him.

Wallis's divorce from Ernest Simpson was still going through the matrimonial court. If collusion might be proved or some other reason concocted to prevent the grant of a decree nisi, could this not present a legal solution to the problem? The ever-sensible Clement Atlee, now leader of the Labour party, told Baldwin that Labour supporters – 'except the intelligentsia, who can be trusted to take the wrong view of everything' – might not object to an American marriage as such, but would not accept Wallis Simpson.[12]

The Trade Union leader Ernest Bevin put it rather more bluntly. 'Our people won't 'ave it.' Some members of the cabinet suggested that if Edward persisted in his desire to marry Wallis, the Government should threaten to resign. But what if Edward called their bluff? Might not Edward then appoint a new Government from his supporters in Parliament, 'one that might get hold of the Executive and act as dictator?'[13] This was precisely the script that Lucy was writing for him. She wrote an article in which she quoted Napoleon Bonaparte as saying 'I saw the crown of France in the gutter. With my sword I raised it up and put it on my own head.'[14] Then she added: 'Is there no patriotic Englishman brave enough to save his country from the political poltroons who are trailing England's heart and pride in the mud and slime of self-interest?'

As the constitutional crisis simmered through the summer of 1936 and into the autumn, Lucy's adoration for Edward remained undimmed. She admired the way he had taken risks by visiting the front line during the Great War, his dashing horsemanship and the fact that he had been prepared to risk his neck by riding in steeplechases and point-to-point races. Wentworth Day described this as 'pathetic', adding that she 'sprang to his defence like a tiger'. She printed a flattering picture of him, wearing shorts and a sweater with a tennis racquet in his hand on the title page of the *Saturday Review* under the headline 'A pattern for his people to copy'.[15] She asked readers to cut this page out and pin it on their wall. 'It is your duty to follow your King's splendid example and to make yourself strong and well, and then England will no longer be under the reproach of being a C.3 nation.' Her article inside described his healthy lifestyle, his strict exercise regime, his love of gardening and his modest daily diet. She would be unaware that he may well have been suffering from what later generations would recognise as anorexia. Nor would she know about his increasing reliance on alcohol.

Another future fascist dictator launched himself onto the world stage in July 1936, when General Franco struck the spark that would ignite the Spanish Civil War. Within weeks, the citizens of Madrid found themselves subjected to the horrors of indiscriminate aerial bombing (by German planes), a precursor to the nightmare that Lucy had foreseen for the Blitz on London. The Basque city of Guernica would fall victim to the same treatment nine months later, and Picasso's iconic painting of the scene, in all its tortured anguish, would leave a lasting memorial of this example of man's inhumanity to his fellow beings. Sir Norman Angell, winner of the Nobel Peace Prize in 1933, addressed meetings of the League of Nations Union across the UK in 1936 declaring: 'War is not made by evil men knowing themselves to be wrong, but by good men passionately convinced that they are right. The real cause of war is international anarchy.'[16] Lucy's riposte, quoted in the 'sayings of the week' column in several newspapers, was blunt: 'None can alter the truth that might is right – and victory is achieved only by the strong. And every creature upon earth has to accept this law.'

Throughout the year her writings became more strident, more hysterical, sounding like a screaming fury aware that time was running out, both for herself and the civilised world. She advocated conscription. She warned that Russia now had the largest fleet of submarines in the world. She published numerous articles in support of General Franco, highlighting the atrocities perpetrated by the left-wing government forces but never those committed by the Fascists. Her rantings may have stiffened the resolve of readers of the *Saturday Review* but others increasingly doubted her sense of balance. To her the deadly enemy was still the 'Red Menace' of Russia and the insidious spread of communism, while she played down the increasing threats posed by Adolf Hitler. This led to an unedifying correspondence in the press between Lucy and her one-time ally and sturdy advocate of true-blue Toryism – and fellow Dame of the British Empire – the Duchess of Atholl. Lucy insisted on publishing a most unflattering portrait of her on the cover of the *Saturday Review*, and when Warner Allen protested that she was losing her sense of proportion she merely giggled.[17]

One interesting example of her later journalism was printed in the *Saturday Review* of 18 July 1936:

> Our congratulations to Germany and Italy, the sanest and most splendidly organised countries in the world today. Their close rapprochement and settlement with Austria make for PEACE. If Frenchmen who love their country were wise, they would invite Hitler to come to France in order to destroy Bolshevism. This would remove the menace of war and give England the breathing space to build up her defences, which have been so shamefully neglected by this accursed National government. *(Author's note: This was achieved later, via a very different route, by Neville Chamberlain's 'Munich Agreement' in 1938.)*

Lucy's article went on to quote a speech by Winston Churchill:

> After the General Election, there was much talk of expenditure of £300 million on defence. In fact the supplementary estimates only amount to £30 million. Sir Thomas Inskip (Minister for Defence Coordination) says that we have now reached the *planning stage* in our defence programme. But Germany had finished her planning stage three years ago, and her whole industry has long been adapted on an unexampled scale.

One man who saw Hitler not as a potential enemy but as a useful ally was Oswald Mosley, who visited Germany in the autumn of 1936 along with Diana Mitford/Guinness. She had previously come over in 1934 to stay with her younger sister Unity, who was by now a constant companion of Hitler, and the two sisters had been his honoured guests at Bayreuth to attend Wagner operas. They were also given privileged, grandstand seats at the Nuremburg rallies and the torch-lit processions that followed. Now they met again and discussed Hitler's theories on eugenics and racial purity, but they also talked politics in a wider sense, often in the presence of his closest associates. Hitler spoke about how he had a great admiration for the British people and how he wished he could persuade British politicians that with his army and the British Royal Navy, the two nations could together rule the world. He would probably have known that the Mitfords were friends of Winston Churchill's family through their cousins the Romillys, the Mitford children having spent several holidays visiting the Churchill's house at Chartwell.[18] So perhaps he hoped that he could use the sisters to establish some line of communication with British politicians. Albert Speer wrote later that Diana in particular pleaded with him to make peace with Britain.[19]

Oswald Mosley's wife Cimmie had died suddenly of peritonitis in April 1933, after which he and Diana blatantly lived together in London. She had deserted her husband Brian Guinness, but he agreed to do 'the decent thing', arranging things so that she could sue him for divorce on the grounds of his adultery. So now Diana and Oswald were in a position to marry, and the ceremony took place on 6 October in the house of Hitler's propaganda minister Dr Joseph Goebbels with Adolf Hitler himself in attendance. Another reason for Mosley travelling to Germany at that time was to explore the possibility of setting up a powerful wireless transmitter on the island of Heligoland. Lying almost directly across the North Sea from East Anglia, the receiving range would not be much further than that of Radio Luxembourg. In this ambition, Mosley was following Lucy in appreciating the valuable role that radio might play in spreading propaganda. (One of Mosley's greatest supporters in this project was a BUF officer called William Joyce, later to become the infamous traitor known as 'Lord Haw-Haw'.)

Away from international politics and the constitutional crisis, Lucy suffered her own personal crisis when her greatest friend, Miss Hoare, died in March.[20] Miss Hoare was a leading figure in the Hampstead Mission Church, visiting the poor in the East End of London every week to distribute food and comfort. She had been appointed MBE in 1917, at the same time that Lucy was made a Dame Commander, and she was the Lady District Officer for St John's Ambulance from 1924. The week before she died she was appointed a Dame of Grace in the Order of St John. Lucy had lost a warm companion and wise counsellor, one who might have been able to make her see a more balanced perspective on the new King.

The late spring of 1936 provided another opportunity for Lucy to make a magnificent gesture of patriotic charity. She was probably at her happiest when she was on board *Liberty* and she relished listening to the tales told by her skipper, an old sea-dog by the name of Captain Gibb. He had been brought up in the age of sail, and although Lucy had by now become entranced by sleek, high-speed aircraft, she could appreciate the romance of the great sailing clippers that raced against each other across the oceans to be the first to bring their cargoes to England. So when she heard that one of the very last of them had run aground off the south coast of Devon she immediately offered to put up the money to salvage the ship on behalf of the nation.

The *Herzogin Cecilie* had been built at Bremerhaven in 1902 and named after the Crown Princess of Prussia. A four-masted, steel-hulled barque 334ft long, she was one of the fastest ever constructed, being logged on one trip at a speed of 21 knots. In 1920 she was handed over as part of German reparations to the French, who promptly sold her to Captain Erikson, a Finn with an English wife, for £4,250. Loaded with 4,200 tons of wheat, the *Herzogin Cecilie* left Port Lincoln in Australia, rounded Cape Horn and reached Falmouth 86 days later.[21] Here she received her orders to unload at Ipswich and so, two days later, she set off on the last leg of her journey. Early on the morning of 25 April, in thick fog and a rough sea, she struck the Ham Stone, close to Soar Mill Cove off the South Hams in Devon, and started taking in water. [see PLATE B23] The Torbay lifeboat was soon on the scene and took off a lady passenger and twenty-one crew members, though Captain Erikson, his wife and son, who was also the first mate, stayed on board with the remaining crew in the hope that the ship might be refloated on a high tide. It was not to be. By the following day three holds were awash and two more were leaking.

On 3 May Lucy offered to pay whatever was needed to salvage the vessel, with the aim of then presenting her to the Admiralty for use as a training ship.[22] Captain Erikson, accompanied by his wife, went up to London for a meeting at Byron Cottage to discuss details, and telephone calls were made to the insurers and a firm of salvage brokers in Liverpool. However, echoing the rejection of her earlier offer to buy fighters for the defence of London, the Admiralty declined on the basis that they would have no possible use for the ship. Lucy told reporters, 'I cannot understand the Admiralty's refusal and am very disappointed. Something must be done quickly as the first storm could break her up.'[23] Instead, a Southampton firm was contracted to take off as much of the cargo as possible and by 6 May they had unloaded 450 tons of dry wheat, but the rest was by now sodden and swelling. Still, there was a market for this in France as pig food and the extraction process continued into June, helped considerably by a number of volunteer students from Cambridge University.[24] Thousands of trippers came to gawp from the cliffs above and the once stately 'Windjammer' became a major tourist attraction for the region. After installing powerful pumps, the ship was finally refloated on 19 June, but the Salcombe Urban Council refused to let it be towed into the harbour 'for fear of odour and disease from the remains of the rotting cargo.'[25] Instead she was beached, temporarily it was hoped, in Starehole Bay at the entrance to the estuary. But successive tides scoured away the sand to leave her stuck on a hidden rock and on 15 July her keel broke, thus ending all salvage attempts. With her masts still erect, she remained a tourist attraction until finally breaking up and sinking during a storm on the night of 17 January 1939. Her fate would have been so different if Lucy's offer had been taken up, an offer that Lord Monsell, First Lord of the Admiralty, later acknowledged as a 'most generous and patriotic gesture'.[26]

Lucy made another such offer that autumn, her last as it turned out, when she donated funds to the Boy Scout's Association. The British National Antarctic Expedition ship *Discovery*, which had conveyed both Captain Falcon Scott and Ernest Shackleton to explore Antarctica in the early 1900s, had been taken over by the Crown Agents for the Colonies as a research vessel during the years between 1923 and 1931. Latterly acquired by the Admiralty, who could find no use for it, *Discovery* had been laid up and allowed to deteriorate until 1936, when the ship was donated to the Sea Scout arm of the Scouting Association as a potential training vessel. Much needed to be done in the way of repairs and refitting before it could be used for this purpose and Lucy agreed to make a large donation towards the cost. *Discovery* is now on display in Dundee.

More intriguing than all the words Lucy had written about her idol King Edward was an incident related by Wentworth Day in his biography. After completing his last political task for Lucy in Scotland in February 1936, he became fully occupied on the *Illustrated Sporting & Dramatic News*, though he 'managed to see a good deal of her from time to time.'[27] At some stage during the summer she summoned a driver to Byron Cottage to undertake a very confidential mission. Wentworth Day claimed he 'knew the man to be of the highest integrity' and it seems that the job was too delicate even to be entrusted to her own loyal chauffeur, Foster, or he would surely have mentioned him by name. Lucy handed the driver a brown paper parcel with the following instruction: 'Drive to Fort Belvedere at once. When you get there, give this signal on your horn and the guards will let you through. Deliver the parcel and wait for an answer from the King.'[28] It seems that Lucy had set up the arrangement in advance via a telephone call to Edward and it may well have been one of many conversations she had with him. As recorded earlier, Lucy had visited him on a number of occasions and he had reciprocated via at least one meeting – that lasted over an hour – at Byron Cottage. Letters may have been exchanged as well, though none are known to have survived. The driver had told Wentworth Day that he had sounded the horn as instructed, been let in and then presented the parcel. 'Some minutes later, King Edward came out himself. He was hatless. He handed me a letter in his own handwriting addressed to Lady Houston. I saluted and drove off.'

So what was in that parcel? The driver asserted that the contents felt like a mass of banknotes and that he could also feel something else under the wrapping paper. Lucy had once mentioned to Wentworth Day that she intended to leave, or give Edward, £250,000,[29] so perhaps this was it. But maybe the parcel also contained something else – a little jewel box containing the engagement ring given to her by Robert Houston with its enormous emerald, as mentioned in chapter 6. It was to be a love-token from Lucy to Edward, and in her accompanying letter she may well have written that she wished him to have it remade into an engagement ring for Wallis. This suggestion must contain an element of conjecture, but the facts are as follows. Once Edward was finally in a position to marry Wallis, he gave her an engagement ring inscribed by Cartier on the inside with the words 'WE are ours now 27.X.36'. The first word is their combined initials and the date is that on which she obtained the first stage, the decree nisi, of her divorce from her second husband Ernest Simpson. The engagement ring that Wallis would wear as Duchess of Windsor was in itself a fairly simple platinum band, but set within it was a truly magnificent Colombian emerald of 19.77 carats.[30] [see PLATE B22]

Charles Higham gives a rather different version.[31] Wallis had heard of the fabled 'Mogul Emerald', one of the finest stones of its kind, whose provenance went back to the ancient rulers of India. She told Edward she had to have it, and so he contacted Jacques Cartier in Paris to obtain it for her. A syndicate in Baghdad were prepared to sell it for a substantial sum and it was brought over to London by special courier, but Edward balked at the price. This account then states that 'Cartier cut it in half and presented the smaller stone to the monarch.' Surely no reputable jeweller would possibly desecrate such a unique specimen, so I contend that the 'Lucy provenance' is much the more likely – and from Edward's point of view much less expensive. Moreover the Mogul Emerald, undamaged and weighing 217.8 carats, was sold by Christie's on 27 September 2001 for £1,543,750 (US$2,272,400). Measuring approximately two inches square by half an inch, it is inscribed on the obverse with Moslem script and the date of 1107 AH (AD 1695–6).

Lucy wrote to Winston Churchill in early November warning that he 'was doing himself immense harm' by trying to revive the League of Nations which was 'as dead as a doornail'. She described Anthony Eden as 'that awful little ass, who isn't fit to black your shoes.' Winston replied that his chief concern was 'the safety of England from the German Nazi menace' and that he shared her regrets for the 'misguided policy of the MacDonald/Baldwin regime in defence affairs' and that 'Britain should be made strong again as fast as possible.'[32] So Lucy would have been delighted by the 'terrible, awe-inspiring words' he used in his next speech to the House of Commons: 'This government have decided only to be undecided, they are resolved to be irresolute; they are adamant for drift, solid for fluidity, all-powerful but impotent.'[33]

Churchill pressed for a Commons debate on whether a morganatic marriage, whereby Wallis would be Edward's wife but not the Queen, might be allowed and even hinted at the desirability of a national referendum. Baldwin insisted that Edward must either give up Wallis completely or renounce the throne, a stance on which he was strongly backed by the Prime Ministers of the Commonwealth nations and the leaders of the Church of England. The final act of Edward's reign was being scripted and the curtain was about to fall.

Back in August the Anglo-Egyptian treaty had been signed, its full title being a 'Treaty of alliance between the United Kingdom and the King of Egypt'. King Fuad had become worried that Italy, after its roughshod treatment of Abyssinia, might turn its attention to invading Egypt, and so needed to formalise his relationship with Britain. Under the terms of the treaty, Britain agreed to train and equip the Egyptian army and 'assist the country in its defence in case of any threat of invasion', but in return would keep its own troops and airmen, the 10,000 or so deemed necessary for the protection of the Suez Canal, penned into a narrow strip of desert – the Canal Zone. The treaty was to be monitored by a subcommittee of the League of Nations, to which Egypt would now be admitted as a full member.

In no way did the treaty satisfy Egyptian nationalists, who wanted full independence and promptly rioted, nor was it welcomed by those people in Britain who saw it as yet another example of loss of British prestige and the dismantling of British authority overseas. Among these Lucy became one of the most vociferous. Her article in the *Saturday Review* opened with the resounding sentence, 'The British negotiators of the Anglo-Egyptian Treaty, signed in London on August 26th, are deserving of impeachment!'[34] Later in the article she posed an awkward question: what might happen to foreign interests in the country and the lives of foreigners living there at the end of the twenty-year treaty period? (The answer would become all too apparent in 1956 with the 'Suez crisis' following the nationalisation of the Suez Canal by Colonel Nasser and Anthony Eden's disastrous, duplicitous conspiracy with France and Israel to go to war.)

Following the signing of the treaty, one of the perhaps more unlikely outcomes was a personal invitation to James Wentworth Day to visit Egypt in December as a guest of King Fuad and the Egyptian Government. This had doubtless come about on the recommendation of Lord Lloyd, who had been impressed by their meeting the previous year. He had particularly admired Wentworth Day's tact and diplomacy, quite apart from his obvious understanding of the tricks needed to navigate through political jungles, clearly believing that someone who could deal with, and even stand up to someone like Lucy would not be browbeaten or intimidated by a Middle-Eastern despot. Lloyd also needed a spy on the inside.

From Wentworth Day's personal point of view, however, the timing was unfortunate because it coincided with his plans to get married that month. So his wedding to Miss Nerina Shute had to be brought forward to 26 November at Caxton Hall, with Lord Mandeville acting as his best man. Lucy was not well enough to attend but sent a present in the form of a magnificent silver loving-cup.[35] After a brief honeymoon in France, Wentworth Day set off on his new mission. He had meetings with all the important Egyptian politicians, studied its parliamentary systems and toured the country from end to end.[36] He sent long, secret reports back to Lord Lloyd, reports that covered his observations on the bribery and corruption among officials, the over-taxation, and the appalling disparity between the poverty of the bulk of the people and the extravagance and irresponsible wealth of the so-called upper classes. He concluded that the country was ripe for Communism and an ideal seedbed for Russian doctrines, pointing out that the number of staff at the Russian Embassy was higher than in any other capital in the world.

It was while he was on a tour of Upper Egypt with the Prime Minister Mohamed Mahmoud Pasha, a man he described as 'a gentleman and a trustworthy friend of Britain', that they alighted from the train at a wayside station to be met by a guard of honour. The captain of the guard was wearing a black armband, on which Wentworth Day commented with suitable words of condolence. 'Oh it is not for any member of my family, Sir, it is for you and your country. You have lost your King.' This was how Wentworth Day heard the news that Edward had announced to the world on 11 December that he had abdicated and handed over the throne to his younger brother, the Duke of York. If the news came as a shock to him, it dealt an even more devastating blow to Lucy. She had sat listening to the wireless in horrified dismay as he said that he 'had found it impossible to carry the heavy burden of responsibility and discharge my duties as King, as I would wish to do, without the help and support of the woman I love.'

Aghast, Lucy could not believe what had happened. Edward had won the hearts of the British people and he had been offered, at a moment of destiny, the opportunity to assert himself and grasp the reins of national leadership. Surely he would not have wanted to let his people down? Not only his loyal subjects, but the very monarchy itself, with its tradition of duty and responsibility. Hidden forces must have been behind the obviously bully-boy tactics of Stanley Baldwin and Archbishop Lang, and in her distraught state Lucy came to the conclusion that the blame must be laid at the door of the 'Red Menace' – Russia. Her beloved Empire was being dismembered and she knew that the world was on the brink of another cataclysmic war. From this moment she decided that she no longer wished to live. She took the fatal decision that she would stop eating.

'Her great and generous heart had been broken,' wrote Wentworth Day, while a close friend, possibly Miss Ritchie, recorded that 'her daemonic energy during that last week was frightening in its intensity … she drove her mind without rest, without mercy.'[37] Reconciled to her own fate, she now clutched at one glimmer of optimism, that Edward could now marry the woman he loved. She wrote her last article for the *Saturday Review* under the heading 'Love Conquers All'.[38]

All through this hectic week I have hardly slept or eaten, my heart has been so full of loving sympathy and indignation for the King during this cruel, heartbreaking trial he has been forced to endure. But what a romance! A true tale of true love! In years to come, when we are all dead and gone, women will weep when they read the tale telling them the love story of King Edward VIII.

Just a few days before she died she penned a long, open letter of devoted loyalty and support to Edward's brother Bertie, the Duke of York and the man who was now King George VI.[39] She was not, however, prepared to pull her political punches. It opened:

I was glad, Sir, to read your rebuke to those who have tried to insinuate that you supplanted the late King *gladly*. Knowing as I do that the moment when you were most unwillingly persuaded to do this was the saddest and blackest moment of your life.

Two paragraphs later, in which she had soundly blamed Stanley Baldwin for the 'dastardly manner' his brother had been driven out, she continued:

> Mr Baldwin has said that a 'Democratic Government' must always be two years behind a country governed by a Dictator. That is why the *Saturday Review* and its readers have for months past tried to persuade King Edward VIII to dismiss Mr Baldwin and his Government and proclaim himself Dictator. These people deceive themselves with the foolish idea that you, Sir, will accept their advice unquestioningly as being the right and proper people to dictate to you the policy you must follow … policy which has – up till now – been against the needs, necessities and welfare of England.

Further on she returned to her themes about the threats of Bolshevism and the impotence of the League of Nations before closing with a final paragraph:

> I send your Majesty this letter as one which is a heart-to-heart talk from a friend, as that I most sincerely am to you and Queen Elizabeth – but I have a faithful heart and I know you will think more and not less of me for this. Your humble servant, Lucy Houston.

By the evening of 29 December Lucy's staff were sufficiently alarmed at her condition to summon Lord Horder to her bedside.[40] He was appalled, though probably not surprised, to find that the windows of her bedroom were wide open, with gusts of squall-laden wind billowing the curtains. Over the years that he had treated her, Horder had become immune to her chiding and her obstinate refusal to take his advice. Tonight would be no different. 'Afraid of a little fresh air are you?' she taunted. He knew that it was now too late to save her from the path she herself had wilfully decided to take. He bade her farewell, leaving a nurse to attend her through her final hours. She lay back on the pillows of her giant bed and began humming her favourite hymns, until the nurse suggested that it was time for her to go to sleep. 'Yes, my dear', Lucy whispered, 'and a damned long sleep it's going to be.'[41]

Chapter 21

Epitaphs and What Happened Afterwards

On 30 December, *The Times* recorded Lucy's death as occurring at 7.30pm the previous evening, adding the fact that her sister Florence Wrey and her husband had been at her bedside. A full obituary appeared the following day. 'Lady Houston was remarkable alike for the wealth she inherited and for the large share of it that she expended on charitable causes,' the extent of her gifts being compared to those of Lord Nuffield. *The Yorkshire Post* wrote, 'The death of Lady Houston removes a picturesque figure who will be remembered more admiringly for the generous help she gave to various causes, rather than her later strivings for political influence.' It went on to mention her great interest in the welfare of women and 'the provocative fervour of her patriotism.'[1] A close friend told Warner Allen that 'she was as many sided as Cleopatra, whose zest and charm she shared', while another admirer stated, 'Implacable in her hatreds, she was insatiable in her kindnesses.' These words resonate with the phrase used by Winston Churchill to describe Field Marshal Montgomery; 'In defeat, unbeatable. In victory unbearable.' Lucy's favourite journalist Collin Brooks, editor of Lord Rothermere's *Sunday Despatch*, wrote: 'My recollection of Lucy Houston is chiefly the memory of her voice on the telephone. We spoke to each other on most days of the week and at all hours of the clock. It bound us in a strange association of friendship, love and conspiracy.'[2]

Warner Allen has left us a very personal assessment of the 'bundle of contradictions' that comprised her character.[3]

As shy and demure as a schoolgirl when she faced a sympathetic audience, she could be as brazen-faced and coarse-mouthed as a fish-wife in controversy. From her days as a Victorian beauty to the time when her ardent spirit wore out her body and cut short her life, her whole existence was one long protest against 'Safety First,' that counsel of defeat dished up as the war-cry by those who should have known better. Much of the bitterness and extravagance of her politics arose from her hatred of indecision and cowardice … She was shrewd, worldly-wise and deeply religious … For her public enemies she had neither pity nor mercy; in her private life she would forgive offences that a far milder soul would never have pardoned.

Lucy was buried on Remembrance Avenue, next door to the Soldiers' Plot in East Finchley cemetery on 4 January 1937. [See PLATE C21] 'It was a cold, bleak morning, and slight drizzle swept across the graveyard as the coffin was borne away. Rich people mingled with working people at the funeral of a woman unique in modern history … many more members of the general public, who had not been able to gain access to the chapel, were grouped around the grave.'[4] The service had been extremely simple; no hymns, no address and merely a single psalm and a few prayers. An anthem was played on the organ while those who crowded into the chapel took their seats. The elaborate coffin carried a simple brass plate – 'Fanny Lucy Houston. At rest. December 29, 1936'. The secret of her age, quite literally, went with her to the grave. Resting on the top of the coffin was a large wreath of yellow chrysanthemums and arum lilies from her sister Florence, 'who was too ill at the time to stand the strain and exposure of the funeral'. Another absentee was Lucy's first husband Sir Theodore Brinckman, who was recovering from an operation but had sent a wreath. Lord Sempill brought another, woven out of laurel leaves, attached to which was the following message:

With love and in memory of a great friend, who never spared herself but thought unceasingly of others and acted courageously in their interest. Her farsightedness and generosity greatly benefited the cause of aeronautics.

Echoing these tributes were those of Air Commodore Fellowes, the leader of the Houston-Mount Everest flight:

The expedition would never have been launched but for the vivid imaginings of the late Dame Lucy Houston … a most remarkable woman. From the moment I took my place in her team, I, as we all did, felt the force of her very human personality. Praise, blame or warm-hearted interest was unstintingly given. She was to me the embodiment of intense patriotism, as she saw it, courage and shrewdness. Her heart was great in its affections, and also in its hates. She cannot but leave a blank to friend or enemy, so vivid was her personality.[5]

Standing shivering around the grave were members of Lucy's family, led by her brother-in-law Arthur Wrey: her nephews Tom Radmall, Colonel Thomas Catty and his brother Hugh Catty, who had come over from America with one of his two daughters; her niece, formerly Cicely Radmall and now Lady Palmer, who was accompanied by her husband Sir Geoffrey Palmer, and another niece, Margaret East, the daughter of Lucy's sister Mary Radmall. Other mourners noted by the press included Miss Meriel Buchanan, Mrs Gilbert Wakefield, the racing correspondent Captain David Livingstone-Learmonth and Mr Hugo Houston.[6] James Wentworth Day was prominent among the mourners, bearing a wreath on behalf of Lord Lloyd who was ill in bed that day. When the service at the graveside was ended, a white-haired man threw a bunch of violets into the grave, while a relation added a posy 'to dear Aunt Poppy, from her grand-nieces Patricia, Margaret, Diana and Barbara.'[7] Another simple bunch of flowers was laid on the coffin by 'a woman who declined to reveal her identity'.

Immediately after the funeral Wentworth Day drove to Portman Square to report to Lord Lloyd. 'She was one of the greatest patriots this country has ever known,' he said. 'A wonderful old lady – and she had second sight. I only hope to heaven that half the disasters she foresaw never strike us.' When he was later appointed by Winston Churchill as a government minister in 1940 and working in the bunkers under his office during the Blitz, he may well have recalled these words.

A 15-year-old schoolgirl, Maud Mason, wrote from Jersey about 'her fairy-godmother'. 'I was very grieved to hear of the death of Lady Houston who I shall always remember with gratitude. She loved England and was always ready to help others who loved their country.'[8]

The next edition of the *Saturday Review* announced that it 'was resuming its position as the leading Conservative weekly,' adding that 'the dictatorship under which its circulation exceeded that in any previous period of its long history is over.' It would 'return to the old traditions that made it a power in the land,' principal members of staff would remain and the new editor expressed the hope that 'the journal could rely on the support of subscribers, old and new, during and after the reconstruction now taking place.' Without 'dictatorial' Lucy, however, it lost its appeal and ceased publication the following year.

Once Lucy was buried, the attention of the newspapers turned to speculations about her will; or rather the fact that an up-to-date version of this document could not be found. How much of her fortune remained? Which individuals or charities might benefit? Her solicitor, Willie Graham, did not have such a document and the will of 1930, mentioned in chapter 10, was rendered void by the fact that Miss Hoare, the sole beneficiary, had died nine months before Lucy. Thorough searches of the house on Jersey and on board *Liberty* proved fruitless. Byron Cottage was actually owned by her sister Florence, and she had already let it to new tenants who refused to cooperate in any search of the building. Cynics might suggest that it would have been in Florence's interest, as next of kin, not to press the matter.

Wentworth Day tells us he informed Graham that he knew Lucy had drafted a revised will after Miss Hoare's death, and that he had seen her stuff it under her mattress when he entered her bedroom unexpectedly.[9] She had told him,

> I have left Lord Lloyd £100,000 because I know he'll use it to fight Communism and Russia. I've left Lord Sempill £30,000 because he is a good, brave man. The air defence of this country ought to be in his hands. You will get £20,000 because you have never jibbed at fighting this country's enemies – but I have tied it up so that no woman can get her hands on it. One day, if you've any sense, you'll marry a nice little home-bird and then you'll be glad of it. And I've left Miss Ritchie and Foster, those two dear things, a nice little fortune apiece.

The fact that she made no mention of a legacy to Edward VIII strengthens the case that she had already sent him the £250,000 mentioned in the previous chapter. When Wentworth Day was working on his biography in

May 1956 he wrote to the Duke of Windsor in Paris to ask whether he could confirm or deny the story. Three weeks later he received a letter from the Duke's secretary stating that the rumour had no foundation whatsoever. Intriguingly, this letter was written on Buckingham Palace letterhead, perhaps implying that the Duke's mail was being intercepted.

With the will still missing, Wentworth Day recounts the strange story of how he had subsequently met a woman with 'the sight', a clairvoyant who could divine people's character without having met them.[10] On being given one of Lucy's handkerchiefs, she said that it had belonged to 'a terrific personality – turbulent, dominant and terribly distressed. She's dead now, but literally turning in her grave with frustration – about a bit of paper, a will I think.' Then she went on to describe where it lay, hidden under a floorboard in a small room like an attic, 'one with a sloping roof and wall-paper patterned in climbing roses'. Miss Ritchie had immediately recognised it as a cupboard off Lucy's bedroom – with a loose floorboard. But when Wentworth Day and Lord Sempill had visited the house to follow this up, the new occupants, 'plagued with vulgar sight-seers', refused to let them in.

The High Court of Justice ruled on 5 April that Lucy had effectively died 'intestate' and that her sister Florence Wrey should be granted letters of administration over Lucy's estate. This was valued at a little over £1.5million, on which duty of £690,000 was payable, leaving £835,500 for distribution to fifteen of Lucy's relations, including 'her sister, two nieces, a nephew and the children of other relatives – some of whom were living in Australia.'[11] (I have failed to trace specific details of the distribution, though the likely candidates are discussed in Appendix II; Lucy's sister Florence Wrey would have been entitled to one half – approximately £400,000 after fees.)

But this was only the portion traced in England, the press speculating that another £3 million lay somewhere in Jersey. The question of Lucy's domicile was still to be determined and contested, though the Jersey authorities claimed that her only asset there was her house, Beaufield.[12] (This property was finally sold on the death of Lucy's nephew 'Tom' Radmall in 1948 for £7,399 on behalf of his son Christopher Thomas Adrian Radmall (1942–84), the 'principal heir' of Lucy's estate.[13] When Florence died in 1959 she left a net estate worth £398,874 before inheritance tax at 64%, and her five-page will gave precise details of the relations still alive whom she wished to receive bequests. These are also given in Appendix II.)

Other people would try to put in a claim on Lucy's money, namely three Liverpool dockworkers by the name of Challiner and their widowed sister, Mrs Crookham, who were second cousins several times removed of Robert Houston.[14] They had remembered that Lucy had been generous to his relations after his death, so they tried again but this time it seems with no success.

On 3 May Christie's held a sale of jewellery that included four of Lucy's most treasured items. An emerald pendant formed of a single square stone was bought by a Paris dealer for £9,500, while a sapphire pendant formerly in the possession of the Russian Imperial family went for £4,800. Two other lots consisting of an emerald single-stone ring and a 15-stone diamond collar made £1,900 and £1,310 respectively.[15]

The fate of the beautiful *Liberty*, the ship that had given Lucy so much pleasure, was tragic. For all her graceful lines and luxurious fittings she was steam-powered, which required a large crew in an age when owners of such vessels demanded the cleanliness, convenience and instant availability of vessels with internal-combustion engines. On the last day of 1937 *Liberty* was bought by the firm of Cashmores to be towed to Newport where she was broken up for scrap.[16]

Of her heroes, Winston Churchill became Prime Minister in May 1940 after Neville Chamberlain, who had taken over on Baldwin's retirement in 1937, lost a vote of confidence in the House of Commons. This strong, obstinate man, with his inspiring gift of oratory, arose out of his wilderness at the time of his country's greatest need, taking up the challenge of leading the fight against Nazi Germany when Britain stood alone after the fall of France. During the Battle of Britain that summer, every fighter-aircraft that fought against the Luftwaffe was powered by a Rolls-Royce Merlin engine, while the Supermarine Spitfire, although outnumbered by the Hawker Hurricane, became the very symbol of the Royal Air Force victory. When Churchill made his famous speech – 'Never in the field of human conflict was so much owed by so many to so few' – he must surely have been including his flirtatious friend Lucy Houston.

Lord Lloyd was made chairman of the British Council in 1937 and also honorary commodore of No. 600 (City of London) squadron RAF. This role he took so seriously that he took up flying again, being awarded his 'wings' at the age of 59. He insisted on flying with his squadron on a reconnaissance raid over Germany in early 1940. One of Churchill's first cabinet appointments in May 1940 was to make Lloyd Minister of State for the Colonies, to which was added the extra burden of Leader of the House of Lords in December. Suffering from overwork and a recurrence of earlier illnesses picked up overseas, he died in harness only nine months later. Churchill wrote of him: 'We championed several causes together which did not command the applause of large majorities; but it is just in that kind of cause, where one is swimming against the stream, that one learns the worth and qualities of a comrade and friend… All the more therefore do we feel the loss of this high-minded and exceptionally gifted and experienced public servant.'

The future for Lord Sempill was more controversial. He became a member of the Anglo-German Fellowship in London and later joined the pro-fascist Right Club, many of whose members, including the founder Major Ramsay, were interned as security risks at the outbreak of war, a fate shared by both Oswald Mosley and his wife Diana. Lord Sempill, however, was given a job in the Department of Air Materiel at the Admiralty. He must have maintained the close links that he had forged in the 1920s with the Japanese aircraft industry, because in 1941, three months before the attack on Pearl Harbour, the code-breakers at Bletchley Park picked up information that he was supplying secret intelligence to the Japanese Embassy in London. Churchill gave orders 'to clear him out while time remains', and the Admiralty told him to resign or be sacked.[17] But Churchill relented somewhat and a charge under the Official Secrets Act was dropped. Sempill retired from public life to his estates in Scotland and died in 1965.

The sad story of Edward and Wallis in exile, she now with the title of Duchess of Windsor but denied the prefix of Her Royal Highness, has been often told.[18] Their marriage in France on 3 June 1937, was not the impressive ceremony that Edward had envisaged, but a very low-key affair indeed with virtually no guests apart from his ADCs 'Fruity' Metcalfe and Dudley Forwood, and Wallis' friends Kathleen and Herman Rogers.

Members of his family refused to attend. Initially Edward believed that he and Wallis could return to England, where he saw himself taking on the role as counsellor to his younger brother, but he utterly underestimated the hatred and animosity engendered by Wallis in the hearts and minds of the women in his own family. Queen Elizabeth, supported by her mother-in-law Queen Mary, blamed Wallis exclusively for ruining her family life and imposing on her husband the burden of duties for which she believed he was ill-equipped and inadequately prepared.

The Windsor's trip to Germany in October 1937, where they were greeted warmly by Adolf Hitler and his ministers, became an acute embarrassment. Hitler clearly believed that Edward still had great influence in his home country and could be manipulated and encouraged to add popular appeal to the political appeasers. Bolstered by this endorsement, Edward planned a visit to America where he would announce his role as the leader of a new International Peace Movement, but when the credentials of his financial sponsor, Charles Bedaux, were found to be extremely dubious, even to the extent of his being a possible German spy, the authorities rang alarm bells and tried to call the venture off. It took a rejection by the US President Franklin D. Roosevelt and withdrawal of any support from the British Embassy to persuade Edward to cancel the trip. When the British Government did grant him an appointment as a liaison officer with the French army, doubts quickly emerged over the security of his staff, with suggestions that secret information about the weak points in France's defences was leaking its way to Berlin. On the declaration of war, Edward resorted to his usual fall-back position and fled to Spain. There the Germans hatched a plot to kidnap them both and hold them to ransom in the hopes of forcing the British Government into peace negotiations, a scheme only thwarted by the couple escaping to Portugal. Their subsequent life, first in the Bahamas when Edward was appointed to the 'non-job' of Governor General and then in Paris after the war, possessed a veneer of glamour and luxury but was in reality an empty shell of loneliness and disappointment, only sustained by their continuing mutual devotion.

In spite of there being nearly 60 years difference in their ages, there are some parallels between Lucy's unblinking adoration of Edward VIII and the obsessive idolatry for Adolf Hitler shown by Unity Mitford, the second youngest of the remarkable Mitford sisters.

Her father, Lord Redesdale, owned a goldmine in Canada and the place of her birth in 1914 was the mining community called Swastika, where her parents christened her with the second name of Valkyrie, the name of the fearsome cavalry-women of Teutonic legend and Wagner's 'Ring Cycle' operas. As a teenager, Unity became fascinated by the ghoulish paintings of Hieronymus Bosch, the poetry of Dante and his exploration of the death cult, and the mystic poems and paintings of William Blake on the same theme. It somehow seems that Unity's destiny to become a rabid fascist and close friend of Adolf Hitler was written in the stars. She developed a passionate determination to meet her hero in person, persuading her mother to send her to a finishing school in Munich where Adolf Hitler had a house. She would sit outside the restaurant where he usually had lunch every day in an effort to gain his notice. Unity was large, blonde-haired and blue-eyed, a perfect specimen of Aryan womanhood, and it was not long before she received an invitation to join Hitler and his henchmen at their table. This was the start of an extraordinary relationship which may have involved as many as 140 instances of time spent together either alone or in company.[19]

Unity's intimacy with Hitler was not of a sexual nature in the normal sense of the word – she derived her sexual satisfaction by ritual orgies with young Nazi storm troopers[20] – but based on a mutual, transcendental fascination with necromancy and the cult of death. Much of Hitler's fanaticism was derived from his knowledge that a single word from him could lead to the slaughter of thousands, as he first proved on the 'night of the long knives' in June 1934. Two women, including his niece, who were believed to have had intimate relationships with him had committed suicide, and it may well have been that he and Unity enjoyed fantasising about the time in the future when they might meet 'on the other side', in some sort of Valhalla after the final, catastrophic destruction of the world. It would prove to be a long-drawn-out suicide pact.

When Hitler invaded Poland in 1939 and Britain declared war on Germany, Unity attempted to commit suicide by shooting herself in the head with a small calibre pistol, supposedly given to her by Hitler. The wound proved not to be fatal, and the German authorities took extraordinary steps to nurse her and then make arrangements for her to be taken on a special train to the frontier where she could be collected and returned to her family. Although she was nursed back to reasonable health, she never made a full recovery either physically or psychologically and died in 1948 aged only 34.

Unity's sister Diana and her husband Oswald Mosley were interned at Holloway prison from 1940 to 1943, when they were released to spend the rest of the war under house arrest. His later efforts to return to the political scene were unsuccessful and he died in France in 1980, 23 years before Diana.

Theodore Brinckman, who had succeeded to his father's title in 1905 and remained friends with Lucy throughout his life, died in September 1937 at the age of 75, the baronetcy passing to his eldest son by his second marriage, Captain Theodore Ernest Brinckman.

Virtually nothing is known about what happened to Lucy's loyal and lifelong friend Miss Bessie Ritchie except that she was still alive in 1956.[21]

Lucy's managing-director, Warner Allen CBE, in spite of being 58 years old when war broke out was gazetted into the Royal Air Force Reserve as an acting Wing Commander, and served as deputy director in the foreign division of the Ministry of Information from 1940 to 1941. After the war he went back to writing more books on wines and spirits, together with a series of works on mystical themes, dying in 1968. His entry in the Oxford Dictionary of National Biography mentions neither his work with Lucy nor the slim biography he wrote about her life.

James Wentworth Day became a prolific author on matters of farming and field sports as well as a biographer of racing drivers and members of the royal family – and Lucy in 1956. His entry in the ODNB lists thirty-eight books. As well as holding senior positions in *The Field* and *Country Life* magazines, he enjoyed a brief and contentious period as a television personality in 1957–58, airing right-wing views on race relations and homophobia. He sought election, unsuccessfully, as the Conservative candidate for Hornchurch in the general elections of both 1950 and 1951. His hasty marriage to the sparkling bisexual Nerina Shute in 1936 was dissolved in 1943, the year he married a New Zealander by the name of Marion McLean and this union was blessed by the birth of a daughter. At the age of 84 he died in 1983, severing the last personal link of anyone with an intimate knowledge of Lucy, as her devoted accomplice and co-conspirator while having to endure her often irrational demands.

Long, long before this, any recognition of Lucy and her achievements had faded into total oblivion. She had been deluded about many things, among them her failure to recognise that the 'winds of change' that were already undermining the foundations of the British Empire as a colonial power were irresistible. She totally failed to understand that the British people, with their long history of democracy and the freedoms enshrined in Magna Carta, would never bow to the will of a dictator, even a home-grown one. Perhaps her worst failing, her greatest misjudgement, had been to believe that Edward VIII should tear up the constitution and exercise political power. His abdication was probably the best and most patriotic thing he ever did in his life. Her admiration of Benito Mussolini and Adolf Hitler in his early days, damned her in the eyes of a generation who had suffered so much at their hands. Victory in the Second World War had been achieved to a large extent through the valour and sacrifices of the Russians, who had been our tough, unyielding allies rather than the 'Red Menace' that Lucy saw as the ultimate threat to civilisation. Therefore to try to see Lucy in the role of a misunderstood heroine in the post-war era would have been to swim against a tide of prejudice.

With the benefit of a longer perspective, I contend that it is high time to revel in the character of this once-so-beautiful, intelligent and outspoken woman, and to reassess all the facets of her extraordinary life. Was she not right to rail against the evils of communism, the doctrine that led to the cold war, the nuclear arms race and the very real possibility of global annihilation? Her unselfish generosity to causes both charitable and patriotic is undeniable, and her insight into the crucial importance of air power in any future conflict was truly prophetic. She had foreseen the horrors of the Blitz on London and other ports and cities in Britain, and had tried to do something practical about it at a time when politicians still believed that our defences were best left to the sham bulwark of the League of Nations. The mass production of allied fighters and bombers during the Second World War had been accepted by the public merely as a result of effective management, and this perception had swamped recognition of the key role played by a few pioneering visionaries, among whom Lucy deserves to have a genuinely heroic status.

A tiny spark was reignited in 1976 by a correspondent to *The Times* who had visited the RAF museum at Hendon and been disappointed to find not a single mention of Lucy and what she had done in financing the development work by the aircraft industry that led to the success of the Schneider Trophy race of 1931 and much, much more.[22] 'Surely, here of all places, a generous tribute should be paid to the lady but for whose timely help there might not even be a Royal Air Force today.' It would be as fitting an epitaph as any.

POSTSCRIPT. Lucy's opinions, however sincerely held, were often misguided and on many occasions her judgement was flawed. But she was absolutely right when she assured the somewhat sceptical Robert Houston about the enduring value and investment potential of the string of black (strictly speaking, grey) pearls that he bought for her birthday in 1924. On Wednesday, 13 June 2012, Christie's held an auction of jewellery in London, including lot 367, 'the rare, natural grey pearl necklace from the Cowdray collection' with an estimate between £200,000 and £350,000.[23] After fiercely competitive bidding, these wonderful pearls realised a world-record price of over £2.2 million, and three years later on 7 October 2015, they were sold again by Sotheby's in Hong Kong for the equivalent of £3.5 million. [see PLATES B14 and C22]

It would be nice to think that these were the gift from Robert Houston that had given Lucy so much pleasure, but the date-trail does not fit. It is not known how or when Lady Cowdray had acquired them but it must have been before 1932, the year she died, and Lucy did not pass hers on to her relation, via Wentworth-Day, until after he had joined her in 1933, as mentioned in chapter 10. However, readers may recall that she already owned some others, described at the time of the coronation of King Edward VII as her 'famous black pearls' (see chapter 4, page 20). So when she was given the necklace by Robert Houston, might she have sold the earlier one to Lady Cowdray? In which case, what did happen to the Houston necklace? Lucy's whole life leaves us with many enigmatic questions unanswered. This is yet another one. [see PLATE B25]

Appendix I

The Racehorses of Frederick Gretton

Frederick Gretton's most outstanding horse by far was a stallion called *Isonomy*, which was bought on Frederick's behalf by his trainer, John Porter, as a yearling in 1876 for 320 guineas. *Isonomy* came with a good pedigree – his sire was *Sterling* and his dam was *Isola Bella*, a half-sister of the Grand Prix de Paris winner *Saint Christophe* – though he had been a late foal and was rather small, only 15.2 hands high. But Porter had been impressed by the colt's 'lively and assertive manner', and as a two-year-old he showed promise, though not appearing to be top class. Instead of contesting the classics the following year, like his three-year-old contemporaries, Frederick held him back till the end of the season and entered him for the Cambridgeshire Handicap at Newmarket on 22 October. He was ranked as a complete outsider, carrying a handicap of only 7 stone 1 pound and being offered by the bookmakers at odds of 40–1.

    The day of the Cambridgeshire was unique in the Newmarket autumn meeting calendar as the last major race of the season, attracting vast crowds, some arriving on special trains and many on foot, who came to watch and usually get drunk. 'The Cambridgeshire is an interesting race, but it certainly attracts a congregation of roughs of the worst description.' This was much to the disgust of the aristocratic punters in their landaus and carriages, who deplored the rowdy behaviour and were unable to see anything of the racing itself. Frederick Gretton had already won the race in 1872 when Playfair had come home at odds of 10–1, though his Sterling had only managed a poor third the following year. In 1878, for some unknown reason, the race was moved to a later slot in the day's programme. There was a very large field of thirty-eight horses, with lots being drawn for position, and Isonomy had the good fortune to draw number 14, almost in the middle of the track. It was not until after 4 o'clock, with the light fading fast, that the starter managed to get them lined up for the 'off', but this was deemed a false start when Shillelagh bolted and the whole procedure had to be repeated. The racing correspondent of The Times wrote:[1] 'To attempt to pick the winner of the Cambridgeshire is always a hazardous experiment; this year, because of the large field, doubly so. No wonder that the most experienced analysts have rather faltered … with nearly all of them going for Macbeth … though Lord Clive was also one of the firmest. The pace told as they came up the hill to the Red Post, where Hampton was going as well as anything, attended by Tallas, Touchet, La Merveille – and Isonomy. The weight began to tell on the top weight and Isonomy, drawing clear, won easily, beating Touchet by two lengths. Backers, as a rule, have lost on the race, which ought to have been a good one for the ring.' What he did not know was that it had been an excellent day for Frederick Gretton, who not only pocketed the prize money of £2,187 but also a betting coup, rumoured to have been in the order of £37,000.

Frederick had another horse running in the first race on the Wednesday, the Second Class Cesarewitch Handicap. 'It was a relief to have the comparative quiet of this afternoon, succeeding the bustle and confusion of the previous day,' wrote the sporting correspondent of the York Herald. Only two horses came to the starting line, with Frederick's Ancient Pistol a very clear favourite at odds of 6–1 on. The jockeys, however, gave the crowd a run for their money right up to the line, with Ancient Pistol finally 'winning comfortably by a neck'. Frederick raced Isonomy successfully as a four- and five-year-old and refused an offer of £25,000 in 1881 when he was retired to stud. In 1886, the Sporting Times conducted a poll among one hundred experts to rank the best British racehorses of the nineteenth century; Isonomy came third. The significance of this particular horse to British flat racing is encapsulated in the following extract from Points of a Racehorse by Major General Sir John Hills RE KC:[2]

Isonomy disputes in many persons' opinion the premiership of the turf. Winner of the Cambridgeshire, Manchester Cup, Ascot Gold Vase and Gold Cup twice, plus other races (a stayer rather than a sprinter). But it is as a sire he has still further distinction. Eleven listed including: *Gellinule* has proved to be a fairly successful sire; *Common*, winner of Triple Crown, 2000 Guineas, Derby and St. Ledger, a horse of extraordinary power. (In the writer's opinion, one of the best racers that ever trod the turf.) *Isinglass*, a perfectly proportioned racehorse. (Most long-lasting source of stamina, which some time ago was not fashionable, so line not much used.) *Seabreeze*, filly – won Coronation Stakes, Oaks and St. Ledger, beautifully made.

Appendix II

Where Did Lucy's Fortune Go?

The residue of Lucy's fortune was distributed after her death amongst her surviving relatives. This appendix gives details of the direct descendants of Lucy's siblings. Relatives still alive in 1937, and therefore likely to benefit from the administration of Lucy's estate after confirmation that she had died intestate, are highlighted in bold, though because not all death dates are known this list cannot be confirmed as being comprehensive. Those who were also still living in 1959 and mentioned in Florence Wrey's will are given in bold italics plus endnotes.

LUCY'S BROTHERS AND SISTERS

A. Lucy's eldest sister Margaret Radmall (1837–1901) had originally married a merchant clerk Alfred Packer, but he died before they had children. Her second husband was a farmer from Pinner called James Vaughn (1822–1902). They had four children, born between 1869 and 1875 (see A2 below).

B. Two years after Margaret, a second sister had been born and christened Mary Elizabeth Radmall (1839–1901), who later married a Monsieur Paul Claudius Steinmann from Montpellier in France in 1865, bearing him two daughters, Isabell and Margaret (see B2 below). (Another sister, Mary Jane Radmall (b.1840) died in infancy.)

C. Lucy's eldest brother Thomas G. Radmall (1843–87) became a wine merchant and married Elizabeth Maria Younghusband, though they never had any children.

D. Next came Sophia Martha Radmall (1845–1922). She married a German bookseller by the name of James Edward Cathy (later changed to Catty) and they had six children (see D2 below).

E. Arthur Clifford Radmall (1850–1927), a stockbroker, married twice and had a daughter by his first wife Rhoda Caroline Allen (1854–1901) and both a daughter and a son by his second, Ethel Nina Taylor (1874–1930) (see E2 below).

F. Walter William Radmall (1852–1928) never married.

G. **Florence Radmall (Wrey) (1862–1959)** married twice but never had any children.

THE SECOND GENERATION

A2. Vaughn children. 1. Margaret C. Vaughn (b.1869) married Francis H.B. King (1867–1915) but there were no known children; 2. Edward Jauncey Vaughn (1870–1906) emigrated to Australia where he married Alma Easton (b.1873) and had seven children (see A3–2 below); 3. *Florence Lillian Vaughn (1871–1960)*[1] married Harold Arthur Cooper (1871–1960) and had three sons and one daughter (see A3–3 below); 4. Elaine B. Vaughn (b.1875) married Richard B. Davis (b.1849) – any children unknown.

B2. Steinmann children. 1. Isabel Steinmann (1866–?); 2. **Margaret Louise Steinmann (1870–1955)** married Alfred Ernest East (b.1868) and had one son (see B3–2 below).

D2. Catty children. 1. James Walter Catty (1873–1929) married twice and had a daughter by his first wife Lilian Baldwin (see D3–1 below); 2. **Florence Catty (1875–1944)**, who never married; 3. Margaret Emmeline Catty (1876–?), who married William Ward Cooper in 1918 – no children; 4. *Thomas Claud Catty (1879–1967)*,[2] who emigrated to South Africa and served during the 1914–18 war as a captain in the 69th Punjabi Regiment, subsequently being promoted to brigadier. In 1933 he married Eileen Cole-Baker (1896–1985) who already had two sons, though names unknown; 5. *Hugh Douglas Catty (1881–1968)* emigrated to the USA, where he married Margaret Gayford of Norfolk, Virginia, and had two daughters (see D3–5 below); 6. *Rose Pauline Catty (1885–post 1959)*[3] emigrated to California. She married twice, first to a wine-grower Henri Jaboulet-Verchère in 1908 by whom she had a daughter (see D3–6 below) and secondly to a Mr Woods.

E2. Arthur Radmall children. 1. Caroline Radmall (1882–?) seems to have remained a spinster; 2. *Cicely Kathleen Radmall (1911–89)*[4] managed to land Sir Geoffrey Frederick Palmer Bt (1893–1951) in 1932 and gave him two sons (see E3–2 below). A year after her husband's death, she married Robert William Banner Newton (1910–62) and had further children; 3. **Clifford Willoughby 'Tom' Radmall (1905–48)** married Barbara Whiting and they had one son (see E3–3 below).

THE THIRD GENERATION

A3-2. Edward Jauncey Vaughn children (Australia). 1. Spencer Vaughn (1896–?); 2. Olive Elaine Vaughn (1897–?); 3. Roger Easton Vaughn (1896–1970) married Kathleen Lynch and had one daughter (see A4-3-3 below); 4. Madge Lillian Vaughn (1901–?); 5. Cecil O. Vaughn (1901–?); 6. Beatrice Alma Vaughn (1903–?); 7. Eileen A Vaughn (1905–?).

A3-3. Harold Arthur Cooper children. 1. *John Vaughn Cooper (1905–post 1959)*;[5] 2. *Vivian Vaughn Cooper (1908–post 1959)*,[6] executor to Florence Wrey's will; 3. Joan Vaughn Cooper (1908–?); 4. *Peter Vaughn Cooper (1911–post 1959)*.[7]

B3-2. Alfred Ernest East child. 1. Philip V. East (1900–?).

D3-1. James Walter Catty children. 1. *Margory Patricia Catty (1908–1997)*[8] married James Newton Rodney Moore (1905–85) in 1947.

D3-5. Hugh Douglas Catty children, both born in New York. 1. *Violet Margaret 'Boo' Catty (1913–82)*[9] married Brian Hutton Dulanty (1910–74) and had one daughter (see D4-3-1 below); 2. *Barbara M Catty (1920–2007)* married firstly James Albert Dew (1915–75) – two children (see D4-3-2 below) and secondly Louis Charles Krauthoff (1917–88) – also two children (see D4-3-2 below).

D3-6. Rose Pauline Catty child. *Diane Henrietta Jaboulet-Verchère (1915–?)*,[10] later Mrs Bierge.

E3-2. Cicely Kathleen Radmall's children. 1. Geoffrey Christopher John Palmer, 12th Baronet (b.1936) who married Clarissa Mary Villiers-Smith; 2. *Jeremy Charles Palmer (b.1939)*;[11] 3. The name of her child by her second husband Robert Newton is known only to the family.

E3-3. 'Tom' Radmall's child. *Christopher Thomas Adrian Radmall (1942–84)*.[12]

THE FOURTH GENERATION

A4-3-3. Robert Easton Vaughn child. **Patricia Grace Vaughn (1927–99)**.

D4-**3**-1&2. The names of these children are only known to their families in the USA.

British General Elections 1920–37 and Changes of Prime Minister

1922 Nov	Cons Majority	Bonar-Law/ Baldwin from May 1923
1923 Dec	Cons <u>Minority</u> -	Baldwin
	Lab <u>Minority</u> from Jan 1924	MacDonald
1924 Oct	Cons Majority	Baldwin
1929 May	Lab <u>Minority</u> [The 'flapper' election]	MacDonald
1931 Oct	National Government – (Cons Majority)	MacDonald/Baldwin from June 1935
1935 Nov	National Government – (Cons Majority)	Baldwin/Chamberlain from May 1937

This table clearly shows how British politics suffered from the 'paralysis' of minority governments at two crucial periods in the interwar years. It was this weakness in the democratic process that was railed against by people such as Lucy and Lord Lloyd.

Appendix IV

The Relative Value of Money

Readers in 2016, when new military aircraft cost several million pounds each and £100 merely buys ten packets of cigarettes, may find it difficult to understand the true value of Lucy's wealth, her donations to charity and her sponsorship of aviation projects. As written, the sums may seem almost paltry by today's standards. How, for example, could £200,000 possible make any significant contribution to the future aerial defence of London? Yet in 1932 this sum could have purchased several squadrons of the most up-to-date fighter aircraft (see chapter 12).

Therefore all the quoted amounts of money have to be 'translated' by a multiplying factor to adjust both for inflation/deflation, changes in taxation and the relative value of non-monetary assets. There is no precise formula for doing this, and the Bank of England's tables of cash-inflation alone understate the necessary multiplier considerably. According to these the following factors should be applied to arrive at 2015 values:

£1 in: 1840 = £92 (yet the cost of a 1st class mail stamp has increased by a factor of 151)

1883 = £109 (eg Lucy's income from Gretton's legacy converts to £760,000 per year.)

1924 = £55 (eg the cost of Black Pearls given by Houston converts to £2.75 million.)

1926 = £54 (eg Lucy's legacy converts to approx £250 million.)

1932 = £63 (eg Lucy's aircraft offer of £200,000 converts to £12.6 million.)

1936 = £64 (eg Lucy's legacy after tax converts to £53 million.)

Notes

Chapter 2 (pages 4–10)
1. Wentworth Day, p14.
2. As imagined by Wentworth Day, p13.
3. The present whereabouts of this photograph is unknown. Wentworth Day uses it in his biography and it doubtless came into his possession after Lucy's death.
4. Wentworth Day, p15. Also Allen, p24.
5. Wentworth Day, p15.
6. Owen.
7. *Oxford Dictionary of National Biography*, 1st edition.
8. Wentworth Day, p17.
9. *ODNB*, H. Yoxall.
10. *The Times*, 23 November 1882.
11. *Morning Post*, 2 January 1883.
12. This became the basis of a rather poor joke published in the '*Pink 'un*'. Apollinaris was the fashionable sparkling water, or seltzer, of the time. The riddle asked the question 'when did Frederick Gretton invent mineral water?', the answer being 'when he made a-Poll-an-heiress.'

Chapter 3 (pages 11–17)
1. Wentworth Day, p24.
2. Wentworth Day, p25.
3. Allen, p29 seq.
4. *Edinburgh Evening News* among others.
5. For reasons of estate inheritance, the family briefly changed its name to Broadhead.
6. *Aberdeen Evening News*, 1 November 1882, among others.
7. *Whitstable Times*, 3 March 1883.
8. *Yorkshire Gazette*, 17 July 1880.
9. *Kentish Gazette*, 30 May 1883.
10. This is the address where Frederick Gretton died, so it may be that he had already given it to Lucy.
11. *Sheffield Evening Telegraph*, 7 May 1895, quoting London Correspondence.
12. *Whitstable Times*.
13. The Marquis must have recovered because he did not die until 1897, though aged only 40.

14. *Aberdeen Journal*, 27 August 1928.
15. Wentworth Day, frontispiece.
16. Allen, p44.
17. *Morning Post*, 3 July 1894.
18. Wentworth Day, p28.
19. *Hastings Observer*, 15 Dec 1894.
20. *London Standard*, 2 July 1894. Also *Morning Post*, 3 July 1894.
21. *Evening Telegraph*, 24 May 1928.
22. *Aberdeen Journal*, 27 August 1928.
23. *Western Daily Press*.
24. *Dundee Courier*, April 29.
25. Wentworth Day, p28. Theodore outlived Lucy by two years, dying in 1938 when the baronetcy passed to his eldest son, Ernest. Like his father, he got married for the first time when he was only 19 in 1921, but this was dissolved within eighteen months. Two further, childless marriages both ended in divorce, and so when he died in 1954 the title passed to his younger brother, Roderick Napoleon 'Naps' Brinckman.
26. Wentworth Day, pp28 and 32.

Chapter 4 (pages 18–27)

1. *Chelmsford Chronicle*, 26 April 1901.
2. *Chelmsford Chronicle*, 3 May 1901.
3. Seymour, pp11–12.
4. *The Times*, 11 August 1902.
5. Wentworth Day, p25. The artist had originally been christened Henry Thaddeus Jones but changed his name around by deed poll to make it more memorable.
6. *ODNB*.
7. *Gloucester Citizen*, 12 September 1902.
8. *Western Daily Press*, 17 October 1902.
9. *Coventry Evening Telegraph*, November 1902. The house in Church Street is now the Shakespeare Centre, a department of Birmingham University.
10. ODN: *Harper's Bazaar*, July 1907.
11. *Locomotive Magazine*, 1911.
12. *Northampton Mercury*, 19 December 1902.
13. *The Times*, 26 April 1905.
14. *Manchester Courier*, 22 May 1908.
15. *The Times*, 4 October 1907 and 12 Aug 1909.
16. *Chelmsford Chronicle*, 30 July 1909. The King's last mistress, Alice Keppel (1868–1947), the great-grandmother of the present (2015) Duchess of Cornwall, was a less flamboyant but far more sympathetic character, respectably married to George Keppel, the third son of the 7th Earl of Albemarle. She was held in sufficient respect by Queen Alexandra that she was invited to attend Edward's deathbed. Alice Keppel was a contemporary of my Scottish grandmother May Violet Dent (née Sellar) and, although I do not know the background to

how and why they met, they became friends. May Dent's great niece, Diana Grove, a bridesmaid at my parent's wedding, would later marry the 9th Earl of Albemarle in 1931. My mother told me that when I was a baby in 1937 I was bounced on Alice Keppel's knee – a minor but amusing incident of Royal association by proxy.

17. Allen, p42.
18. 1911 census.
19. Wentworth Day, pp28–9.
20. *The Times*, 26 April 1910.
21. Wentworth Day p29.
22. Allen, p63.
23. Wentworth Day, p26.
24. Wentworth Day, p30.
25. In private correspondence, she has told me that Thrumpton contains not a single trace of George Byron; not a portrait, nor a letter or any single item of memorabilia.
26. Seymour, pp21–23. Anna finally married him in 1921, by which time he was the 10th Baron Byron. The marriage was childless. When he died in 1949, he left Thrumpton to his nephew, George FitzRoy Seymour, an eccentric bisexual who had developed an obsessive liking for the house since visiting it as a small boy.
27. *Dundee Courier*, 31 October 1912.
28. *Manchester Evening News*, 6 June 1914.
29. Allen, p65.
30. Mitra.
31. The *Gentlewoman*, quoted in the *Coventry Evening Telegraph* and the *Liverpool Echo*, 2 January 1914.
32. *Aberdeen Journal*, 2 March 1914. Regrettably, I have not been able to trace a copy of this.

Chapter 5 (pages 28–34)
1. *The Times*, 19 September 1914.
2. *The Times*, 19 October 1914.
3. *Hull Daily Mail*, 4 September 1917. Referring to the donation of a surviving sample to the National Museum.
4. The ancient kingdom of Galicia lay between Hungary to the south, Poland to the north and Russia to the east. It is now largely within Ukraine.
5. *The Times*, 14 January 1915.
6. Lord Byron the poet had gone out to fight for the Greeks in their War of Independence against the Ottoman Empire. He had been masterminding an attack on the Turkish fortress of Lepanto when he went down with some illness, which was treated by the standard procedure of 'bleeding'. As a result of this barbaric practice he developed blood poisoning and died of sepsis on 19 April 1824, aged 36.

7. *The Times*, 2 April 1915.
8. *The Times*, 14 February 1916.
9. *Dundee Courier*, 16 January 1916.
10. For his work, he was awarded the Imperial Russian Order of St Anne.
11. Powell. Flora Sandes dressed in male uniform and was given the rank of sergeant major in the Serbian army.
12. *The Times*, 10 June 1915. Also *British Journal of Nursing*, 19 June (with photograph).
13. *The Times*, 12 July 1915.
14. *The Times*, 16 March 1916.
15. *Newcastle Journal*, 12 October 1916.
16. *Nottingham Evening Post*, 18 April 1916.
17. The full version was printed in the *Hull Daily Mail*, 28 September 1916.
18. My own father-in-law used to tell the story that one rather 'unusual' little boy preferred doing this to playing football and could be bribed with sweets to make up the quota for his more macho form-mates. The boy in question never married, and later in life founded a very successful department store in Birmingham.
19. *Bath Chronicle*, 23 June 1917.
20. *Aberdeen Journal*, 26 January 1918.
21. *Western Times*, 2 March 1918.
22. *Hull Daily Mail*, 15 October 1918.

Chapter 6 (pages 35–43)
1. *Dundee Courier*, 7 November 1919.
2. *Aberdeen Journal*, 13 September 1920.
3. *Western Gazette*, 17 September 1920.
4. *Nottingham Evening Post*, 'Echoes from Town', 19 April 1926.
5. *Sunday Times*, quoted in the *Jersey Evening Post*, 20 April 1926.
6. *Jersey Evening Post*, 20 April 1926.
7. *Liverpool Echo*, 10 March 1916.
8. *Liverpool Echo*, 2 December 1916.
9. *The Times*, 31 December 1936.
10. *Sunday Times*, quoted in the *Jersey Evening Post*, 20 April 1926.
11. An article in the *Jersey Morning News*, 17 April 1926, quoting the *London Evening Standard*, claimed that Houston had commanded the ship as a Captain RNVR between 1914 and 1915 when it had initially been used by the Royal Navy as an auxiliary patrol vessel, before its conversion to a hospital ship. I can find no confirmation of this claim.
12. Couling, p113. On his death in 1911, *Liberty* passed to James Ross and then to Lord Tredegar for the first few months of 1914.
13. He also donated the 'Sir Thomas Lipton Trophy' for an international soccer competition prior to the establishment of the FIFA World Cup in 1930.
14. Wentworth Day, pp34–39.

15. Wentworth Day, pp40–42.
16. *Jersey Morning News*, 17 April 1926.
17. Wentworth Day, pp44–45.

Chapter 7 (pages 44–49)
1. Wentworth Day, p45.
2. *Jersey Evening Post*, Saturday, 17 April.
3. Clifford Willoughby 'Tom' Radmall (1905–48)
4. Wentworth Day, p44.
5. *The Times*, 26 November 1926.
6. Allen pp77–78.
7. *Daily Express*, 20 April 1926.
8. Probate office records.
9. *Daily Express* lobby correspondent, 26 April 1926.
10. *Exeter & Plymouth Gazette*, 24 April 1926.
11. *Derby Daily Telegraph*, 20 August 1926.
12. *Dundee Courier*, 30 September 1926.
13. *Dundee Courier*, 28 October 1926.
14. Wentworth Day, pp46–47; Allen pp78–79.

Chapter 8 (pages 50–59)
1. Allen, p84.
2. Pugh, p112.
3. Pugh, p39.
4. *Western Daily Press*, 13 December 1928.
5. *Saturday Review*, 3 February 1934.

Chapter 9 (pages 60–68)
1. *The Times*, 28 July 1927.
2. *The Times*, 1 August 1927.
3. *The Times*, 11 August 1927.
4. *The Times*, 31 October 1927.
5. Allen, p83.
6. Wentworth Day, p53–4.
7. Wentworth Day, p54.
8. *Aberdeen Journal*, 16 November 1927.
9. Article by Winston Churchill in the *Illustrated Sunday Herald*, 2 February 1920, 'Zionism versus Bolshevism'. In this, he picks up on her theme that 'there are three main lines of political conception among the Jews, two of which are helpful and hopeful in a high degree to humanity, and the third absolutely destructive.' The latter, International Jewry, he describes as a 'sinister confederacy … largely of atheistic Jews'.
10. Europe correspondent for the *Milwaukee Sentinel*, 10 November 1928. It seems that this unknown writer was the only journalist who bothered to track her down during this period.

11. *The Times*, 3 May 1928.
12. *Cheltenham Chronicle*, 1 September 1928.
13. Wentworth Day, p55.
14. Allen, p90.
15. *Nottingham Evening Post*, 6 July 1928.
16. *Evening Telegraph*, 26 July 1928.
17. Allen, p89.
18. *Evening Telegraph*, 13 November 1928.
19. *Gloucester Citizen*, 28 January 1929.
20. *Western Morning News*, 25 January 1929.
21. *Aberdeen Journal*, 17 December 1929.
22. *Western Morning News*, 21 December 1929.
23. *Dundee Courier*, 16 December 1929.
24. Wentworth Day, p55. Lucy was not officially stated to be the author, the title page merely attributing it to 'the compiler'.
25. Wentworth Day, p55.
26. Urbach, p171.
27. Speech in Rome, 20 January 1927. Quoted in Urbach, p173.
28. *Western Daily Press*, 30 December 1929.

Chapter 10 (pages 69–72)
1. Allen, p139.
2. Wentworth Day, pp114–5.
3. Wentworth Day, p180.

Chapter 11 (pages 73–86)
1. The superiority of the Farman brothers' designs persuaded the emerging British Royal Flying Corps to purchase examples for use as primary trainers.
2. Biard reported that he had encountered 'wing-flutter' on earlier turns, so bracing wires were reintroduced onto all later models of the Supermarine S series.
3. Setright. The Air Ministry was hedging its bets by encouraging Bristol to show how much power could be derived from a light radial engine, one that went on to be the highly successful 'Mercury'.
4. Mondey, p252.
5. Quoted in Allen, pp14–15.
6. Wentworth Day, p68.
7. Wentworth Day, p69.
8. Replicas of the trophy and another Supermarine S6 can be viewed in the Solent Sky Museum, Southampton.
9. TS 28/217.

Chapter 12 (pages 87–100)
1. Pugh, pp119–20.
2. Wentworth Day, p77.

3. Ditto.
4. As recounted by Miss Ritchie to Wentworth Day and quoted by him on page 106.
5. James. Contemporary fighters, like the Gloster Gamecock, cost about £2,700 each, while the new all-metal prototypes such as the Gloster Gauntlet, would have been around £3,000.
6. Ditto, page 107.
7. Gunston.
8. Andrews & Morgan. This was probably a correct decision. The thick aerofoil wing section of both the Dornier X and the Type 179, with the tandem engines mounted on pylons above, was inherently unsound, inevitably resulting in poor lift and a high drag coefficient. The range of the Type 179 at the expected cruising speed of 145 mph would have been only 700 miles, though this could have been extended to 1,300 at the reduced speed of only 108 mph.
9. Wentworth Day, p115.
10. *Saturday Review*, 16 December 1933.
11. I am indebted to Blythe and Tucker (see bibliography) for much of the following account, including the direct quotations.
12. Wentworth Day, pp74–6.
13. This could have been either Patricia Davidson (b.1911) or even the youngest daughter, Pamela, then only 13.

Chapter 13 (pages 101–118)
1. Wentworth Day, p83.
2. Ditto.
3. Wentworth Day, p85–6.
4. Lloyd papers, 19/2, Churchill College, Cambridge.
5. *Saturday Review*, October 1933.
6. Wentworth Day, p125.
7. They were divorced in 1934. His second marriage to Nerina Shute (1936–43) also failed. In 1943 he married a New Zealander, Marion McLean, a marriage that produced one daughter and lasted until his death in 1983.
8. Wentworth Day, p131.
9. Wentworth Day, p162.
10. *Dundee Courier*, 6 Jan 1933.
11. *Dundee Courier*, 9 Jan 1933.
12. *Dundee Evening Telegraph*, 9 Jan 1933.
13. Wentworth Day p138.
14. Ditto.
15. The National Conservatives retained the seat though with a sharply reduced majority.
16. *Yorkshire Post*, 25 February 1933.
17. Not be confused with the distinguished cavalry officer Cecil Blacker (1916–2002) who was only commissioned in 1936. As Sir Cecil Blacker, he later became Vice Chief of the Imperial General Staff in 1970 and the Adjutant General of

the Forces in 1973. Nor with Latham Valentine Stewart Blacker (1887–1964), another army officer and weapons inventor who will appear in a later chapter.
18. Wentworth Day's memory let him down in his recollections, naming the footballer incorrectly as Hugh Gallagher.
19. Wentworth Day, p148.
20. Wentworth Day, p162.

Chapter 14 (pages 119–132)

1. The mountain was named after an officer in the Royal Artillery, Lieutenant George Everest, who was later knighted for his services as Surveyor General of India.
2. Allen, p128.
3. Fellowes.
4. In the film, the producers make it appear that Lucy recorded her conversation with Lord Clydesdale at her hunting lodge, Kinkara.
5. Readers interested in exploring these aspects in more detail are referred to the book *First over Everest*, a compilation of essays by Fellowes and three other members of the team.
6. Fellowes, chapter XIII.
7. Blacker, 2006, p164–5.
8. Blacker, p165.
9. *Gloucester Echo*, 20 May 1933.
10. Allen, p133.
11. *The Times*, 30 November 1933.
12. Allen, p137.
13. Allen, p138.
14. *The Times*, 1 June 1934. A copy of the film is held in the archives of the British Film Institute and may be viewed by appointment. No copy has been made available on DVD.

Chapter 15 (pages 133–143)

1. *Yorkshire Post*, 19 April 1933.
2. *Western Gazette*, 26 May 1933.
3. Wentworth Day, p82. Founded by the Duke of Northumberland.
4. Wentworth Day, p95.
5. Wentworth Day, p103.
6. *Saturday Review*, 14 July 1934.
7. Allen, p 97.
8. Wentworth Day, pp170–1.
9. *Saturday Review*, 18 November 1933.
10. Wentworth Day, p171.
11. Allen, p100.
12. Allen, p125.
13. Allen, p111.

14. Wentworth Day, p165.
15. *Yorkshire Evening Post*, 27 June 1934.
16. Wentworth Day, p161.
17. Wentworth Day, p195.
18. Wentworth Day, p122.
19. Wentworth Day, p123.
20. Wentworth Day, p169.

Chapter 16 (pages 144–150)
1. Wentworth Day, p177.
2. Allen, chapter 21.
3. *Yorkshire Post* & *Leeds Intelligence*, 19 April 1934.
4. *Saturday Review*, 14 November 1936.
5. Wentworth Day p97. Letter undated.
6. *Saturday Review*, 30 June 1934.
7. Private communication from Sir Roderick Brinckman Bt., 2012.
8. Wentworth Day, pp182–3
9. Allen, p122.
10. Reproduced in the *Saturday Review*, 14 November 1936.
11. *The Patriot*, February 1933.

Chapter 17 (page 151–165)
1. 27 November 1930. Quoted in Wentworth Day, p 91. This book gives no sources, so it is unclear how Wentworth Day knew about it, since it was before his employment by Lucy. It is possible that Oscar Pulvermacher gave him access to his personal correspondence files.
2. Quoted in Wentworth Day, p93.
3. Quoted in Wentworth Day, p96.
4. Charmley, p10.
5. Pugh, p17.
6. Charmley shows a delightful picture of the two of them, both in Arab costume, as they are about to blow up another railway bridge. [see PLATE B21]
7. Charmley, p127.
8. Charmley, p111.
9. Papers of Blanche Lloyd.
10. Charmley, p116. On becoming Prime Minister in June 1940, Winston Churchill appointed him as Colonial Secretary, the post he held until his premature death in February 1941.
11. Charmley, p141.
12. Lloyd papers, 19/2, October 1933.
13. Wentworth Day, p176.
14. *Daily Herald*, 20 November 1933.
15. Lloyd papers, 22/1, November 1933.
16. Charmley, p192.

17. *The Times*, 25 May 1934.
18. Wentworth Day, p184. Much of what follows was recounted by Day on the next four pages.
19. Lloyd papers, 19/2, 25 June 1934.
20. It seems that Lloyd's obstinacy prevented him from accepting Lucy's offer.
21. Lloyd papers, 1/22.

Chapter 18 (pages 166–179)
1. Churchill papers, CHAR 2/246/74–5.
2. Reproduced in *Saturday Review*, 2 March 1935.
3. *Saturday Review*, 6 April 1935.
4. *Saturday Review*, 3 October 1936.
5. *Saturday Review*, 6 April 1935.
6. National Archives, PRO 30/69/1558.
7. *Saturday Review*, 2 March 1935.
8. Wentworth Day, p192.
9. *Saturday Review*, 9 November 1935.
10. *Saturday Review* supplement, 21 September 1935.
11. Wentworth Day, p190.
12. Macnair, 2014.
13. Moorehead, 1972.
14. Farwell, p175.

Chapter 19 (pages 180–193)
1. *The Times*, 31 May 1935.
2. *Yorkshire Post*, 4 June 1935.
3. *Saturday Review*, April 1935.
4. Including the *Lincolnshire Echo*, April 21.
5. *Gloucester Citizen*, 14 June 1935.
6. Allen, p144. *Saturday Review*, 21 July 1934.
7. Various editions of *The Times*, 1935.
8. *The Times*, 18 August 1934.
9. *Burnley Express*, 5 June 1935.
10. *Sunderland Daily Echo*, 1 January 1935.
11. *Dundee Evening Telegraph*, 10 October 1935.
12. *Hull Daily Mail*, 25 May 1935.
13. *Western Times*, 4 May 1935.
14. Allen, pp161–3.
15. Stonor, pp88–9.
16. Skidenski, p255, quoting Nicholson diaries MS, 20 July 1931.
17. Wentworth Day, p157.
18. Allen, pp148–9.
19. Barnes, p257.
20. *Hull Daily Mail*, 17 August 1935.

21. Wentworth Day, p239.
22. Ziegler.
23. Wentworth Day, p120.
24. Urbach.
25. Urbach.
26. peer.
27. Ziegler chapter 15, quoting Michael Bloch.
28. Ziegler chapter 15, quoting PRO FO 371/20734.
29. What follows is largely based on Wentworth Day, chapter 15.
30. *Nottingham Evening Post*, 8 January 1936.
31. *Dundee Courier*, 13 January 1936.
32. The result was McDonald (National Labour) 8,949; Labour 5,967; Randolph Churchill (Unionist) 2,427; Liberal 738.
33. *Dundee Courier*, 10 January 1936.
34. National Archives, LO 2/32.

Chapter 20 (pages 194–210)
1. *Saturday Review*, 30 March 1937.
2. Higham, pp65–6, quoting the 'Chinese Dossier' later discovered in US Intelligence files.
3. Higham, p72.
4. Higham, p77.
5. Higham, p75.
6. Norwich. Entry for 20 January 1936.
7. Ziegler, Williams and others.
8. For this paragraph, I am indebted to Andrew Rose author of *The Prince, the Princess and the Perfect Murder*, 2014, and his subsequent research which became the subject of a TV documentary, *Prince Edward's Murderous Mistress*, Yesterday channel, 28 May 2015.
9. Morton, chapter 1.
10. Morton.
11. *The Guardian*, 30 January 2003, based on files released from the Home Office.
12. Ziegler, p304.
13. Ziegler, p302.
14. *Saturday Review*, 22 August 1936.
15. *Saturday Review*, 21 October 1936.
16. *Nottingham Evening Post*, 27 October 1936.
17. Allen, pp114–17.
18. Diana and Unity's sister Jessica, the communist in the family, married her cousin Esmond Romilly, whose aunt Clementine Hozier was married to Winston Churchill.
19. Speer.
20. *Saturday Review*, 14 March 1936.
21. Farr, pp84–5.

22. *Western Daily Press*, 4 May 1936.
23. *Western Morning News*, 5 May 1936.
24. McDonald, p82.
25. Farr, p85.
26. *The Times*, 31 December 1936.
27. Wentworth Day, p232.
28. Wentworth Day, p247.
29. Ditto.
30. In 1958, the Duchess of Windsor returned the ring to Cartier, asking for it to be brought up to date with a more opulent mount in yellow gold set with diamonds.
31. Higham, pp204–5.
32. Churchill Papers, CHAR 2/260/10,65,113–15.
33. Allen, p85. *Saturday Review*, 21 November 1936.
34. *Saturday Review*, 24 October 1936.
35. *Chelmsford Chronicle*, 27 November 1936.
36. Wentworth Day, pp235–6.
37. Allen, p171.
38. *Saturday Review*, 12 December 1936
39. *Saturday Review*, 26 December 1936.
40. Wentworth Day, pp249–50 and Warner-Allen, p172.
41. Wentworth Day, p250.

Chapter 21 (pages 211–222)
1. *Yorkshire Post*, 30 December 1936.
2. Allen pp108–9.
3. Allen p11.
4. London daily newspaper, quoted in Wentworth Day, p252.
5. Allen, p173.
6. This name would suggest that he might be some relative of Robert Houston but further details are unknown.
7. *Hull Daily Mail*, 4 January 1937. These were all descendants of Lucy's sister Sophia Radmall (Catty): Marjory Catty (1908–97), Margaret Catty (Dulanty) (1913–80), Barbara Catty (Kraufmann) (1920–2007) and Diana Jaboulet-Verchère (b.1915).
8. *Jersey Weekly Post*, 9 January 1937. Lucy had set up a trust for Maud Mason which paid £1 a week until she was 18 so that she could train to be a dressmaker.
9. Wentworth Day, pp255–6.
10. Wentworth Day, p256.
11. *Nottingham Evening Post*, 9 April 1937.
12. *The Times*, 9 April 1937.
13. Jersey Public Registry.
14. *Dundee Evening Telegraph*, 6 January 1937. This report must be wrong in one aspect; none of Lucy's brothers were alive by 1937.

15. *The Times*, 4 May 1937.
16. *The Times*, 31 December 1937.
17. *ODNB*.
18. Including Ziegler, Higham, Morton etc.
19. Litchfield.
20. Litchfield, chapter 1.
21. Wentworth Day, p55.
22. *The Times*, 19 May 1976.
23. The family had previously put them up for auction in 1937, but on that occasion they failed to reach the reserve of £7,500. *The Times*, 2 July 1937.

Appendix I (pages 223–224)
1. *The Times*, 23 October 1878.
2. Published by William Blackwood & Sons, 1903. General Hills (1834–1902), known in his family as 'Jack', was my great-grand-uncle, the third son of James Hills, indigo planter of Neechindepur in East Bengal. He was in command of the Royal Engineer Division at Kandahar, Afghanistan, alongside his brother Colonel 'Jimmy' Hills VC during the Afghan Wars of 1879–81. Of his contribution to this campaign, Sir Henry Cotton recalled that he 'was burly, brusque and good-natured ... and won fame and honour at the time when all in authority were not so level-headed as himself.' (Macnair, p54)

Appendix II (pages 225–227)
1. £200.
2. £5,000. Also one fifth of residual estate.
3. Income for life from £5,000 in trust. Capital then to pass to her daughter Diane Henrietta Bierge.
4. £500 plus clothes. One fifth of residual estate.
5. £500.
6. Executor's fees, plus £500. Also authority to sell all jewellery.
7. £5,000 plus a large sofa. One fifth of residual estate.
8. £500 plus an oil painting and a fur coat. One fifth of residual estate.
9. £2,000.
10. £500.
11. £1,000 in trust until reaching 21.
12. £200 in trust until reaching 21.

Bibliography

Adam, Colin Forbes, *The Life of Lord Lloyd*, Macmillan, 1947.

Allen, Warner, *Lady Houston DBE*, Constable, 1947.

Andrews, C. & Morgan, E. *Supermarine Aircraft since 1914*, Putnam, 1981.

Blacker, Barnaby, *The Adventures and Inventions of Stewart Blacker*, Pen & Sword, 2006.

Blythe, R. *The Age of Illusion; England in the Twenties and Thirties*, Penguin, 1964.

Charmley, J. *Lord Lloyd and the Decline of the British Empire*, Weidenfeld, 1987.

Crawford, R & A. *Michael & Natasha; the life and love of the Last Tsar of Russia*, Weidenfeld & Nicholson, 1997.

Farr, G. *Wreck and Rescue on the Coast of Devon*, Bradford Barton, 1968.

Farwell, B. *Queen Victoria's Little Wars*, Wordsworth Editions, 1973.

Fellowes, P. *First over Everest*, Cherry Tree, 1933, republished by Pilgrim Publishing, 2004.

Gottlieb, J. *Feminine Fascism*, I.B. Tauris, 2000.

Gunston, B. *Giants of the Sky*, PSL, 1991.

Higham, C. *Wallis; Secret lives of the Duchess of Windsor*, Pan Books, 1988.

Hills, General Sir John, *Points of the Racehorse*, 1903.

James, D. *Gloster Aircraft*, Putnam & Co, 1971.

Lentin, A. 'The Treaty of Versailles', *History Today*, January 2012.

Linehan, T. *British Fascism 1918–1939; Parties, Ideology & Culture*, Manchester University Press, 2000.

Litchfield, D. *Hitler's Valkyrie*, The History Press, 2013.

Lovell, M.S. *The Mitford Girls*, Abacus, 2001.

McDonald, K. *Shipwrecks of the South Hams*, Wreckwalker Books, 1998.

Macnair, M. *Indigo and Opium*, Brewin Books, 2014.

Mitra, S.M. *Voice for Women – without votes*, Billing & Sons, 1914.

Mondey, D. *The Schneider Trophy*, Robert Hale, 1975.

Moorehead, A. *The Blue Nile*, Harper & Rowe, 1972.

Morton, Andrew, *17 Carnations: The Windsors, the Nazis and the Cover-up*, Michael O'Mara books, 2015.

Norwich, J.J. (editor), *The Duff Cooper Diaries*, Phoenix, 2006.

Owen, C. *The Greatest Brewery in the World*, Derbyshire Record Society, 1992.

Powell, Anna, *Women doctors and nurses on the Western and Eastern Fronts during the First World War. (Article)*

Pugh, M. *Hurrah for the Blackshirts! Fascists and Fascism between the Wars*, Pimlico, 2005.

Rose, A. *The Prince, the Princess and the Perfect Murder*, Coronet, 2013.

Setright, L.J.K. *The Power to Fly*, Allen & Unwin, 1971.

Seymour, Miranda, *In my Father's House*, Simon & Schuster, 2007.

Shelton. J. *Schneider Trophy to Spitfire; the design career of R.J. Mitchell*, Haynes Publishing 2008.

Skidelsky, R. *Oswald Mosley*, Macmillan, 1975, 1981.

Smith, V.A. *The Oxford History of India*, OUP 4th edition, 1999.

Speer, A. *Inside the Third Reich*, Phoenix, 1995.

Stonor, Julia, *Sherman's Wife*, Desert Hearts, 2006.

Thaddeus, T.H. *Recollections of a Court Painter*, The Bodley Head, 1912.

Tucker, J. *The Troublesome Priest*, Michael Russell, 2007.

Urbach, K. *Go-Betweens for Hitler*, Oxford University Press, 2015.

Wentworth-Day, J. *Lady Houston, DBE*, Allan Wingate, 1958.

Williams, S. *The People's King: The True Story of the Abdication*, Penguin, 2003.

Ziegler, P. *King Edward VIII*, Knopf, 1991.

Index